A SURE
FOUNDATION

A SURE FOUNDATION

ANSWERS TO DIFFICULT GOSPEL QUESTIONS

Deseret Book Company
Salt Lake City, Utah

©1988 Deseret Book Company

All rights reserved. No part of this book may be reproduced
in any form or by any means without permission in writing
from the publisher, Deseret Book Company, P.O. Box 30178,
Salt Lake City, Utah 84130.

Deseret Book is a registered trademark of Deseret Book Company.

Library of Congress Cataloging-in-Publication Data

A Sure foundation : answers to difficult gospel questions.
    p.   cm.
   Includes index.
   ISBN 0-87579-149-2
   1. Church of Jesus Christ of Latter-day Saints—Doctrines—
Miscellanea.   2. Mormon Church—Doctrines—Miscellanea.
BX8637.S87   1988
289.3—dc19   88-25629
                                   CIP

Printed in the United States of America

10   9   8   7   6   5   4   3

CONTENTS

PREFACE xi

BOOK OF MORMON

Why does the Book of Mormon say that Jesus would be born in Jerusalem? (See Alma 7:10.) — D. Kelly Ogden. 3

Some passages in the Book of Mormon seem to indicate that there is only one God and that he is a spirit only. How can we explain this? — Roy W. Doxey. 5

Why do we say that the Book of Mormon contains "the fulness of the gospel" (D&C 20:9) when it doesn't contain some of the basic teachings of the Church? Why doesn't it include such doctrines as the three degrees of glory, marriage for eternity, premortal existence of spirits, and baptism for the dead? — Daniel H. Ludlow 11

Why are the words *adieu, Bible,* and *baptize* used in the Book of Mormon? These words weren't known in Book of Mormon times. — Edward J. Brandt 16

A friend of mine says he has prayed about the Book of Mormon but has not received a testimony of its truthfulness. Shouldn't Moroni's promise *always* work? — Daniel H. Ludlow 18

Since the Book of Mormon is largely the record of a Hebrew people, is the writing characteristic of the Hebrew language? — John A. Tvedtnes... 21

What are the best evidences to support the authenticity of the Book of Mormon? — Ellis T. Rasmussen............................. 27

Why have changes been made in the printed editions of the Book of Mormon? — Robert J. Matthews 33

Did Oliver Cowdery, one of the three special witnesses of the Book of Mormon, express doubt about his testimony? — Richard Lloyd Anderson 39

What is the meaning of the Book of Mormon passages on eternal hell for the wicked? — H. Donl Peterson....................... 45

What is the approximate weight of the gold plates from which the Book of Mormon was translated? — Roy W. Doxey 50

Why were the Book of Mormon gold plates not placed in a museum so that people might know Joseph Smith had had them? — Monte S. Nyman... 52

Would you respond to the theories that the Book of Mormon is based on the Spaulding manuscript or on Ethan Smith's *View of the Hebrews?* — Bruce D. Blumell 54

What is B. H. Roberts's "Study of the Book of Mormon" and how have critics used it to discredit the Book of Mormon? — John W. Welch... 60

DOCTRINE AND COVENANTS

What are the features of the 1981 edition of the Doctrine and Covenants that can aid us in our scripture study? — Bill Applegarth . 77

Does Doctrine and Covenants 84:19–22 mean that a person has to have the Melchizedek Priesthood in order to see God? Joseph Smith didn't have the priesthood at the time of the First Vision. — Melvin J. Petersen 78

Why does Doctrine and Covenants 104:1 say that the united order is an everlasting order until the Lord comes, yet it is not practiced today? — Stephen K. Iba 83

More than a century and a half ago, the Prophet Joseph Smith learned from the Lord that tobacco is not good for us. Since then, medical science has determined the same thing. How has society responded to this information? — Dr. James Mason 85

NEW TESTAMENT

How do we reconcile the passage "God is a spirit" with God's being a personage of flesh and bones? — William O. Nelson 93

How do we support the position that Christ organized a church with various officers, particularly in view of Matthew 18:19–20 and 1 Corinthians 12:12–14? — Robert J. Woodford 99

How do we interpret scriptures in the New Testament that seem to condemn genealogy? — George H. Fudge..................... 103

Does the practice of baptism for the dead (see 1 Corinthians 15:29) refer to a non-Christian practice, or was it a practice of the gospel of Jesus Christ? — Robert L. Millet........................... 106

Were the blessings of the temple available to the Saints of Jesus' time, or did they become available after his death? — Robert J. Matthews 110

Inasmuch as Latter-day Saints believe in marriage for eternity, how do we explain Jesus' teachings in Matthew 22:29–30? — David H. Yarn, Jr. 113

I get the impression from reading 1 Corinthians 7:7–9 that Paul was not married and was against marriage in general. How can his views be reconciled with the revealed truths of eternal marriage? — C. Wilfred Griggs 116

Will you explain these references in the Bible in view of the Latter-day Saint doctrine that works are necessary for salvation: Ephesians 2:8–9, Titus 3:5, and Romans 4:5?—Robert E. Parsons......... 120

OLD TESTAMENT

Did Ezekiel's prophecy about two "sticks" foretell the coming forth of the Book of Mormon, or have Latter-day Saints misinterpreted Ezekiel 37:15–20?—Keith Meservy 129

How much emphasis is found in the writings of the Old Testament prophets on the subjects of the Restoration and the last days?— Brent Bulloch 143

THE CHURCH

What is an appropriate way to respond to unfriendly questions about the Church?—Steve F. Gilliland 151

When nonmembers say we're not Christians, what is the best way to respond?—Jack Weyland 155

How can I explain the Church's attitude toward the Bible? A friend of mine objects to the fact that we have additional scriptures and that we believe in the Bible only "as far as it is translated correctly."— Robert J. Matthews... 159

CHURCH HISTORY

Do the various accounts by the Prophet Joseph Smith of his first vision demonstrate the validity of that event, or do they cast doubt on the Prophet's integrity?—Milton V. Backman, Jr. 169

Did Joseph Smith's contemporaries provide accounts of the First Vision as given to them by Joseph Smith, and, if so, are these accounts consistent with his own accounts of the First Vision?— Milton V. Backman, Jr.. 183

What is the historical context of Joseph Smith's concern about which church was true? Did Joseph write a reliable account of that historical setting?—Milton V. Backman, Jr. 192

What changes have been made in the name of the Church? Its full designation does not appear in the revelations until 1838. (See D&C 115:4.) — Richard Lloyd Anderson 194

Was the Church legally incorporated at the time it was organized in the state of New York? — Larry C. Porter 196

I've been reading the *Journal of Discourses* with a great deal of interest and pleasure, but I notice that they are not printed by the Church. How authoritative should I consider them to be? — Gerald E. Jones 199

DOCTRINES AND PRINCIPLES

The Savior said that we should be perfect, even as he and our Father in Heaven are perfect. (See 3 Nephi 12:48.) Are we expected to achieve perfection in this life? If so, how can I avoid becoming discouraged with myself while I try to achieve it? — Gerald N. Lund 205

What was in the creeds of men that the Lord found abominable, as he stated in the First Vision? — Hoyt W. Brewster, Jr. 210

How do Latter-day Saints support the doctrine of Melchizedek Priesthood authority from the Bible? — James A. Carver 215

Why do we observe the Sabbath on Sunday when the biblical Sabbath seems to have been observed on the seventh day? — Robert J. Matthews 220

How can Jesus and Lucifer be spirit brothers when their characters and purposes are so utterly opposed? — Jess L. Christensen ... 223

How do we endure to the end? The idea seems to imply putting up with a bad situation (life) until death brings release. What do the prophets really mean when they speak of enduring to the end? — Gordon M. Thomas 226

INDEX 229

PREFACE

Be ready always to give an answer to every man that asketh you a reason of the hope that is in you with meekness and fear. —1 Peter 3:15

The articles in this book provide a doctrinal perspective for members of The Church of Jesus Christ of Latter-day Saints to draw from to answer questions about the Church and to respond to misrepresentations or charges against the Church. Answers proffered to questions in this book are for guidance only and do not represent official statements of Church policy.

Previously published in other publications, these articles are now published together to provide the reader with the convenience of having the information in one place. Appreciation is extended to the authors who prepared the articles.

The articles are arranged in the following general categories: questions that pertain to the Book of Mormon, to the Doctrine and Covenants, to the New Testament, to the Old Testament, to the Church, to Church history, and to the doctrines and principles of the restored gospel.

It is hoped that this book will strengthen the faith of every individual who reads it.

BOOK OF
MORMON

QA

Why does the Book of Mormon say that Jesus would be born in Jerusalem? (See Alma 7:10.)

D. Kelly Ogden, professor of historical geography and ancient scripture at the Jerusalem Center for Near Eastern Studies

Let's look more closely at Alma's wording: "He shall be born of Mary, at Jerusalem which is the land of our forefathers." (Alma 7:10.) Notice two points: First, Jerusalem is referred to as a land rather than as a city; second, Jesus' birth would occur *at* Jerusalem.[1]

The Land of Jerusalem

Towns and villages that surrounded larger demographic or political centers were regarded in ancient times as belonging to those larger centers. For a major city center such as Jerusalem to be called not only a city but also a land was standard practice.

El Amarna letter 287, an ancient Near Eastern text, mentions the "land of Jerusalem" several times.[1] And, like Alma, the ancient writer of El Amarna letter 290 even referred to Bethlehem as part of the land of Jerusalem: in this letter is recorded the complaint of Abdu-Kheba of Jerusalem to Pharaoh Akhenaton that "the land of the king went over to the Apiru people. But now even a town of the *land of Jerusalem*, Bit-Lahmi [Bethlehem] by name, a town belonging to the king, has gone over to the side of the people of Keilah."[2] Hebron, almost twenty miles south of Bethlehem, was also considered part of the "land of Jerusalem."[3]

The Book of Mormon is internally consistent in using the wording "the land of Jerusalem" to refer to the place from which Lehi and his family had left, to which the Savior would appear as a mortal, and to which the people of Judah would eventually return.[4]

Modern revelation given through the Prophet Joseph Smith perpetuates the expression and its ancient meaning. In Doctrine and Covenants 133:24, we read that when the continents are reassembled and again become one land mass, "the land of Jerusalem and the land of Zion shall be turned back into their own place."

3

Several other scriptural cities are also labeled at times as lands. Ammonihah was a city (see Alma 8:6), but it was also a land (see Alma 14:23). The area surrounding the city of Ur was also known as Ur. We read that an idolatrous shrine stood by Potiphar's Hill, which "was in the land of Ur, of Chaldea." (Abraham 1:20.) And in Abraham 2:4, we learn that Abraham and his family left "the land of Ur, of the Chaldees" and transferred to the "land" of Haran. The Damascus Rule (also known as the Zadokite Document, part of the Dead Sea Scrolls) twice refers to the "land of Damascus."[5]

At Jerusalem

Alma stated that Jesus would be born of Mary, not *in* Jerusalem, but *at* Jerusalem. Dictionary definitions of *at* include "close by" and "near." Thus "at Jerusalem" could mean "near Jerusalem."

There is another example in the Book of Mormon in which the word *at* may mean "near." The record does not say that Lehi and his family lived *in* Jerusalem, but *at* Jerusalem: "My father, Lehi, . . . dwelt at Jerusalem in all his days" (1 Nephi 1:4); "he returned to his own house at Jerusalem" (1 Nephi 1:7); and "I, Nephi, . . . have dwelt at Jerusalem" (2 Nephi 25:6). That Lehi and his family may indeed have lived outside of Jerusalem proper is evidenced in the account of the sons' attempt to secure the brass plates with their abandoned wealth: "We went *down* to the *land* of our inheritance, and we did gather together our gold, and our silver, and our precious things. And after we had gathered these things together, we went *up* again unto the house of Laban." (1 Nephi 3:22–23; italics added.) Lehi could have lived several miles away and still lived *at* Jerusalem, just as Jesus could be born several miles away in Bethlehem but still be born *at* Jerusalem.

Joseph Smith, of course, knew well that Jesus was born in Bethlehem. If he had been the author of the Book of Mormon, he would have so stated the fact, since any deviation from the well-known setting would certainly draw objection and accusation. But Joseph Smith was translating a geographical note from an ancient writer, a note which in itself is another evidence that the Book of Mormon derives from a Semitic background.

Thus, Alma's prophetic preview of the setting of the Savior's birth is not erroneous or contradictory. It is compatible with similar biblical and extrabiblical figures of speech—it is evidence, in fact, of the passage's authentic ancient origin.

Notes

1. See Hugh Nibley, *An Approach to the Book of Mormon*, vol. 6 of *The Collected Works of Hugh Nibley* (Salt Lake City: Deseret Book Co., 1988), pp. 101–2.

2. See James B. Pritchard, ed., *Ancient Near Eastern Texts Relating to the Old Testament*, 3d ed. (Princeton, N.J.: Princeton University Press, 1969), p. 488.

3. Ibid., p. 489; italics added. Translation by W. F. Albright and George E. Mendenhall. See also Yohanan Aharoni and Michael Avi-Yonah, *Macmillan Bible Atlas* (New York: Macmillan, 1974), map 39.

4. See Yohanan Aharoni, *The Land of the Bible, a Historical Geography* (London: Burns and Oates, 1974), p. 195.

5. It is recorded at least thirty-three times throughout the Book of Mormon that Lehi and Nephi went out from "the land of Jerusalem." (1 Nephi 2:11; 3:9, 10; 5:6; 7:2, 7; 16:35; 17:14, 20, 22; 18:24; 2 Nephi 1:1, 3, 9, 30; Jacob 2:25, 31, 32; Omni 1:6; Mosiah 1:11; 2:4; 7:20; 10:12; Alma 3:11; 9:22; 10:3; 22:9; 36:29; Helaman 5:6; 7:7; 8:21; 3 Nephi 5:20; Ether 13:7.) The scene of significant events in the Savior's ministry is referred to four times as "the land of Jerusalem." (Helaman 16:19; 3 Nephi 16:1; Mormon 3:18, 19.) The place to which the people of Judah would return and which they would receive as an inheritance is four times identified as "the land of Jerusalem." (2 Nephi 25:11; 3 Nephi 20:29, 33, 46.)

6. Geza Vermes, *The Dead Sea Scrolls in English*, 2d ed. (Harmondsworth, Middlesex, England: Penguin Books Ltd., 1975), 6:102–3; italics added.

QA

Some passages in the Book of Mormon seem to indicate that there is only one God and that he is a spirit only. How can we explain this?

Roy W. Doxey, assistant in the office of the Quorum of the Twelve and dean emeritus of Religious Instruction, Brigham Young University

Readers of the Book of Mormon are sometimes concerned with passages that seem to contradict Latter-day Saint doctrine on the Godhead. But when we look at these passages in context, along with teachings found throughout the book, we find that the Book of Mormon does indeed teach that God the Father, his Son Jesus

5

Christ, and the Holy Ghost are three separate beings and that the Father and the Son are not personages of spirit.

Is There More Than One God?

The question of whether there is more than one God is often raised in response to Alma 11, in which Zeezrom, a critic, is contending with the missionary Amulek:

"Now Zeezrom was a man who was expert in the devices of the devil, that he might destroy that which was good; therefore, he said unto Amulek: Will ye answer the questions which I shall put unto you?

"And Amulek said unto him: Yea, if it be according to the Spirit of the Lord, which is in me; for I shall say nothing which is contrary to the Spirit of the Lord. And Zeezrom said unto him: Behold, here are six onties of silver, and all these will I give thee if thou wilt deny the existence of a Supreme Being. . . .

"And Zeezrom said unto him: Thou sayest there is a true and living God?

"And Amulek said: Yea, there is a true and living God.

"Now Zeezrom said: Is there more than one God?

"And he answered, No.

"Now Zeezrom said unto him again: How knowest thou these things?

"And he said: An angel hath made them known unto me." (Vv. 21–22, 26–31.)

In order to understand Amulek's statement, we must look at the full context. Throughout most of their history, many Israelites (forefathers of the Nephites) were eager to accept the numerous pagan gods of the Egyptians and Canaanites. Although the Book of Mormon is silent about the specific apostate notions held by the people in Zeezrom's city of Ammonihah, it is clear that some apostate Nephites of Alma's time were idolatrous, as some of their Israelite fathers had been. When Alma, Amulek's missionary companion, was chief judge as well as high priest over the Church, he helped to establish a strong and faithful body of church members. Nevertheless, "those who did not belong to their church did indulge themselves in sorceries, and in idolatry." (Alma 1:32.) Apostasy was such a problem that Alma later gave up the judgment seat, "that he himself might go forth among his people, or among the people of Nephi, that he might preach the word of God unto them." (Alma 4:19.)

As a missionary, Alma found that many of the people were steeped in idolatry. He discovered, for example, that the people in the city of Zoram "were perverting the ways of the Lord, and that Zoram, who was their leader, was leading the hearts of the people to bow down to dumb idols." (Alma 31:1.)

This is the context, then, of the discussion Alma and Amulek had with Zeezrom. Seen in this light, Amulek's answer is completely understandable and, of course, correct: There is only one "true and living God," who shares none of his godhood with the hosts of false gods invented by man.

Of course Amulek knew that there are three separate personages in the Godhead and that they are one in purpose. He declared to Zeezrom that in time all will be brought before the judgment bar of "Christ the Son, and God the Father, and the Holy Spirit, which is one Eternal God." (Alma 11:44.) Since the Son and the Holy Spirit are one in purpose, mission, and glory with the "true and living God," the three are indeed "one Eternal God."

Following Amulek's discussion with Zeezrom, Alma, "seeing that the words of Amulek had silenced Zeezrom, . . . opened his mouth and began to speak unto him, and to establish the words of Amulek, and to explain things beyond, or to unfold the scriptures beyond that which Amulek had done." (Alma 12:1.) In the course of explaining "things beyond" to Zeezrom, Alma made the concept of Godhead even clearer:

"God did call on men, *in the name of his Son,* (this being the plan of redemption which was laid) saying: If ye will repent, and harden not your hearts, then will I have mercy upon you, *through mine Only Begotten Son;*

"Therefore, whosoever repenteth, and hardeneth not his heart, he shall have claim on mercy *through mine Only Begotten Son,* unto a remission of his sins." (Alma 12:33–34; italics added.)

Here is clarification of the truth that God and his Only Begotten Son are separate and distinct from each other, and it is found within Alma and Amulek's discussion with Zeezrom.

It is interesting that Amulek's statement about one "true and living God" is similar to one given by Paul in a similar context. "We know that an idol is nothing in the world," Paul told the Corinthians, "and that there is none other God but one.

"For though there be that are called gods, whether in heaven or in earth, (as there be gods many, and lords many,)

"But to us there is but one God, the Father, of whom are all things, and we in him; and one Lord Jesus Christ, by whom are all things, and we by him." (1 Corinthians 8:4–6.) Like Amulek, Paul declared that there is only one God—the Father. But he also testified of the divinity of the Lord Jesus Christ.

Elsewhere in the Book of Mormon, the distinction between the Father and the Son is clearly illustrated. For example, immediately before Christ's appearance to the Nephites after his resurrection, the people heard the voice of the Father proclaiming: "Behold my Beloved Son, in whom I am well pleased, in whom I have glorified my name—hear ye him." Then they "cast their eyes up again towards heaven; and behold, they saw a Man descending out of heaven"—the Son, Jesus Christ. (3 Nephi 11:7–8.) This experience is similar to experiences at the Savior's baptism and at his transfiguration, in which the Father spoke from the heavens, acknowledging his Beloved Son, who was on earth. (See Matthew 3:17; 17:5.)

The oneness of the Godhead in purpose (the salvation of man) is also illustrated in both the Book of Mormon and the Bible. In the Book of Mormon, the resurrected Christ prayed:

"Father, I pray not for the world, but for those whom thou hast given me out of the world, because of their faith, that they may be purified in me, that I may be in them as thou, Father, art in me, that we may be one, that I may be glorified in them." (3 Nephi 19:29.)

The Bible records a similar prayer that the Savior uttered during his ministry in Palestine. (See John 17:11, 21–22.) On both occasions Jesus was praying for a oneness in purpose for all the disciples as the Father and he were one in purpose—not in essence or substance.

Is the Son of God the Eternal Father?

Zeezrom sought to confuse the issue by asking, "Is the son of God the very Eternal Father?

"And Amulek said unto him: Yea, he is the very Eternal Father of heaven and of earth, and all things which in them are; he is the beginning and the end, the first and the last;

"And he shall come into the world to redeem his people; and he shall take upon him the transgressions of those who believe on his name." (Alma 11:38–40.)

The Book of Mormon makes it clear that although Jesus Christ is the Son of God, there are some ways in which he is our Father. In one way, he is the Father of the earth, since he created it under the Father's direction. King Benjamin declared, for example, that the Savior "shall be called Jesus Christ, the *Son* of God, the *Father* of heaven and earth, the *Creator* of all things from the beginning." (Mosiah 3:8; italics added.)

This doctrine is not new. Biblical prophets also testified that the Son was the Creator of the heaven and earth. John bore witness that "all things were made by him; and without him was not any thing made that was made." (John 1:3.) Paul declared that by the Son "were all things created, that are in heaven, and that are in earth." (Colossians 1:16.) But it is also clear that the Son acted as the Father's agent; Paul wrote to the Ephesians of "God, who created all things by Jesus Christ." (Ephesians 3:9.)

Jesus Christ is the Father in another way as well. For those who accept the gospel, he becomes their Father by adoption and covenant in their new relationship with him. Abinadi alluded to this relationship when he spoke of the *seed* of Jesus — the prophets and "those who have hearkened unto their words." (See Mosiah 15:10–13.) King Benjamin also made this relationship clear: "Because of the covenant which ye have made," he told a group of repentant Nephites, "ye shall be called the children of Christ, his sons, and his daughters; for behold, this day he hath spiritually begotten you; for ye say that your hearts are changed through faith on his name; therefore, ye are born of him and have become his sons and his daughters." (Mosiah 5:7.) Thus, Jesus Christ becomes the Father of the righteous through adoption.

Jesus Christ is also the Father because the Eternal Father gave him authority to represent him. The resurrected Christ taught the Nephites that they should pray to the Father in his name because he and the Father are one. (See 3 Nephi 20:31, 35.) Jesus had also taught his disciples in Palestine that "I and my Father are one" (John 10:30); yet he declared that "my Father is greater than I" (John 14:28) and that "I am come in my Father's name" (John 5:43).

Is God a Spirit?

Some readers of the Book of Mormon have been concerned that in two passages God is called a "Great Spirit." Again, it is important to see these passages in context.

When Ammon was teaching the Lamanite king Lamoni, he asked: "Believest thou that there is a God?

"And he answered, and said unto him: I do not know what that meaneth.

"And then Ammon said: Believest thou that there is a Great Spirit?

"And he said, Yea.

"And Ammon said: This is God." (Alma 18:24–28.)

On another occasion, when Ammon's brother Aaron was teaching Lamoni's father, the king said: "Is God that Great Spirit that brought our fathers out of the land of Jerusalem?

"And Aaron said unto him: Yea, he is that Great Spirit, and he created all things both in heaven and in earth." (Alma 22:9–10.)

In these instances, Ammon and Aaron simply accepted the king's definition of God as sufficient until the king could be taught a broader basis of truth, upon which further information could be built.

But were the missionaries teaching false doctrine? No. Both kings were taught that the "Great Spirit" was the creator of all things in heaven and in earth—Jesus Christ. As Jehovah, the premortal Jesus Christ was a spirit being who, at that time, could properly have been referred to as a Great Spirit, the Creator of all things.

The Book of Mormon makes known the doctrine of the physical reality of the Father and the Son, dispelling any notion that they are spirit beings. For example, when the brother of Jared saw the spirit body of the premortal Christ, the Lord said, "Seest thou that ye are created after mine own image? Yea, even all men were created in the beginning after mine own image.

"Behold, this body, which ye now behold, is the body of my spirit; and man have I created after the body of my spirit; and even as I appear unto thee to be in the spirit will I appear unto my people in the flesh." (Ether 3:15–16.)

Two millennia later, Jehovah entered earth life, his spirit joining his mortal body, thus taking upon himself the physical image of God, the same "image after which man was created in the beginning." (Mosiah 7:27.)

When the resurrected Christ appeared to his disciples in Jerusalem and in America, he invited them to thrust their hands into his side and to feel the prints of the nails in his hands and feet. (See John 20:27; 3 Nephi 11:14.) Then, at the close of his visits with the Nephites, the physically resurrected Lord said, "And now I go unto the Father." (3 Nephi 27:28.)

Although the Book of Mormon is an abridgment containing not even "the hundredth part" of what could have been included (Words of Mormon 1:5), it contains the fulness of the gospel of Jesus Christ, including the true doctrine of the Godhead.

QA

Why do we say that the Book of Mormon contains "the fulness of the gospel" (D&C 20:9) when it doesn't contain some of the basic teachings of the Church? Why doesn't it include such doctrines as the three degrees of glory, marriage for eternity, premortal existence of spirits, and baptism for the dead?

Daniel H. Ludlow, director of Correlation Review, The Church of Jesus Christ of Latter-day Saints

Jesus Christ himself defined the word *gospel* to the Nephites: "Behold I have given unto you my gospel, and this is the gospel which I have given unto you—that I came into the world to do the will of my Father, because my Father sent me." The Savior then reviewed for the Nephites the facts of the Atonement, including the need to repent, be baptized, receive the Holy Ghost, and endure to the end. (See 3 Nephi 27:13–22.)

Gospel means "good news," the good news that Jesus Christ has made it possible for us to return to the presence of our Heavenly Father. Through his perfect, sinless life and his suffering in Gethsemane and on the cross, Jesus Christ atoned for the original transgression of Adam and Eve and made it possible for us to be redeemed from spiritual death, which is the consequence of sin. Also through his atonement, including his crucifixion and resurrection, he has saved us from the permanent effects of physical death.

In addition to these aspects of the Atonement, which apply to all mankind, the "good news" also includes things that we must do in order to reenter God's presence. Peter mentioned some of these principles when he and other apostles were asked on the day of Pentecost, "Men and brethren, what shall we do?" His reply was, "Repent, and be baptized every one of you in the name of Jesus Christ for the remission of sins, and ye shall receive the gift of the Holy Ghost." (Acts 2:37–38.)

11

Peter's answer parallels our fourth article of faith: "We believe that the first principles and ordinances of the Gospel are: first, Faith in the Lord Jesus Christ; second, Repentance; third, Baptism by immersion for the remission of sins; fourth, Laying on of hands for the gift of the Holy Ghost."

One of the best summaries of the gospel was given by the Savior to the Nephites:

"And no unclean thing can enter into his kingdom; therefore nothing entereth into his rest save it be those who have washed their garments in my blood, because of their faith, and the repentance of all their sins, and their faithfulness unto the end.

"Now this is the commandment: Repent, all ye ends of the earth, and come unto me and be baptized in my name, that ye may be sanctified by the reception of the Holy Ghost, that ye may stand spotless before me at the last day.

"Verily, verily, I say unto you, this is my gospel; and ye know the things that ye must do in my church; for the works which ye have seen me do that shall ye also do." (3 Nephi 27:19–21.)

The essentials of the "fulness of the gospel" are contained in this one brief statement in the Book of Mormon, although they are also discussed in greater detail throughout this sacred scripture. In these verses, the Book of Mormon clearly emphasizes and explains the doctrine of the Atonement and the basic principles and ordinances of the gospel. (See the many references to these topics in the index of the Book of Mormon.) If these principles and doctrines are observed, a person may regain the presence of God in the celestial kingdom. Thus, the Book of Mormon can appropriately be said to contain the fulness of the gospel—the "good news"—even though it might not discuss all the ordinances necessary for exaltation.

Now let's look at the second part of the question—why the Book of Mormon doesn't contain information on all the doctrines of the Church.

An effective author has an audience and a purpose in mind when he prepares his material. Thus, it is important to understand the purpose of the authors of the Book of Mormon in order to understand why it contains what it does and why it doesn't contain other information.

The four major writers (engravers and/or compilers) of the Book of Mormon are Nephi (117 pages), Jacob (19 pages), Mormon (338 pages), and Moroni (50 pages). All four of these authors were personal witnesses of Jesus Christ. Nephi and Jacob were visited by the premortal Jesus Christ (see 2 Nephi 11:2–3), and Mormon and Moroni were visited by the resurrected Jesus Christ (see Mormon 1:15; Ether 12:22–39). Moroni also provided us with the testimony of the brother of Jared concerning the premortal Christ. (See Ether 3:9–16.) Thus, the writings of these four brethren constitute a strong witness for the divinity of Christ.

All four of these authors indicated that the major purpose of their writings is to lead people to Christ. Some of them also indicated that they intended their writings to serve as a second witness of the teachings of the Bible (the "record of the Jews"). At *no time* did any of them indicate that they would include *all* the teachings and ordinances of the gospel. In fact, they frequently mentioned they would include only those things that are necessary to a belief in Christ or those things that they had been inspired or commanded to write. (See 1 Nephi 19:2; 28:2; 31:1; 32:7; Jacob 1:19; 3 Nephi 26:12; 30:1; Mormon 5:9–13; 8:1; Ether 8:20; 13:13.)

Note the following statements of these four authors concerning their knowledge of Christ:

Nephi: "We labor diligently to write, to persuade our children, and also our brethren, to believe in Christ. . . .

"We talk of Christ, we rejoice in Christ, we preach of Christ, we prophesy of Christ, and we write according to our prophecies, that our children may know to what source they may look for a remission of their sins." (2 Nephi 25:23, 26.)

Jacob: "For this intent have we written these things, that they [the readers] may know that we knew of Christ, and we had a hope of his glory many hundred years before his coming; and not only we ourselves had a hope of his glory, but also all the holy prophets which were before us." (Jacob 4:4.)

Mormon: "Know ye that ye must come to the knowledge of your fathers, and repent of all your sins and iniquities, and believe in Jesus Christ, that he is the Son of God. . . .

"Therefore repent, and be baptized in the name of Jesus, and lay hold upon the gospel of Christ, which shall be set before you, not only in this record but also in the record which shall come unto the Gentiles from the Jews, which record shall come from the Gentiles unto you.

"For behold, this [the Book of Mormon] is written for the intent that ye may believe that [the Bible]; and if you believe that ye will believe this also; and if ye believe this ye will know concerning your fathers, and also the marvelous works which were wrought by the power of God among them." (Mormon 7:5, 8–9.)

Moroni: "I exhort you to remember these things; . . . for ye shall see me at the bar of God; and the Lord God will say unto you: Did I not declare my words unto you, which were written by this man? . . .

"Yea, come unto Christ, and be perfected in him. . . .

"And again, if ye by the grace of God are perfect in Christ, and deny not his power, then are ye sanctified in Christ by the grace of God, through the shedding of the blood of Christ, which is in the covenant of the Father unto the remission of your sins, that ye become holy, without spot." (Moroni 10:27, 32–33.)

These four writers also understood that their writings would come forth in the last days during a period of unbelief, when the true Church had been taken from the earth. (See 2 Nephi 25:3–23; 26:16–24; Jacob 4:4, 13–16; Mormon 8:25–35; Moroni 10:24–34.) Thus, their stated purpose was to help lead us to Christ and to the true Church, rather than to provide all the doctrines and ordinances of the gospel that we might receive after becoming members of the Church.

Explaining some of the procedures he followed in abridging the plates, Mormon indicated that it wasn't possible to record everything: "I cannot write the hundredth part of the things of my people." (Words of Mormon 1:5.) Nevertheless, he and the other major writers of the plates were faithful to their express mission of testifying of Jesus Christ.

The Lord has indicated that he works with his children by providing them information "line upon line, precept upon precept, here a little and there a little." (2 Nephi 28:30.) Thus, even on 6 April 1830, when the Church was restored in this dispensation, many of the ordinances we now have were not available to the early Church members. For example, the revelations providing much of the information on the three degrees of glory, eternal marriage, the premortal existence, and baptism for the dead were not received until later:

1. A wealth of information on the three degrees of glory is contained in Doctrine and Covenants 76, which was not received until 16 February 1832.

2. Major teachings and instructions pertaining to marriage for eternity date from May 1843 (D&C 131) and July 1843 (D&C 132).

14

3. Teachings pertaining to the premortal existence of spirits were not given by the Prophet Joseph Smith until well after the establishment of the Church. Some of his most significant statements on this subject were made at the April conference of the Church in 1844. (See *Teachings of the Prophet Joseph Smith,* sel. Joseph Fielding Smith [Salt Lake City: Deseret Book Co., 1938], pp. 342–62.)

4. Instructions on baptism for the dead were given in January 1841 (D&C 124) and September 1842 (D&C 127–28).

When Jesus Christ was on the earth, he also was given the gospel "line upon line." (D&C 98:12.)

"And he received not of the fulness at first, but continued from grace to grace, until he received a fulness;

"And thus he was called the Son of God, because he received not of the fulness at the first." (D&C 93:13–14.)

Concerning this principle of learning line upon line and precept upon precept, the Lord has said:

"I give unto you these sayings that you may understand and know how to worship, and know what you worship, that you may come unto the Father in my name, and in due time receive of his fulness. . . .

"And no man receiveth a fulness unless he keepeth his commandments." (D&C 93:19, 27.)

These principles are consistent with the concept of a living prophet who is entitled to receive the mind and will of the Lord by the power of the Holy Ghost for the members of the true Church. (See D&C 68:4.) This idea is also expressed in our ninth article of faith: "We believe all that God has revealed, all that He does now reveal, and we believe that He will yet reveal many great and important things pertaining to the Kingdom of God."

These teachings and doctrines are in accord with the statement of the Prophet Joseph Smith that the principles of the gospel are "according to the Holy Scriptures, and the Book of Mormon; and the only way that man can enter into the celestial kingdom." (*Teachings of the Prophet Joseph Smith,* p. 16.) The fulness of the gospel as contained in the Book of Mormon means that it contains those instructions a person needs to observe in order to be worthy to enter the presence of God in the celestial kingdom.

QA

Why are the words *adieu, Bible,* and *baptize* used in the Book of Mormon? These words weren't known in Book of Mormon times.

Edward J. Brandt, instructor, LDS Institute of Religion, University of Utah, Salt Lake City, Utah

A similar question could be asked about the Bible: Why, for example, is the word *book,* which comes from Old English and was not known in Old Testament times, found in the Old Testament?

The answer to both questions is simply that the Book of Mormon and the King James Version of the Bible are translations from ancient languages through the function of translators, who diligently endeavored to convey the intended meaning of the original writers.

The challenge faced by translators is a very difficult one. As Elder John A. Widtsoe wrote, "To convert the ideas recorded in Hebrew or Greek [or any language] into another language is not an easy task. The translator at best is only an interpreter of the text." (*Evidences and Reconciliations,* 3 vols. in 1, arr. G. Homer Durham [Salt Lake City: Bookcraft, 1960], p. 119.)

The language of the Book of Mormon plates was an altered Hebrew, expressed in "reformed Egyptian" characters. (See Mormon 9:32–33.) Although the Prophet Joseph Smith acted under the powers and gifts of God to receive and translate the anciently recorded message, he could transmit the meaning of what he received only through his own expression.

Speaking of the revelations given through the Prophet after the coming forth of the Book of Mormon, the Lord said, "These commandments are of me, and were given unto my servants in their weakness, *after the manner of their language,* that they might come to understanding." (D&C 1:24; italics added; see also 2 Nephi 31:3; Ether 12:39.) This same principle had governed the Prophet's translation of the Book of Mormon. Much of the translation is quite literal, reflecting Semitic idiom and structure; however, the choice of words came through the manner of the language of Joseph Smith, so that we might have understanding. That is why words not known in Book of Mormon times are found in the translated text.

The word *adieu* is defined in a dictionary of Joseph Smith's day as "a farewell; an expression of kind wishes at the parting of friends." (Noah Webster, *An American Dictionary of the English Language,* 1828.)

16

Although the word is of French origin, it appears to have found common usage in early nineteenth-century New England. This evidence may suggest the possible common use of the word *adieu* in the Smith family. When the Prophet received the concept or idea of a farewell at the conclusion of the portion of the record known as the book of Jacob, he used an expression he felt would convey the message to our understanding: "Brethren, adieu." (Jacob 7:27.)

The various forms of the word *baptize* are found 145 times in the Book of Mormon. It comes from the Greek *baptizein,* meaning "to immerse" or "to dip." The Hebrew *rachts,* "to wash" or "to bathe," or other ancient expressions such as "the burial," "the anointing," and even "to go down in water" do not convey the full meaning that the historical Christian term *baptize* does. The ordinance of baptism was one of the "plain and precious things" lost or tampered with in the ancient records. (See 1 Nephi 13:26–36; Moses 6:59–60, 64; JST Genesis 17:3–7.) In order that this generation might understand the significance of this important ordinance, the Prophet used the word *baptize* in the translation.

The word *Bible* is used eleven times in the Book of Mormon, all within four verses of one chapter. It comes from the Greek *biblion,* meaning "books," and other similar ancient roots. In Joseph Smith's time, as well as today, it was the title or synonym for the Hebrew and Greek scriptural record.

The primary word for a record or book in the ancient Hebrew is *Sepher.* It is translated 185 times in the Old Testament as "book," which, as mentioned earlier, comes from Old English. Thus, in the Bible we read of the "book of the generations" (Genesis 5:1), "book of the covenant" (Exodus 24:7), "book of the law" (Joshua 1:8), "book of the chronicles of the kings of Israel" (1 Kings 14:19), and "a roll of a book" (Jeremiah 36:2). Even though the word *book* was not known in Old Testament times, it was used in the translation to communicate an idea best understood by the use of that expression.

The word *book* is found seventy-eight times in the Book of Mormon, and the noun *record* is used ninety-eight times. In some instances, these words are used to describe what we know as the Bible — the "book" brought by the "Gentiles" to this land was "a record of the Jews, which contains the covenants of the Lord" (1 Nephi 13:20–23) and "the book which thou beheld proceeding out of the mouth of the Jew" (1 Nephi 14:23). The fact that Joseph Smith used the word *Bible* at one point should not be surprising; he undoubtedly wanted to make sure there would be no misunderstanding about which specific record was being referred to.

"And because my words shall hiss forth—many of the Gentiles shall say: A Bible! A Bible! We have got a Bible, and there cannot be any more Bible.

"But thus saith the Lord God: O fools, they shall have a Bible; and it shall proceed forth from the Jews, mine ancient covenant people. And what thank they the Jews for the Bible which they receive from them? . . .

"Thou fool, that shall say: A Bible, we have got a Bible, and we need no more Bible. Have ye obtained a Bible save it were by the Jews?

"Wherefore, because that ye have a Bible ye need not suppose that it contains all my words; neither need ye suppose that I have not caused more to be written." (2 Nephi 29:3–4, 6, 10.)

The intent of the message in the ancient record is clear, because it is after the manner of our language so we might understand.

QA

A friend of mine says he has prayed about the Book of Mormon but has not received a testimony of its truthfulness. Shouldn't Moroni's promise *always* work?

Daniel H. Ludlow, director of Correlation Review, The Church of Jesus Christ of Latter-day Saints

To understand the promise found in Moroni 10:4, a person should read and ponder the verses immediately before and after. In fact, in the first edition of the Book of Mormon (1830), Moroni 10 was all written as one paragraph. Let us examine carefully and individually verses 1 through 5.

Verse 1: "Now I, Moroni, write somewhat as seemeth me good; and I write unto my brethren, the Lamanites; and I would that they should know that more than four hundred and twenty years have passed away since the sign was given of the coming of Christ."

Although Moroni is addressing himself specifically to "the Lamanites," these words, as well as all of the other words in the Book of Mormon, apply also to the Jews and the Gentiles. (See Book of Mormon title page.)

Verse 2: "And I seal up these records, after I have spoken a few words by way of exhortation unto you."

The words *these records* refer to the records upon which Moroni was then writing (the plates of Mormon), which were later received by Joseph Smith and translated as the Book of Mormon.

Verse 3: "Behold, I would exhort you that when ye shall read these things, if it be wisdom in God that ye should read them, that ye would remember how merciful the Lord hath been unto the children of men, from the creation of Adam even down until the time that ye shall receive these things, and ponder it in your hearts."

Too frequently this verse is not quoted in connection with verse 4 and when it is quoted, it is often misinterpreted. Nonetheless, verse 3 is a key to understanding the full promise of Moroni 10:1–5. When analyzed thoroughly, this verse indicates that the honest seeker after truth must do two things:

1. Read the Book of Mormon. The words *these things* in verse 3 refer to the words *these records* in verse 2, the records from which our present Book of Mormon was translated.

2. "Ponder" the dealings of God with men as recorded in the Book of Mormon, and then compare them with the dealings of God with men as recorded in the Bible. Although the word *Bible* is not found in verse 3, Moroni indicates that the person should—"remember how merciful the Lord hath been unto the children of men, from the creation of Adam even down until the time that ye shall receive these things." The Bible contains a story of the Creation and the history of events from that time forward; however, an account of the Creation and subsequent happenings are *not* contained in the Book of Mormon. In fact, Moroni had earlier acknowledged that the Book of Mormon would not include this information. In explaining his abridgment of the book of Ether, Moroni wrote:

"And now I, Moroni . . . take mine account from the twenty and four plates which were found by the people of Limhi, which is called the Book of Ether.

"And as I suppose that the first part of this record, which speaks concerning the creation of the world, and also of Adam, and an account from that time even to the great tower, and whatsoever things transpired among the children of men until that time, is had among the Jews—

"Therefore *I do not write those things which transpired from the days of Adam until that time.*" (Ether 1:1–4; italics added.)

Thus, if a sincere person hasn't gained a testimony of the Book

19

of Mormon after reading it, he should—as Moroni seems to suggest here—read the Bible as well, pondering in his heart *both* scriptural accounts of God's dealings with his children.

Verse 4: "And when ye shall receive these things, I would exhort you that ye would ask God, the Eternal Father, in the name of Christ, if these things are not true; and if ye shall ask with a sincere heart, with real intent, having faith in Christ, he will manifest the truth of it unto you, by the power of the Holy Ghost."

Note that the word *read* is not even included in this verse; rather, the verb is *receive*. In other words, after the person has, first, read the Book of Mormon and, second, pondered the dealings of God with the peoples of the Book of Mormon and the Bible, he must then put himself in a frame of mind where he would be willing to "receive" or "accept" all these things. Then he must ask "with a sincere heart, with real intent, having faith in Christ." Sincere pondering of the scriptures helps put a person in an appropriate frame of mind to ask for—and receive—divine guidance.

The *things* we should be in a position to receive (accept) may refer not only to the Book of Mormon but also to everything mentioned in verses 2 and 3. Similarly, the word *it* near the end of verse 4 ("he will manifest the truth of *it* unto you") may refer to the process of God's dealing with men, along with referring to the Book of Mormon itself. In either case, if a person receives "the truth of *it*," he will believe in (accept) the Book of Mormon.

Verse 5: "And by the power of the Holy Ghost ye may know the truth of all things."

This verse indicates that the principles contained in the formula for learning truth as explained in verses 1 through 4 can also be applied to areas other than learning the truth of the Book of Mormon.

About whether this promise is Moroni's or the Lord's, we learn from Doctrine and Covenants 68:4:

"And whatsoever they [the Lord's chosen servants] shall speak when moved upon by the Holy Ghost shall be scripture, shall be the will of the Lord, shall be the mind of the Lord, shall be the word of the Lord, shall be the voice of the Lord, and the power of God unto salvation."

When Moroni "speaks" or writes by the power of the Holy Ghost, his writings represent the "will . . . mind . . . word . . . [and] voice of the Lord." Thus it is appropriate to say this promise comes *from* the Lord *through* the writings of Moroni.

When a person follows this divine formula, the results are certain: that person will gain a testimony of the Book of Mormon. God cannot and does not lie, and his promises made through his prophets are sure. Therefore, anyone who claims to have followed the various requirements but says he has not gained a testimony should check to see which step has not been followed faithfully or completely. The person should —

1. Read and ponder the Book of Mormon — all of it.

2. Remember the methods God has used in working with the peoples of both the Book of Mormon and the Bible — and ponder these things in his heart.

3. Put himself in a frame of mind to be willing to accept (receive) all of "these things" — the Book of Mormon, the Bible, and the way God works with his children.

4. Pray "with a sincere heart, with real intent, having faith in Christ," and "ask God, the Eternal Father, in the name of Jesus Christ, if these things are not true."

5. Be able to recognize the promptings and feelings that will be evidences to him of the truth of "these things" (including the Book of Mormon) as they are made manifest unto him "by the power of the Holy Ghost."

QA

Since the Book of Mormon is largely the record of a Hebrew people, is the writing characteristic of the Hebrew language?

John A. Tvedtnes, specialist in Near Eastern studies and former instructor at the Jerusalem Center for Near Eastern Studies

Nephi described the writing system of his people as a combination of "the learning of the Jews and the language of the Egyptians." (1 Nephi 1:2.) A thousand years later, Moroni recorded that his people still spoke Hebrew but that the plates were being written in a script called "reformed Egyptian." (See Mormon 9:32–34.) Years ago, Sidney B. Sperry, followed by other Latter-day Saint scholars, suggested that the Book of Mormon writers may have used this "reformed Egyptian" script as a sort of shorthand to record their modified Hebrew language.[1]

Although it is not presently entirely clear what the actual writing system of the Nephites was, a number of factors support the idea that the language from which Joseph Smith translated the Book of Mormon was, in fact, Hebrew, though recorded in a "reformed Egyptian" writing system.

Hebrew Idioms and Syntax

The Book of Mormon contains numerous idioms and syntax that are not typically English but that would be perfectly normal in a Hebrew setting. For example:

Construct state. In Hebrew a noun in construct state is immediately followed by another noun to which it bears a close grammatical relationship. We would say in Hebrew, for example, "altar stone." This construction is most accurately translated into English as "altar of stone," even though the normal English usage is "stone altar." The Book of Mormon frequently reflects the Hebrew construction in such expressions as "plates of brass/gold" (rather than "brass/gold plates") and "mist of darkness" (rather than "dark mist").

Prepositional phrases where English would prefer adverbs. Typically Hebrew are phrases in the Book of Mormon such as "with harshness" (rather than "harshly"), "with joy" (rather than "joyfully"), "with gladness" (rather than "gladly"), and "in diligence" (rather than "diligently").

Cognate accusative. A verb accompanied by a direct object derived from the same root is a common Hebrew idiom. Some examples are "I *dreamed* a *dream,*" "*cursed* with a sore *cursing*" (rather than "cursed sorely"), "*work* all manner of fine *work*" (rather than "work well"), and "*judge* righteous *judgment*" (rather than "judge righteously").[2]

Word-Play and Range of Meaning

Some passages of the Book of Mormon can be better understood in Hebrew than in English because the Hebrew reflects word-play or a range of meaning that gives more sense to the passage.

A classic example is found in 1 Nephi. Having arrived at a valley in the Arabian peninsula, Lehi named the valley after his son Lemuel, exhorting him to "be like unto this valley, *firm* and *steadfast, and immovable.*" (1 Nephi 2:10.) Lehi similarly named the valley's river after Laman, pleading that he might "be like unto this river, continually *running* into the fountain of all righteousness." (1 Nephi 2:9.)

One of the Hebrew words for "river," *nahar*, has a verbal root meaning "to flow." The Hebrew word *'eytan*, which means "valley," is actually an adjective meaning "perennial, ever-flowing, enduring, firm." Another word for "valley" is *'aphiq* (which actually means "a stream-bed or a ravine"), from the verb meaning "to be strong." It is possible that Lehi deliberately patterned his speech to reflect the meanings of these Hebrew words.

Many other passages in the Book of Mormon take on richer meaning if the passages are read as translations of Hebrew. For example, in 1 Nephi, we read that as Lehi "prayed unto the Lord, there came a pillar of fire and *dwelt* upon a rock before him." (1 Nephi 1:6; italics added.) Here, English usage would prefer the verb *sat* rather than *dwelt*. But the Hebrew verb, in fact, has *both* meanings.

Similarly, Nephi wrote of the wicked who "seek deep to hide their counsel(s) from the Lord." (2 Nephi 27:27; 28:9.) If Hebrew was indeed the language of the Book of Mormon, the Hebrew word here translated as "counsel" may have been *sod*, which can also mean "secret."

New Words

The Book of Mormon introduces a number of new words to the English language, including words for animals, monetary values, and even honeybees. A study has shown that many of these Nephite, Lamanite, and Mulekite names suggest a Hebrew origin.[3] In fact, a fair number of Nephite names appear to be Hebrew in form and would thus have valid meanings in that language. Of course, this is to be expected of those names that also appear in the Bible, such as Lehi, Jeremiah, or Isaiah. But it is the nonbiblical names that make the strongest case for a Hebrew background of the Nephite record.

For example, many Book of Mormon names end in *-i*, which in most cases probably serves as the Hebrew *nisbeh*, or gentilic suffix, rendered in English as "-ite." Thus, *Moroni* could be rendered "Moronite" — from the land of Moron known in the Book of Mormon. Similarly, *Lamoni* could be rendered "Lamanite," *Muloki* could be written "Mulekite," and *Amaleki* probably means "Amalekite."

Some other probable meanings of Nephite names read as Hebrew are as follows:

Mulek, Melek may mean "king" (Hebrew *melek*). That the son of Zedekiah, the last king of Judah, should be named Mulek, or "king," is significant. There is also a city/land named Mulek and another named Melek.

Zarahemla may mean "seed of compassion" (Hebrew *zera^c-hem-lah*).

Sariah may mean "princess of the Lord" (Hebrew *sar-yah*).

Nahom probably means "consolation, comfort" (Hebrew *nahum*). The Arabic cognate, or related word, means "sigh, moan,"[4] reminding us that this was the place of Ishmael's burial, where his daughters "did mourn exceedingly." (1 Nephi 16:35.)

Jershon may mean "place of inheritance" (Hebrew *yershon*). In Alma 27:22, we read that the Nephites gave the land of Jershon to the converted Lamanites "for an inheritance."

Ziff may quite possibly mean "splendor, brightness" (Hebrew *ziw*), from a Hebrew root meaning "to shine." Ziff is listed with silver, iron, brass, and copper—materials used by King Noah to ornament buildings. (See Mosiah 11:3, 8.) It is therefore likely a shiny metal, possibly a copper alloy.

Isaiah Variants

Large portions of the book of Isaiah are quoted by the Nephite scribes in the Book of Mormon. Where these agree with the King James Version of the Bible, we are inclined to believe that the Prophet Joseph Smith merely employed the language and text known to the people of his time. It is where these portions differ from those in the King James Version, however, that we find some of the best evidence for the authenticity of the Book of Mormon as an ancient Hebrew text.[5]

Of the 478 Isaiah verses quoted by the Nephite historians, more than 200 have a reading different from that in the King James Version. These differences support a Hebraic background for the Book of Mormon.

Use of abbreviations. Abbreviations appear to have been used by some scribes when copying biblical scrolls. Isaiah 2:6 is an example. The Masoretic Text begins with the Hebrew word *ky*, which means "therefore" and was evidently understood to be an abbreviation of *k"y*—used by some scribes and representing either *ky Y^cqb* ("therefore, O Jacob") or *ky Ysr'l* ("therefore, O Israel"), as reflected in versions of the Septuagint translation of that passage.

The parallel passage in the Book of Mormon (see 2 Nephi 12:6) may reflect the original intent, for it reads, "Therefore, O Lord" (Hebrew would read *ky Yhwh*). Note that the letters *k* and *y* (of the abbreviation postulated by scholars) are at the beginning of the two words in both the Isaiah and the Book of Mormon versions.

Accidental dropping of letters or words because of their dual occurrence in the text (haplography). A comparison of Isaiah variants shows how ancient biblical scribes could easily have dropped letters — and how the Book of Mormon restores sense to these passages. A good example is Isaiah 13:3 and its parallel passage in 2 Nephi 23:3.

King James Version:

"I have commanded my sanctified ones, I have also called my mighty ones, for mine anger, *even* them that rejoice in my highness."

Book of Mormon:

"I have commanded my sanctified ones, I have also called my mighty ones, for mine anger *is not upon* them that rejoice in my highness."

In the Masoretic Text, from which the King James Version of the Bible comes, the latter part of the verse reads: *l-'py ᶜlyzy g'wty,* which, literally translated, means "to/for mine anger, the rejoicers of my highness." In this example, both the King James Version and the Masoretic Text require clarification. It is likely that this is a case of double haplography, which can best be examined by comparing the Hebrew of the Masoretic Text with a Hebrew translation of the Book of Mormon:

Masoretic Text: *l-'py ᶜlyzy g'wty*

Book of Mormon: *l' 'py ᶜl ᶜlyzy g'wty*

Notice how the Book of Mormon translation reveals the two important deletions that the Masoretic scribe or a predecessor probably made: (1) the Hebrew letter *aleph* (here transliterated ') from the negative particle *l',* resulting in the preposition *l-,* and (2) the preposition ᶜl ("upon"). Both could easily have been deleted because of their proximity to identical letters in the text. (Such a mistake would probably have been made at an early stage, before the introduction of spaces to divide words in Hebrew.) Once again, a Hebrew origin for the language of the Book of Mormon makes sense.

Conclusions

A large body of research, published and unpublished, by numerous scholars provides abundant evidence for the ancient Near Eastern origin of the original text of the Book of Mormon. Although there is still some uncertainty about the actual writing system in which the text was recorded — probably because Hebrew is related to a number of other languages of Lehi's time (including Egyptian) that

25

display some of the same linguistic features[6] — a fair number of Latter-day Saint scholars think that the Nephite record evidences the book's Hebraic origin.

This modern research corroborates the Prophet Joseph Smith's testimony of the origins of the Book of Mormon and is all the more stunning because Joseph Smith had not received any training in Hebrew or its cognate languages at the time he translated the record.

Notes

1. *Our Book of Mormon* (Salt Lake City: Bookcraft, 1950), pp. 28–38. See also John A. Tvedtnes, *New Era*, May 1971, p. 19, an abbreviated version of "Linguistic Implications of the Tel Arad Ostraca," *Newsletter & Proceedings of the Society for Early Historic Archaelogy* (hereafter *NPSEHA*), Oct. 1971; John L. Sorenson, *An Ancient Setting for the Book of Mormon* (Salt Lake City: Deseret Book Co. and Foundation for Ancient Research and Mormon Studies [hereafter FARMS], 1985, pp. 74–78.)

2. For further examples, see John A. Tvedtnes, *BYU Studies*, Autumn 1970, pp. 50–60. See also Thomas W. Brookbank, *Improvement Era*, Dec. 1909-Apr. 1910, July-Oct. 1914, and Dec. 1914; Sidney B. Sperry, *Improvement Era*, Oct. 1954; E. Craig Bramwell, *Improvement Era*, July 1961; and M. Deloy Pack, "Possible Lexical Hebraisms in the Book of Mormon (words of Mormon-Moroni)," Master's thesis, Brigham Young University, 1973.

3. John A. Tvedtnes, "A Phonemic Analysis of Nephite and Jaredite Proper Names," *NPSEHA*, Dec. 1977. Reprints available from FARMS.

4. This fact was pointed out by Hugh Nibley in *Lehi in the Desert and the World of the Jaredites* (Salt Lake City: Bookcraft, 1952), p. 90. Dr. Nibley's writings on the ancient Near Eastern background of Book of Mormon names and idioms are too numerous to cite here. For more information, refer to the FARMS preliminary report by Gary P. Gillum and John W. Welch, "Comprehensive Bibliography of the Book of Mormon."

5. See John A. Tvedtnes, "Isaiah Variants in the Book of Mormon," in Monte S. Nyman, ed., *Isaiah and the Prophets* (Provo, Utah: Religious Studies Center, Brigham Young University, 1984). The author's exhaustive study, "The Isaiah Variants in the Book of Mormon," is circulated in photocopy form by FARMS.

6. Chiasmus, for example, is also a feature of Egyptian, Sumerian, Akkadian, and even Greek writings.

QA

What are the best evidences to support the authenticity of the Book of Mormon?

Ellis T. Rasmussen, professor emeritus of Religious Education at Brigham Young University

The best support for the authenticity of the Book of Mormon is the testimony of the Holy Spirit. In fact, the Lord has exhorted us to seek that witness not only of the Book of Mormon as a whole but also of its parts. When Moroni, the last author in the Book of Mormon, gave the promise of spiritual confirmation, he spoke especially of particulars:

"When ye shall receive *these things,* I would exhort you that ye would ask God, the Eternal Father, in the name of Christ, if *these* things are not true; and if ye shall ask with a sincere heart, with real intent, having faith in Christ, he will manifest the truth of it unto you, by the power of the Holy Ghost.

"And by the power of the Holy Ghost ye may know the truth of *all things."* (Moroni 10:4–5; italics added.)

The essence of the witness of the Holy Ghost is the witness of the book itself. Great concepts impressively written bear within them a witness of validity and divine origin more convincing than any clues that external evidences can provide, however helpful they may be. Such is the case with the Book of Mormon.

Attempts to prove or disprove the book's authenticity by focusing on Joseph Smith's description of how he obtained the gold plates, or on anthropological and archaeological evidence, though interesting, can be only marginally successful. Reconstructing history is difficult at best. The evidence is always incomplete—a clay inscription and a bit of pottery here, or a journal entry and a newspaper account there—so any picture that researchers develop will be, by nature, fragmentary. That picture will change as new information becomes available.

In contrast to the indecisive nature of external evidence, the Lord has provided a way to obtain decisive support for the book's authenticity: "the Spirit of truth . . . will guide [us] into all truth." (John 16:13.) This search is of necessity an individual matter. No matter how many millions have found the gospel and the scriptures true, and no matter how many people have joyfully lived the commandments, each new candidate must gain his own testimony. The Spirit's witness comes only after individual effort and sincere seeking.

God the Father has set up a system of witnesses for the Book of Mormon. The book openly claims that it is the word of God. Joseph Smith and eleven other witnesses also testified of the book. The Bible itself serves as a witness of the Book of Mormon, and to all this is added the witness of the Father himself through the Holy Ghost.

Furthermore, the individual parts of the ancient record — the doctrines, teachings, prophecies, and narratives — carry within themselves a spirit of authenticity. For me, this internal evidence, as corroborated by the witness of the Holy Spirit, has been most convincing. I have chosen seven key concepts that I feel are especially compelling:

The Book of Mormon authors intended to bring us to Christ. Nephi, the young prophetic author of the first books in the record, stated clearly that "the fulness of mine intent is that I may persuade men to come unto the God of Abraham, and the God of Isaac, and the God of Jacob, and be saved." (1 Nephi 6:4; see also 2 Nephi 26:33.)

Moroni, the last person who kept the record, wrote: "Again I would exhort you that ye would come unto Christ. . . . Yea, come unto Christ, and be perfected in him, and deny yourselves of all ungodliness." (Moroni 10:30, 32.)

Without a single exception, every prophet between these two teaches us about Christ in some way, and nearly every page of the book contains some reference to him. The overriding intention of the book fits fully the intention of authentic scripture.

Nephi teaches that the condescension of God — the gift of the Savior's ministry and the saving sacrifice of the Atonement — demonstrates God's love. In one revelation, an angel asked Nephi, "Knowest thou the condescension of God?" (1 Nephi 11:16.) One meaning of the word *condescension*, "patronizing someone," has a negative connotation, but the other meaning is positive: "to waive dignity or superiority voluntarily and assume equality with an inferior." (*Random House Dictionary of the English Language*, 1971 unabridged edition.)

To the angel's question, Nephi replied that he knew that God loved his children but that he didn't know the meaning of all things. He had just been shown in vision the town of Nazareth, and in it he had seen a beautiful virgin. After the angel's question, Nephi saw her again with a baby in her arms.

The angel identified the baby as the Lamb of God, the Son of the Eternal Father, proffering the gift of Jesus as evidence of the love of God. Then the angel declared, "Look and behold the condescension of God!" and Nephi saw the Redeemer of the world teaching the gospel and offering himself as a sacrifice. (See 1 Nephi 11:17–33.)

Eight chapters later, Nephi wrote again of Jesus' sacrifice: "The world, because of their iniquity, shall judge him to be a thing of naught; wherefore they scourge him, and he suffereth it. Yea, they spit upon him, and he suffereth it, because of his loving kindness and his long-suffering towards the children of men. . . .

"[He] yieldeth himself, according to the words of the angel, as a man, into the hands of wicked men, to be lifted up, according to the words of Zenock, and to be crucified, according to the words of Neum, and to be buried in a sepulchre, according to the words of Zenos." (1 Nephi 19:9–10.)

This is a moving statement of divine condescension, of how God lovingly came to earth and accepted persecution, crucifixion, and suffering so great he bled from every pore. The concept of God's condescension, unique to the Book of Mormon, is a powerful witness of the truth of the Book of Mormon.

The Book of Mormon identifies the roles of "the Holy Messiah." The Old Testament prophets spoke often of a divinely appointed future king, of a Davidic branch with great power, and of a suffering servant who would save Israel. Despite the many messianic prophecies, the use of different titles for the Messiah has caused confusion over who the Messiah was to be and what he was to do.

The Book of Mormon, however, is explicit about the name of the deliverer—Messiah and Christ are synonymous terms—and his work. Lehi, for example, taught his son Jacob that "redemption cometh in and through the Holy Messiah." He went on to talk of the Messiah's grace and truth, his sacrifice and mercy, and his intercession for all. (See 2 Nephi 2:6–10.)

In addition to this teaching, other Book of Mormon prophets discussed why Christ's sacrifice had to be infinite in its outreach (see 2 Nephi 9:7; 25:16); how man would always be subject to the devil—carnal, sensual, and devilish—without the Atonement (see 2 Nephi 9:8–9; Mosiah 16:3; Alma 42:9–10); and what relationship the Mosaic law has to the Atonement (see Mosiah 3:15).

These teachings clarify the role of the Messiah, and their insights bear within them the stamp of divine authenticity.

The Book of Mormon views the Bible as a great religious heritage from the Jews. The band of Lehi that fled Jerusalem took with them a copy of the Law and the Prophets on brass plates. So valuable was the record that they risked their lives to obtain it. Even 450 years after the time of Lehi, King Benjamin spoke of the importance of these plates containing Old Testament writings:

"I would that ye should remember that were it not for these plates, which contain these records and these commandments, we must have suffered in ignorance, even at this present time, not knowing the mysteries of God." (Mosiah 1:3.)

Nephi saw in vision the effect the Bible would have in the future. He saw that the Bible would "go forth from the Jews in purity unto the Gentiles, according to the truth which is in God" and that the record of his people and the Bible would verify each other and become established as one. (See 1 Nephi 13:25, 40–41.)

At a later time, Nephi prophesied that most would not acknowledge or thank the Jews for their record:

"What thank they the Jews for the Bible which they receive from them? . . . Do they remember the travails, and the labors, and the pains of the Jews, and their diligence unto me, in bringing forth salvation unto the Gentiles?

"O ye Gentiles, have ye remembered the Jews, mine ancient covenant people? Nay; but ye have cursed them, and have hated them, and have not sought to recover them." (2 Nephi 29:4–5.)

These are but a few samples from the Book of Mormon on the worth of the Bible, a theme whose validity rings true and which can easily be tested.

The Book of Mormon prophesies of its role as a companion witness with the Bible. When the Book of Mormon was first published in 1830, it boldly declared on its title page that its purpose was "the convincing of the Jew and Gentile that Jesus is the Christ, the Eternal God, manifesting himself unto all nations." Many felt then that the claim was presumptuous, yet the millions of readers who have since believed in Christ because of the Book of Mormon have proved that the purpose was valid.

The role of the Book of Mormon as a companion witness of Christ was explained to Nephi by an angel. Nephi learned that the scriptures of his descendants would "come forth unto the Gentiles, by the gift and power of the Lamb. . . .

"And the words of the Lamb shall be made known in the records of [Nephi's] seed, as well as in the records of the twelve apostles of the Lamb; wherefore they both shall be established in one." (1 Nephi 13:35, 41.)

The Book of Mormon performs a complementary role with that of the Bible, declaring that the "whole meaning of the law of Moses" is to point our souls to Christ, our divine Redeemer. (See Alma 34:13–14.)

In our day, when billions of people do not know the gospel of the Lamb of God, and when many doubt the Bible and the divinity of Jesus, a second witness of the Savior is sorely needed so mankind can know the truth and obtain the blessings of the gospel. This witness is provided by the Book of Mormon and serves as one more mark of its truth and authenticity.

The Book of Mormon is full of valuable warnings and admonitions about the last days. Oftentimes the warnings in the Book of Mormon are more detailed and clear than those in the Bible. One example is a warning in 2 Nephi 27, the Book of Mormon rendering of Isaiah 29. Many readers of Isaiah 29 have difficulty understanding who is being warned and what the warning is. Nephi's account, however, is a clear warning to the people who fight against Zion—the people of the Lord in the last days. It follows a chiastic realignment of phrasing:

a "In the last days . . . all the nations of the Gentiles and also the Jews . . . will be drunken with iniquity and all manner of abominations.

b "They shall be visited of the Lord of Hosts" with great catastrophes.

c "All nations that fight against Zion . . . shall be as a dream of a night vision; . . . even as unto a hungry man which dreameth, and behold he eateth but he awaketh and his soul is empty.

c¹ "Or like unto a thirsty man which dreameth, and behold he drinketh but he awaketh and behold he is faint . . . ; yea, even so shall . . . the nations be that fight against Mount Zion.

b¹ "All ye that doeth iniquity, stay yourselves and wonder, for ye shall cry out, and cry" [apparently because of the catastrophes].

a¹ "Ye shall be drunken but not with wine, ye shall stagger but not with strong drink." (2 Nephi 27:1–4.)

Through study and prayer, a critical reader may test such statements of warning and admonition. In this area of scripture, too, the Book of Mormon bears witness that it is valid, valuable, realistic, and authentic.

The authors of the Book of Mormon were deeply concerned with the welfare of individual souls. The word *soul* in the Book of Mormon most

31

frequently denotes the eternal self. Worship centers in the soul, and the devil seeks to cheat the souls of men. If one yields to the devil, it is the soul that is racked with torment until repentance takes place. When communication comes from heaven, it pierces the very souls of men and women.

In his farewell address, Nephi urged his people to adopt a way of life that will be good for the welfare of their souls: "I say unto you that ye must pray always, and not faint; that ye must not perform any thing unto the Lord save in the first place ye shall pray unto the Father in the name of Christ, that he will consecrate thy performance unto thee, that thy performance may be for *the welfare of thy soul.*" (2 Nephi 32:9; italics added.)

These seven topics are taken almost wholly from the books of Nephi. There are many more, as the following list illustrates:

From the book of Jacob:
On the matter of seeking riches. (See Jacob 2:17–19.)
On the dangers of sin and spiritual indifference. (See Jacob 3:11.)
On prophetic Christianity. (See Jacob 4:4–5.)

From the book of Enos:
On the quest for salvation. (See Enos 1:1–6.)
On having hope in Christ. (See Enos 1:27.)

From the book of Mosiah:
On the Law and the gospel, types and redemption. (See Mosiah 13:27–35.)
On understanding prophecy. (See Mosiah 15:5–13, on Isaiah 53:7–10; Mosiah 15:14–18, on Isaiah 52:7.)
On losing the boon of redemption. (See Mosiah 16:5.)

From the book of Alma:
On the saving power of pure testimony. (See Alma 4:19.)
On being spiritually born of God. (See Alma 5:14–40; 36:1–30.)
On gaining more or losing all revelation. (See Alma 12:9–11.)
On Melchizedek, the missionary king, and his priesthood. (See Alma 13:1–19.)
On the Lord's revelations to other nations. (See Alma 29:4–8.)
On death, the spirit world, and resurrection. (See Alma 40–42.)

From the book of 3 Nephi:
On the blessings in the Beatitudes. (See 3 Nephi 12.)
On the essence of "the gospel." (See 3 Nephi 27:13–21.)

From the book of 4 Nephi:
On the effects of the gospel on a whole community. (See 4 Nephi 1:10–18.)

From the book of Mormon:
On the effects of apostasy on a community. (See Mormon 6:16–22; 8:33–41.)

From the book of Ether and the book of Moroni:
On the powers of faith. (See Ether 12; Moroni 7:21–48.)

These points are only a brief sampling of the internal evidences that the Book of Mormon is true and authentic scripture. But the real burden of proof of its authenticity lies with each reader. In each instance of doctrine, in each narrative passage, in each great personality of the Book of Mormon, the Lord has challenged us to ask the Father in the name of Christ whether these things are true, and he will manifest the truth unto us by the power of the Holy Ghost.

QA

Why have changes been made in the printed editions of the Book of Mormon?

Robert J. Matthews, dean, Religious Education, Brigham Young University

Changes and corrections have been necessary to correct copying and printing errors and to clarify the message of this book of scripture. Corrections of this sort are normal whenever new editions of a book are printed. Mistakes such as typographical errors, misspellings, misplaced or dropped words, and ambiguities noted in one edition are usually corrected in the next. Errors like these multiply when one language is translated into another. And if the source of the communication is divine revelation, the process becomes even more complex.

The Prophet Joseph Smith and Sidney Rigdon, for example, said they saw and heard things they could not communicate in the language they had:

"Great and marvelous are the works of the Lord, and the mysteries of his kingdom which he showed unto us, which surpass all understanding in glory, and in might, and in dominion;

"Which he commanded us we should not write while we were

yet in the Spirit, and are not lawful for man to utter;

"Neither is man capable to make them known, for they are only to be seen and understood by the power of the Holy Spirit, which God bestows on those who love him, and purify themselves before him." (D&C 76:114–16.)

President John Taylor told of an occasion when he and the Prophet Joseph Smith were discussing the second coming of the Savior and the role of various prophets who held priesthood keys: "He wished me to write something for him on this subject, but I found it a very difficult thing to do. He had to correct me several times. . . . It is very difficult to find language suitable to convey the meaning of spiritual things." (*Journal of Discourses*, 18:330.) President Taylor was a man of considerable intelligence, very gifted in the use of language. His discourse and writing flowed smoothly and clearly, but he experienced, as have others, the difficulty mortals have when they attempt to write the things of God.

The Prophet Joseph Smith was well aware of this problem. During his lifetime, three editions of the Book of Mormon were printed. Each time, he amended the text in a few places to more correctly convey the intended meaning of his translation. Other changes in these and successive editions were made to correct typographical errors, improper spelling, and inaccurate or missing punctuation and to improve grammar and sentence structure to eliminate ambiguity. None of these changes, individually or collectively, alters the message of the Book of Mormon.[1]

Let us survey the corrective literary process that took place from the original translation of the gold plates by the Prophet Joseph Smith to the printing of the various editions. Here we will deal particularly with changes in the original manuscript, in the handwritten copy of the original, and in the printed editions of 1830, 1837, 1840, and 1981.[2] The first three editions are especially valuable because they were printed during the Prophet Joseph Smith's lifetime; some copies contain his editorial comments.

Corrections took place at every stage—while transcribing and editing the original manuscript, while copying the manuscript, and while setting type from that manuscript. As each edition was prepared for printing, the errors that had been noted in the preceding edition or editions were corrected.

The Book of Mormon Documents

The Prophet Joseph Smith did not leave us a detailed account of the daily translation process of the Book of Mormon but said it was accomplished through the "mercy of God, by the power of God." (D&C 1:29.) His usual procedure was to dictate to a scribe while he translated from the plates. Oliver Cowdery was the principal scribe and was assisted by Martin Harris, Emma Smith, probably John Whitmer, and an additional unidentified person. The words on the manuscript were essentially the Prophet's, but each scribe wrote them down in his or her own spelling variations.

Spelling was not as standardized in those days as it is now, and many felt at liberty to vary the way they formed words.[3] For example, in what is now 1 Nephi 7:20, *ware sorraful* in the manuscript was changed to *were sorrowful* in the first printed edition. *Plaits* in the manuscript (1 Nephi 13:23) became *plates* in the printed edition. These and similar changes show why editing was necessary to make the manuscript more understandable.

The document these several scribes produced as they wrote at the Prophet's dictation is the original manuscript of the Book of Mormon in English translation. It was completed about 1 July 1829.

Then Oliver Cowdery was directed by the Prophet to make a second copy. This he did, writing most, but not all, of it himself. This manuscript is called the "printer's" or "emended" manuscript. It was made before any printing was attempted.

The original manuscript has not survived intact; it became water-soaked while stored in the cornerstone of the Nauvoo House, and about two-thirds of it rotted away. The 144 remaining pages, in the Church vaults in Salt Lake City, contain most of 1 Nephi; a portion of 2 Nephi 1; portions of Alma 11 and 19; Alma 22–63; parts of Helaman 1–3; and part of 3 Nephi 26.[4] The printer's manuscript, on the other hand, is in good condition. It is a part of the collection of the Reorganized Church of Jesus Christ of Latter Day Saints in Independence, Missouri.

As one might expect, any handwritten copy will differ in some ways from its original. The printer's manuscript of the Book of Mormon differed from the original for two principal reasons. First, unintentional variations are impossible to avoid in a transcription of 464 pages. Second, there is evidence of some deliberate editing, such as smoothing out phrases, substituting one word for another, correcting spelling errors, adding of punctuation, and other intended improvements. It was this "emended" manuscript that was taken to the printer for typesetting for the first edition of the Book of Mormon.

Printed Editions

The first edition of the Book of Mormon was printed in 1830 in Palmyra, New York, by the E. B. Grandin Company. The principal typesetter and compositor was John H. Gilbert, who also provided most of the punctuation and paragraphing. Production was slow and fraught with the possibility of making errors, both of sight and of judgment. A comparison of first edition copies shows that corrections were made even during the press run, a practice common in those days.[5]

Seven years later, the second edition—a minor revision—of the Book of Mormon was printed in Kirtland, Ohio, by O. Cowdery and Company for P. P. Pratt and J. Goodson. Brothers Pratt and Goodson served as editors and caretakers and made the following explanation about the efforts of the Prophet Joseph Smith and Oliver Cowdery to prepare this revised edition (spelling and punctuation are original):

"Individuals acquainted with book printing, are aware of the numerous typographical errors which always occur in manuscript editions. It is only necessary to say, that the whole has been carefully reexamined and compared with the original manuscripts, by elder Joseph Smith, Jr. the translator of the book of Mormon, assisted by the present printer, brother O. Cowdery, who formerly wrote the greatest portion of the same, as dictated by brother Smith.

"Parley P. Pratt,

"John Goodson

"Kirtland, Ohio 1837."

In 1840, the third edition was printed in Nauvoo, Illinois, by Ebenezer Robinson and Don Carlos Smith. Here the title page notes that this edition has been "Carefully Revised by the Translator," again letting the reader know that the Prophet Joseph Smith was directly involved with the editorial changes in both this edition and its 1830 and 1837 predecessors.

Over the next 140 years, various other editions containing adjustments and refinements were published, resulting in considerable format change but not in many textual revisions. Then, in 1981, the Church published an edition with approximately 160 corrections. Although most are grammar and spelling improvements, several significant corrections and additions to the text were made. A detailed account of these corrections may be found in the *Ensign* (Sept. 1976, pp. 77–82; Oct. 1981, pp. 8–19) and in *BYU Studies* (Fall 1982, pp. 387–423). Two examples follow.

In Alma 16:5 two words sound similar, but the spelling is slightly different, and the meaning is vastly different. The Lamanites had taken Nephite prisoners of war. Zoram, chief Nephite army captain, went to Alma the prophet and asked him to inquire of the Lord concerning the prisoners. Until 1981, all printed editions read, "therefore they went unto him to know *whether* the Lord would that they should go . . . in search of their brethren." (Italics added.) The original manuscript reads *whither* rather than *whether,* and it was corrected to read so in the 1981 version. For years the interpretation had been whether (if) the Nephites should go in search of their brethren. The true meaning is, rather, *whither* (where) they should go. The printer's manuscript contains a rather awkward correction from *whether* to *whither,* showing that this had been discovered long ago, but the correction was not assimilated into the scripture until the 1981 edition.

An interesting correction has been made in Alma 57:25, which deals with the remarkable preservation of 2060 young soldiers: "And to our great astonishment, and also the *joy* of our whole army, there was not one soul of them who did perish." Until 1981, all editions of the Book of Mormon read *foes;* however, careful examination of the printer's manuscript shows that the correct word is *joy.* The error occurred in earlier editions because the handwriting on the manuscript is peculiarly formed at this point, and typesetters and proofreaders simply misread it. The word *foes* does make sense as used in the passage, but it is not as appropriate as *joy.*

Editing Bible Texts

The same kind of editorial effort that has been exerted to correct and refine the Book of Mormon over the past 158 years has been occurring for centuries with the Bible. Students familiar with biblical research know that the reason there are several versions of the Bible in print today is that there are literally thousands of biblical manuscripts available, none of them originals, and all differ in various ways. They are grouped in "families" because they appear to come from several major textual ancestors. Hence, the Catholic Vulgate Bible represents a different textual lineage than the New English Bible. The King James Version represents still another.

Typographical errors have occurred in many editions of the Bible, especially in the sixteenth, seventeenth, and eighteenth centuries, when typesetting was done by hand. Since the first printing of the King James Version in A.D. 1611, many revisions and modifications have been made by British scholars. This process has resulted in an increasing number of words being set in italics, which indicates an editorial attempt to enlarge or round out a thought that was poorly expressed in the manuscripts or was difficult to translate exactly. Readers of today's King James Version may think that it is an exact duplicate of what was printed 375 years ago, but it is not. The number of italicized words in Matthew alone increased from 43 in 1611 to 583 in 1870 because of revisions to the text.[6]

It is no secret that many changes and omissions occurred during the development of modern Bible texts. This creates a particularly serious situation because neither the originals nor even a complete second- or third-generation document of the Bible is available for comparison. In this respect, the text of the Book of Mormon is on a much stronger footing because the entire printer's manuscript is available as well as parts of the original dictated manuscript and the 1837 and 1840 editions, which were revised by the translator himself. Because comparison with these early versions was possible, the 1981 edition of the Book of Mormon is the most correct ever published by the Church.

Notes

1. Several individuals have sought out with great care the variants that exist among the printed editions of the Book of Mormon, and some have also made comparison with the prepublication manuscripts. These studies have shown that most of the changes have been grammatical, punctuational, and explanatory, but not substantive.

2. Readers wishing to know more will find the following documents informative: Jeffrey R. Holland, "An Analysis of Selected Changes in Major Editions of the Book of Mormon — 1830–1920," Master's thesis, Brigham Young University, 1966; Stanley R. Larson, "A Study of Some Textual Variations in the Book of Mormon Comparing the Original and Printer's Manuscripts and the 1830, the 1837, and the 1840 Editions," Master's thesis, Brigham Young University, 1974; Richard P. Howard, *Restoration Scriptures: A Study of Their Textual Development* (Independence, Mo.: Herald Publishing House, 1969); Daniel H. Ludlow, "Selected Changes in the Book of Mormon Since the First Edition," Special Collections, Brigham Young University Library, n.d.; Dean C. Jessee, "The Original Book of Mormon Manuscript," *BYU Studies*, Spring 1970, pp. 259–78.

3. For an interesting discussion of the varieties of spelling that were common and even acceptable in the period immediately preceding Joseph Smith's time, see George A. Horton, Jr., "Changes in the Book of Mormon

and How to Handle Them," report of the Sixth Annual Church Educational System Religious Educators' Symposium on the Book of Mormon, Aug. 1982, pp. 36–39.

4. Jessee, "Original Book of Mormon Manuscript," pp. 259–78.

5. For an informative discussion on this matter, see Janet Jenson, "Variations between Copies of the First Edition of the Book of Mormon," *BYU Studies,* Winter 1973, pp. 214–22.

6. P. Marion Simms, *The Bible in America* (New York: Wilson-Erickson, 1936), p. 97.

QA

Did Oliver Cowdery, one of the three special witnesses of the Book of Mormon, express doubt about his testimony?

Richard Lloyd Anderson, professor of ancient scripture, Brigham Young University

Oliver Cowdery's strong testimony of the Book of Mormon is well documented throughout his life, and his decisive return to the Church before he died backs up his words.

In 1838 Oliver challenged the Prophet Joseph Smith's leadership and spent the next ten years out of the Church. But in 1848 he returned to Kanesville, Iowa, the base camp of Mormon migration, and wintered in Richmond, Missouri, where his health failed. He was unable to fulfill his desire to go west with the Saints, and he died in Richmond in early 1850.

Two people who knew Oliver Cowdery best were his wife, Elizabeth Ann Whitmer, and her brother David Whitmer, also a Book of Mormon witness. David took pride in his role as the last survivor of the three witnesses, and in 1887, a year before his death, he reiterated his testimony:

"I also testify to the world, that neither Oliver Cowdery or Martin Harris ever at any time denied their testimony. . . . I was present at the death bed of Oliver Cowdery, and his last words were, *'Brother David, be true to your testimony to the Book of Mormon.' "*[1]

Elizabeth first got acquainted with Oliver at her house in 1829, while the Book of Mormon was being translated there. After their 1832 marriage, she was with him constantly, except for temporary separations because of Church assignments. She later reviewed his testimony:

"He always without one doubt or shadow of turning affirmed the divinity and truth of the Book of Mormon."[2]

These plain summaries of Oliver Cowdery's views really settle the matter, since they come from those with firsthand, intimate knowledge.

Nevertheless, the importance of "the second elder" (D&C 20:3) has stimulated vicious attempts to neutralize his powerful support of the Restoration. Besides seeing an angel and the plates from which the Book of Mormon was translated, Oliver was with Joseph Smith when John the Baptist and later Peter, James, and John restored the Aaronic and the Melchizedek priesthood. Evidently some have wanted a Cowdery denial enough to invent two documents that contradict history.

A dozen major archives in the United States have a strange typescript headed "A Confession of Oliver Overstreet," in which the above-named character claims that he was bribed to impersonate Oliver Cowdery in a return to the Church. That claim is fairly easy to dismiss, for if it were so, the whereabouts of the real Oliver Cowdery could be traced somewhere else. But some two dozen Latter-day Saints, half of them Oliver's former close friends, detail his return in their journals and in the Church's official minute books. Moreover, sale of Oliver's Wisconsin property before he returned appears in recorded deeds.

There is also a problem with the Oliver Overstreet manuscript itself. An important clue in identifying spurious documents is the vagueness of a document's origin—the impossibility of going past a late copy to an original from a known person. And the Overstreet document exists in a late typescript with no hint of who generated it.

Similar faults appear in a better-known historical forgery claiming to come from Oliver Cowdery the year after he left the Church. In 1906 the "mountain evangelist" R. B. Neal, a leader in the American Anti-Mormon Association, published a document with much fanfare but without evidence of the document's authenticity. Reverend Neal claimed that the publication was a reprint of an 1839 document explaining Oliver Cowdery's apostasy: *Defence in a Rehearsal of My Grounds for Separating Myself from the Latter Day Saints.*[3]

"No more important document has been unearthed since I have been engaged in this warfare," R. B. Neal asserted.[4]

With such convictions, we can be sure that Reverend Neal would have produced evidence if he could have proved that the original actually existed. But all we have is his 1906 first printing, which is silent about why no one had ever heard of the document until a half century after Oliver Cowdery's death.

The introduction simply puffs, "This real and original 'Defence' is a 'rare find,' and should be speedily sent on its mission to the thousands already deluded."[5]

Informed historians, however, are more skeptical. The standard bibliography of Mormon-related works first notes that Reverend Neal's 1906 tract is "the version from which all copies have been taken," and then conservatively adds, "whether the pamphlet ever existed is doubtful."[6]

The second half of the *Defence* is built on a supposed vision of Christ to Oliver, in which Oliver was told, "Thou shalt withdraw thyself from among them."[7] If such an event took place, why did the Second Elder violate divine instruction and return to the Church afterward?

Nothing is said about the angel and the gold plates, but the *Defence* challenges the restored priesthood, "about which," the pamphlet's author writes, "I am beginning to doubt." One reason is that John the Baptist's voice "did most mysteriously resemble the voice of Elder Sidney Rigdon."[8] Such words were apparently written by someone pushing the theory that Rigdon was the brain behind Book of Mormon work in 1829, but he always insisted that he never knew about Joseph Smith until the missionaries came to his Ohio home the next year.

Predictably, none of the twenty Cowdery letters from the period of his apostasy express such doubts. For instance, Oliver's spirited resignation letter to his high council court closed by saying that he questioned Church government only, not its spiritual foundations.[9] Indeed, a private letter during his estrangement speaks feelingly of the responsibility he felt after standing "in the presence of John, with our departed brother Joseph . . . and in the presence of Peter."[10]

Moreover, the 1906 tract falls into a major historical trap by paralleling mistakes David Whitmer made in his 1887 *An Address to All Believers in Christ,* written after Oliver's death. In doing so, the *Defence* identifies Whitmer's *Address* as one of its probable sources of information.

David, the witness who never returned to the Church, justified

41

his view of Joseph Smith as a fallen prophet by remembering a revelation in the winter of 1829–30 that authorized Oliver Cowdery and Hyrum Page to "go to Toronto, Canada, and . . . sell the copyright of the Book of Mormon" for that country.[11]

The revelation and trip did occur, but David, in remembering them fifty-seven years later, missed several important details. We know this because Hyrum Page outlined what happened only eighteen years afterward, a firsthand source because he went on the journey with Oliver, whereas David did not. Hyrum Page clarifies that the revelation instructed the brethren to sell Canadian rights to purchasers "if they would not harden their hearts," making clear the conditional command.[12]

The most glaring mistake perpetrated in the *Defence* is the true destination, for Hyrum Page says that "we were to go to Kingston," and he relates that they did.[13] Thus, in real life, Oliver Cowdery went to a location 150 miles away from Toronto, the place that David Whitmer erroneously mentioned in his address. Yet the *Defence* mistakenly has Oliver Cowdery say that the "revelation . . . sent Bro. Page and me so unwisely to . . . Toronto."[14]

Before the microfilm-photocopy era, which has made in-depth local history possible, the 1906 pamphlet was often accepted as legitimate, even by Latter-day Saint historians. Now, however, with modern methods of verification, the pseudo-Cowdery *Defence* fails every specific test that a genealogist or historian can set up. Following are four examples, presented in a question-answer format to highlight issues:

Q. Doesn't the *Defence* sound like Oliver Cowdery's prose?

A. It sounds too much like Oliver Cowdery. More than fifty striking phrases and sentences match passages from eight letters of his that appeared in the *Messenger and Advocate* during 1834 and 1835. A full 35 percent of the *Defence* is word for word what was first recorded in these published letters. Yet the hundred or so letters and editorials that exist from the Second Elder show a creative style that never mechanically repeats elements from earlier writing.

Q. Could not the original manuscript and all 1839 copies of the *Defence* have accidentally perished?

A. That would be odd, since the 1906 pamphlet, if it were authentic, would have to have been published from an earlier document, which R. B. Neal never produced. Furthermore, the *Defence* states that its purpose is to explain Cowdery's position to Latter-day Saints. Even if all copies had perished by 1906, the Saints living during the mid to late 1800s would have been aware of the work, but no one recorded such an awareness.

In Oliver's lifetime, Latter-day Saint journalists noticed major publications against the faith and refuted them, as in the cases of the attacks of E. D. Howe in 1834 or John C. Bennett in 1842. But the early Nauvoo press did not mention any printed attack from Oliver Cowdery. Instead, the year after the supposed 1839 pamphlet, Church editors who had worked with Cowdery at the Kirtland press reprinted several of Oliver's letters in the *Messenger and Advocate*. The editors announced that the letters answered the questions of "the coming forth of the Book of Mormon . . . and the restoration of the Priesthood . . . from the pen of a living witness."[15]

Q. Would not Church officials, when Oliver returned to the Church, suppress mention of his early opposition?

A. Actually, the opposite is the case. Three sets of minutes at Kanesville in 1848 show that Oliver was examined carefully to see whether he really supported the mission of Joseph Smith. William E. McLellin had published a letter of Oliver Cowdery to David Whitmer, implying that Oliver held keys higher than those of the Twelve, and Oliver was questioned on his motives in that matter. If Oliver had really written the *Defence,* Church leaders would have at least asked him about it to clarify his worthiness to be rebaptized.

Q. The *Defence* claims that it was printed at Pressley's Job Office, Norton, Ohio. Does this detail check out?

A. Ohio experts know of no such press, and gazetteers of the time indicate that the village of Norton in Delaware County was too small to have a press. There was a Norton township some thirty-five miles from Kirtland, but townships are merely geographical jurisdictions, like small counties, and are rarely given as places of publication.

My book *Investigating the Book of Mormon Witnesses* gives some other statements that opponents of the Church have used to throw doubt on Oliver's testimony.[16] One is an 1841 poem by Joel H. Johnson, making the point that God's revelations are true no matter who opposes them:

> Or prove the gospel was not true
>   Because old Paul the Saints could kill?
> Because the Jews its author slew,
>   And now reject their Saviour still? . . .

Or Book of Mormon not his word
Because denied by Oliver?[17]

The poem is a secondary comment, not a primary source. It is rhetoric, not history. To qualify for the latter, it would have to be based on demonstrable knowledge Joel Johnson had of Oliver outside the Church, which it is not. Johnson may simply have meant that Oliver had withdrawn from the Church and did not then stand openly for the ancient record.

Attacks on Oliver Cowdery typically add a statement by Brigham Young, although it clearly was not intended to refer to Oliver. President Young said that "some of the witnesses of the Book of Mormon" had received visitations but were yet "left to doubt and to disbelieve that they had ever seen an angel."[18] President Young then followed with an example of "one of the Quorum of the Twelve" of his day. His description fits none of the Three Witnesses, particularly not Oliver Cowdery. Indeed, on another occasion Brigham Young expressly declared, "Oliver Cowdery . . . never denied the Book of Mormon, not even in the wickedest days he ever saw, and came back into the Church before he died."[19]

When Oliver returned to the Saints, and as he approached the last year of his life, he reiterated his witness of the plates and the priesthood—the same testimony that he had held since the beginning of the Restoration:

"I beheld with my eyes, and handled with my hands, the gold plates. . . . I was present with Joseph when an holy angel . . . conferred, or restored, the Aaronic Priesthood. . . . I was also present with Joseph when the Melchisedek Priesthood was conferred by the holy angels of God."[20]

Notes

1. David Whitmer, *An Address to All Believers in Christ* (Richmond, Mo.: David Whitmer, 1887), p. 8.

2. Elizabeth Cowdery to David Whitmer, 8 March 1887, published in the religious periodical *The Return* 3, no. 5 (Dec. 1892): 7. I have changed *shudder* to *shadow,* the probable reading of the original.

3. R. B. Neal, *Oliver Cowdery's Defence and Renunciation, Anti-Mormon Tracts, No. 9* (Ashland, Ky.: Independent Publishing Co., 1906), p. 3.

4. R. B. Neal, *Oliver Cowdery's Defence; "Sword of Laban" Leaflets, No. 11* (n.p., n.d.), p. 1.

5. Neal, *Defence and Renunciation,* p. 2.

6. Chad J. Flake, *A Mormon Bibliography, 1830–1930* (Salt Lake City: University of Utah Press, 1978), p. 455 (entry 5744) and p. 182 (entry 2544).

7. Neal, *Defence and Renunciation*, p. 7.

8. Ibid., pp. 4–5.

9. Joseph Smith, *History of the Church*, 7 vols., 2d ed. rev., ed. B. H. Roberts (Salt Lake City, Utah: The Church of Jesus Christ of Latter-day Saints, 1932–51), 3:18; passage reproduced from the *Far West Record.*

10. Oliver Cowdery to Phineas Young, 23 March 1846, Tiffin, Ohio, original at Archives of The Church of Jesus Christ of Latter-day Saints, Salt Lake City, Utah. For a photo of this letter, see Richard L. Anderson, *Improvement Era*, Sept. 1968, pp. 15–24.

11. Whitmer, *Address*, p. 31.

12. Hyrum Page to William McLellin, 2 February 1848, Fishing River, Mo., original at Archives of the Reorganized Church of Jesus Christ of Latter Day Saints, Independence, Missouri.

13. Ibid.

14. Neal, *Defence and Renunciation*, p. 5.

15. *Times and Seasons* 2 (1 Nov. 1840): 204, ed. Ebenezer Robinson and Don Carlos Smith.

16. See Richard Lloyd Anderson, "The Case against the Witnesses" (chap. 11), *Investigating the Book of Mormon Witnesses* (Salt Lake City: Deseret Book Co., 1981).

17. *Times and Seasons* 2 (15 July 1841): 482. See also Anderson, *Book of Mormon Witnesses*, pp. 153–55.

18. In *Journal of Discourses*, 26 vols. (London: Latter-day Saints' Book Depot, 1855–86), 7:164. See also Anderson, *Book of Mormon Witnesses*, pp. 161–63.

19. In *Journal of Discourses*, 2:257–58.

20. Journal of Reuben Miller, 21 October 1848, Archives of The Church of Jesus Christ of Latter-day Saints, Salt Lake City, Utah. See also Richard Anderson, "Reuben Miller, Recorder of Oliver Cowdery's Reaffirmations," *BYU Studies* 8 (Spring 1968): 277–93.

QA

What is the meaning of the Book of Mormon passages on eternal hell for the wicked?

H. Donl Peterson, professor of ancient scripture, Brigham Young University

In the Book of Mormon, "hell" is the destination of the wicked following death. Among these are "the wise, and the learned, and the rich, that are puffed up in the pride of their hearts, and all those who preach false doctrines, and all those who commit whore-doms, and pervert the right way of the Lord." (2 Nephi 28:15; see also 2 Nephi 9:34, 36; Luke 16:19–25.) Matthew indicated that hell awaits those who habitually turn away from their fellowmen in need. (See Matthew 25:40–46.)

Nephi called hell "spiritual death" (2 Nephi 9:12), a place where the wicked are "cast off . . . as to the things which are spiritual, which are pertaining to righteousness. . . . Wherefore there must needs be a place of filthiness prepared for that which is filthy." (1 Nephi 15:33–34.)

Two Hells

The prophet Alma explained that the wicked "shall be cast out into outer darkness; there shall be weeping, and wailing, and gnashing of teeth, and this because of their own iniquity, being led captive by the will of the devil." (Alma 40:13.)

On the other hand, "the spirits of those who are righteous are received into a state of happiness, which is called paradise, a state of rest, a state of peace, where they shall rest from all their troubles and from all care, and sorrow." (Alma 40:12.)

These statements may seem to reflect the traditional Christian view of heaven and hell. (See Matthew 13:36–43.) But the Book of Mormon takes us a step farther. It describes these conditions as being, for most of mankind, temporary. Alma, for example, stated: "Now this is the state of the souls of the wicked, yea, in darkness, and a state of awful, fearful looking for the fiery indignation of the wrath of God upon them; thus they remain in this state, as well as the righteous in paradise, *until the time of their resurrection.*" (Alma 40:14; italics added.)

The Bible alludes to that fact in a number of places. David was promised that his soul would not remain in hell (see Psalm 16:10; Acts 2:27, 31), and it was promised that others would be delivered from spirit prison (see Isaiah 49:8–9; John 5:25). This, in fact, happened when Christ opened the doors of hell to missionary work among the dead. (See 1 Peter 3:18–19; 4:6; D&C 138:6–37.)

Those who hear and accept the message of salvation, whether in this life or in the spirit world, are raised "unto the resurrection of life; and they that have done evil, unto the resurrection of damnation." (John 5:29.) At their resurrection, Nephi explained, all people "must appear before the judgment seat of the Holy One of Israel;

and then . . . must they be judged according to the holy judgment of God.

"And assuredly, as the Lord liveth, for the Lord God hath spoken it, . . . that they who are righteous shall be righteous still, and they who are filthy shall be filthy still; wherefore, they who are filthy are the devil and his angels; and they shall go away into everlasting fire, prepared for them; and their torment is as a lake of fire and brimstone, whose flame ascendeth up forever and ever and has no end." (2 Nephi 9:15–16; see also Revelation 22:11.)

In the Book of Mormon, as in the Bible, two distinct states are referred to as "hell." One is the temporary condition of the wicked between death and the resurrection. The other is the never-ending state of the wicked for whom there is no mercy because they, "like unto the son of perdition" (3 Nephi 29:7; John 17:12), have rejected the mercy of Christ and would sell him "for silver and for gold, and for that which moth doth corrupt" (3 Nephi 27:32). These are they, called perdition and the sons of perdition, who come out "in open rebellion against God" and who "listeth to obey the evil spirit, and becometh an enemy to all righteousness. . . . Therefore [their] final doom is to endure a never-ending torment." (Mosiah 2:37, 39; see also 2 Peter 3:7; Revelation 20:13–15; D&C 76:31–46.) For the most part, it is this second hell, or "second death," to which the Book of Mormon prophets referred when they spoke of eternal hell and damnation. (See Jacob 3:11; Alma 12:16–18; Helaman 14:16–18.)

The Lord has used such phrases as "eternal damnation" and "endless torment" to refer to the kind of punishment he administers: "every man must repent or suffer, for I, God, am endless. . . .

"Nevertheless, it is not written that there shall be no end to this torment, but it is written *endless torment*.

"Again, it is written *eternal damnation*; wherefore it is more express than other scriptures, that it might work upon the hearts of the children of men, altogether for my name's glory.

"Wherefore, I will explain unto you this mystery, for it is meet unto you to know even as mine apostles. . . .

"For, behold, the mystery of godliness, how great is it! For, behold, I am endless, and the punishment which is given from my hand is endless punishment, for Endless is my name. Wherefore —

"Eternal punishment is God's punishment.

"Endless punishment is God's punishment." (D&C 19:4–12.)

These verses help clarify some statements in the Book of Mormon and the Bible that refer to the temporary hell as being endless.

The Spirit World

As Latter-day Saints we have four books of scripture, as well as latter-day prophets, to help us understand doctrines that have confused apostate Christianity for centuries. We understand, for example, that the spirits of all who die enter the spirit world to await their resurrection. But even though the righteous enter a state of happiness, rest, and peace, they feel confined. The large assemblage of spirits who awaited Christ's visit to them shortly after his crucifixion were anxiously anticipating their "deliverance." The Doctrine and Covenants explains that "the dead had looked upon the long absence of their spirits from their bodies as a bondage." (D&C 138:49–50.)

Thus, the peace that the righteous experience in the spirit world is not the ultimate state of happiness most of Christianity think of as heaven. It is only when the spirit and body are "inseparably connected" that mankind can "receive a fulness of joy. And when separated, man cannot receive a fulness of joy." (See D&C 93:33–34.) In this context, all spirits between death and resurrection are in confinement.

Release for the righteous spirits comes at the beginning of the Millennium. At this time, the heirs of the celestial kingdom will come forth from paradise and receive glorified, celestial bodies of flesh and bone in the "morning" of the first resurrection, the resurrection of the just. (See 1 Corinthians 15:20–42; D&C 88:97–98; 76:17; *Teachings of the Prophet Joseph Smith,* sel. Joseph Fielding Smith [Salt Lake City: Deseret Book Co., 1938], pp. 295–96.) Following the glorious resurrection of the celestial candidates, the heirs of the terrestrial glory will be resurrected. Their resurrection too, though later, is still considered a part of the first resurrection. (See D&C 76:71–80; 2 Nephi 9:26.) Elder Bruce R. McConkie stated that the terrestrial heirs will come forth in "the afternoon of the first resurrection" which takes place after the "Lord has ushered in the millennium." (*Mormon Doctrine,* 2d ed. [Salt Lake City: Bookcraft], 1966, p. 640; see also D&C 88:99.)

The Temporary Hell

Among those at death who are assigned to hell are the heirs of the telestial kingdom and the sons of perdition. These spirits will remain in hell, or spirit prison, suffering "the wrath of Almighty God" until the millennial reign is over. (See D&C 76:106.) At that time, they will be resurrected in the last resurrection, the resurrection of the unjust. (See D&C 76:16–17, 81–85; John 5:28–29.)

Those who inherit the telestial kingdom constitute the filthy of the earth—the sorcerers, the adulterers, the whoremongers, "and whosoever loves and makes a lie." (D&C 76:103.) But through the mercies of God, even these people will be given a degree of glory. They will be "heirs of salvation," capable of being instructed by the Holy Spirit and by ministering angels. (D&C 76:88.)

Elder Bruce R. McConkie wrote that even most murderers will come out of hell, or the spirit prison, in the last resurrection to live in telestial glory: "When the Lord paraphrases the language of Revelation 21:8 in latter-day revelation (D&C 63:17–18 and 76:103–6) he omits murderers from the list of evil persons. Their inclusion here by John, however, coupled with the fact that only those who deny the truth after receiving a perfect knowledge of it shall become sons of perdition, is a clear indication that murderers shall eventually go to the telestial kingdom, unless of course there are some among those destined to be sons of perdition who are also murderers." (*Doctrinal New Testament Commentary,* 3 vols. [Salt Lake City: Bookcraft, 1965–73], 3:584.)

Hell, then, is a temporary part of the spirit world where the wicked are restrained in order for justice to be served and to give them a chance to repent. The Lord's promise is that all who do repent will receive a kingdom of glory, according to his judgment of their works. Even those who merit no kingdom of glory will be resurrected, for Christ's atonement broke the bands of death for all mankind. (See 1 Corinthians 15:22; 2 Nephi 9:14–16.) Following the resurrection, then, that temporary quarter of the spirit world called hell will no longer be necessary. "After all men are resurrected," wrote Elder McConkie, "the [post-earthly] spirit world will be without inhabitants." (*Mormon Doctrine,* p. 762.)

The Hell That Has No End

The three degrees of glory provide eternal homes for the vast majority of God's children who merited earth life. There is a fourth destination, however, for those "comparatively few" who cannot abide even a telestial glory. The Lord explains that the destiny of the sons of perdition is a kingdom without glory (see D&C 88:24), and "the end thereof, neither the place thereof, nor their torment, no man knows," only those "ordained unto this condemnation" (see D&C 76:43–49). These are they who "cannot repent." They "sin against the Holy Ghost" and "put Christ to open shame." (Joseph Fielding Smith, *Doctrines of Salvation,* comp. Bruce R. McConkie, 3 vols. [Salt Lake City: Bookcraft, 1954–56], 1:47–49.)

"All who partake of this, the greatest of sins, sell themselves as did Cain to Lucifer. They learn to hate the truth with an eternal hatred, and they learn to love wickedness. They reach a condition where they cannot repent. The spirit of murder fills their hearts and they would, if they had the power, crucify our Lord again, which they virtually do by fighting his work and seeking to destroy it and his prophets. . . .

"Before a man can sink to this bitterness of soul, he must first know and understand the truth with a clearness of vision wherein there is no doubt. *The change of heart does not come all at once,* but is due to transgression in some form, which continues to lurk in the soul without repentance, until the Holy Ghost withdraws, and then that man is left to spiritual darkness. Sin begets sin; the darkness grows until the love of truth turns to hatred, and the love of God is overcome by the wicked desire to destroy all that is just and true. In this way Christ is put to open shame, and blasphemy exalted.

"How fortunate it is that in the mercy of God there will be comparatively few who will partake of this awful misery and eternal darkness." (Ibid., p. 49.)

Thus, hell has an end for all consigned to it except the sons of perdition. They alone remain in that hell which has no end.

QA

What is the approximate weight of the gold plates from which the Book of Mormon was translated?

Roy W. Doxey, assistant in the office of the Quorum of the Twelve and dean emeritus of Religious Instruction, Brigham Young University

The Prophet Joseph Smith described the gold plates as follows: "These records were engraven on plates which had the appearance of gold, each plate was six inches wide and eight inches long, and not quite so thick as common tin. They were filled with engravings, in Egyptian characters, and bound together in a volume as the leaves of a book, with three rings running through the whole. The volume was something near six inches in thickness, a part of which was sealed. The characters on the unsealed part were small, and beautifully engraved. The whole book exhibited many marks of antiquity in its construction, and much skill in the art of engraving."[1]

Although no specific mention of weight is made in this description, several references to the weight can be found in accounts by Joseph's acquaintances who personally handled the plates. Joseph's wife, Emma, recorded that she moved the linen-wrapped plates while cleaning. Martin Harris declared, "I hefted the plates many times, and should think they weighed forty or fifty pounds."[2] William Smith, brother of the Prophet, reported that he "was permitted to lift them as they laid in a pillow case; but not to see them, as it was contrary to the commands he [Joseph Smith] had received. They weighed about sixty pounds according to the best of my judgment."[3] The eight men who testify that they examined the plates say that they each lifted them.

Variations in the estimation of the weight of the plates by those who "hefted" them are due to the experience of each in judging weight. But these accounts indicate that the plates were light enough to be carried without undue difficulty. Joseph Smith, for example, carried them some distance when he was forced to flee from some men seeking the plates shortly after he received them.[4]

Critics of the Prophet Joseph Smith have claimed that the plates may have weighed as much as two hundred pounds. Such estimates, however, are based on computation of a solid 24-karat gold object with the dimensions described by the Prophet; this estimation does not allow for the weight reduction that would naturally result from cutting the engravings, from unevenness of the leaves wrinkled by hammering, and from air space between each leaf.[5]

Referring to the Prophet's statement that the plates "had the appearance of gold," some have speculated that the metal of the plates was probably tumbaga, the name given by the Spaniards to a versatile alloy of gold and copper which could "be cast, drawn, hammered, gilded, soldered, welded, plated, hardened, annealed, polished, engraved, embossed, and inlaid."[6]

Tumbaga can be treated with a simple acid such as citric acid to dissolve the copper on the surface. What is then left is a shiny layer of 23-karat gold on top of a harder, more durable copper-gold alloy sheet. This process was widely used by the pre-Columbian cultures of central America in making religious objects.[7] Tumbaga plates of the dimensions Joseph Smith described would weigh between fifty-three and eighty-six pounds.[8]

Though we may never know the exact weight of the plates, the statements of others who handled them, as well as the scriptural references to their mobility, substantiate that weight was no barrier to conveying the plates in accordance with the purposes of God.

Notes

1. *History of the Church,* 7 vols., 2d ed. rev., ed. B. H. Roberts (Salt Lake City: The Church of Jesus Christ of Latter-day Saints, 1932–51), 4:537.

2. *Tiffany's Monthly,* May 1859, p. 166.

3. *William Smith on Mormonism* (Lamoni, Iowa: Herald Steam Book and Job Office, 1883), p. 12.

4. See Lucy Mack Smith, *History of Joseph Smith,* ed. Preston Nibley (Salt Lake City: Bookcraft, 1958), pp. 104–9.

5. See B. F. Cummings, "Weight of the Plates," *Liahona: The Elders' Journal,* 18 July 1908, pp. 108–10.

6. Reed H. Putnam, *Improvement Era,* Sept. 1966, p. 789.

7. See H. Lechtman, "Pre-Columbian Surface Metallurgy," *Scientific American,* June 1984, pp. 56–63.

8. See Putnam, pp. 830–31.

QA

Why were the Book of Mormon gold plates not placed in a museum so that people might know Joseph Smith had had them?

Monte S. Nyman, professor of ancient scripture, Brigham Young University

The scriptures suggest two reasons the Book of Mormon gold plates were not made available to the public: the first is that the Lord refused to allow men to use these sacred plates for commercial or personal benefit; the second, and most important, was so the Lord could test the faith of all who receive the record.

As Moroni concluded his father Mormon's record, he wrote: "And I am the same who hideth up this record unto the Lord; the plates thereof are of no worth, because of the commandment of the Lord. For he truly saith that no one shall have them to get gain; but the record thereof is of great worth; and whoso shall bring it to light, him will the Lord bless." (Mormon 8:14.)

Because the plates were made of precious metal, their monetary value was undoubtedly impressive, but they would be of still greater value to those who would attempt to publicize them by displaying them. The Lord obviously knew that the presence of the plates would cause men to attempt to use them to obtain money or personal notoriety. That may be one reason he commanded the plates to be taken from the earth following their translation.

We can see the wisdom of the Lord's commandment when we study Moroni's vision of the day when the Book of Mormon was to come forth. He saw that pride had corrupted the churches of that day and that the members of those churches loved money, their fine apparel, "and the adorning of your churches more than ye love the poor and the needy, the sick and the afflicted." (Mormon 8:37.) He witnessed "murders, and robbing, and lying, and deceivings, and whoredoms, and all manner of abominations." (Mormon 8:31.) Such conditions would require constant vigilance over the plates were they to be placed on display.

Furthermore, those who would dismiss the truths taught in the Book of Mormon would also dismiss the plates themselves as genuine even if they were available for display. Such people would undoubtedly insist that Joseph Smith or one of his associates had made the plates or that the Prophet's translation was only pretended. In this respect, the physical presence of the plates would not convince anyone of the truth of the Book of Mormon.

In short, it is not necessary that the plates be physically present to bless the lives of the covenant people. It is the content of the plates that is important. Those who are of the people of Israel, or those who are adopted into the covenant, will know of the truth of the plates' content through the power of the Holy Ghost without seeing the plates. This brings us to the second reason the plates were not made available to the public—the test of faith.

Moroni testified that the plates and their message would be brought forth by the power of God and warned that those who condemn the message will be judged on the same basis. (See Mormon 8:16–22.) He further commented that it would be because of the prayers and the faith of the ancient Nephites that the record would be translated and disseminated. The Lord had assured that the record would come even as Isaiah had prophesied, although it would "be said that miracles are done away." (Mormon 8:23–26.)

After the record was brought forth, the Lord provided two sets of witnesses: three men who had a spiritual manifestation, and eight who saw the plates in a purely temporal setting. These men fit the law of witnesses which the Lord revealed in both Old and New Testament times. (See Deuteronomy 19:15; Matthew 18:16.) Their testimonies serve to bolster the faith of readers. (See D&C 5:11–16; 17:1–4; Ether 5:2–4; 2 Nephi 27:12–14.)

Since it was by faith that the record was brought forth, why would the Lord not require the same kind of faith from readers as he did from the recorders of the plates? Earlier the Savior had told Mormon to write only the lesser part of the Nephite record first to try the faith of the latter-day readers; if they believed in Book of Mormon teachings, greater things would be manifest to them. (See 3 Nephi 26:6–11.) Nephi concluded his record with this warning testimony to the unbeliever:

"And you that will not partake of the goodness of God, and respect the words of the Jews, and also my words, and the words which shall proceed forth out of the mouth of the Lamb of God, behold, I bid you an everlasting farewell, for these words shall condemn you at the last day.

"For what I seal on earth, shall be brought against you at the judgment bar; for thus hath the Lord commanded me, and I must obey." (2 Nephi 33:14–15.)

Mormon and Moroni bore a similar testimony. (See Mormon 3:17–22; Moroni 10:27, 34.) An acknowledgment of the truth of the plates at Judgment Day, however, will be, in the words of Samuel the Lamanite, "everlastingly too late." (Helaman 13:38.)

Those who lack faith are usually the same ones who want or expect material or physical evidence. That evidence will come, but only after they have passed the test of faith.

QA

Would you respond to the theories that the Book of Mormon is based on the Spaulding manuscript or on Ethan Smith's *View of the Hebrews*?

Bruce D. Blumell, attorney, Calgary, Alberta, Canada

Historically, the most popular anti-Mormon or non-Mormon explanation of the origin of the Book of Mormon has been that it was based on a manuscript written by Solomon Spaulding. In spite of its weaknesses, this theory continues to surface from time to time even in our day. Another more recent theory, also open to criticism, suggests that Joseph Smith used Ethan Smith's (no relation) *View of the Hebrews,* which was published during the 1820s, to help him write the Book of Mormon.

Solomon Spaulding was born in 1761 in Connecticut and lived in New England and New York until he moved to Conneaut, Ohio, in 1809. Because his business there was unsuccessful, he decided to write a story about some of the original inhabitants of America that he hoped he might be able to publish and sell. While working on the story he read extracts of it to several of his neighbors from time to time. In 1812 he moved to the Pittsburg, Pennsylvania, area where he died in 1816, never having found a publisher for his manuscript.

In 1833, Philastus Hurlbut, a former member of the Church who had been excommunicated for immorality, was employed by an anti-Mormon committee in Ohio to collect derogatory evidence against Joseph Smith and the Book of Mormon. In the process of attempting to secure such information, Hurlbut interviewed a number of people who claimed to have known Joseph Smith or known of him. Among those Hurlbut said he talked to were eight people from the Conneaut, Ohio, area who signed affidavits claiming that the Book of Mormon was based on Solomon Spaulding's unpublished manuscript written more than twenty years previously. Hurlbut sold these affidavits to Eber D. Howe, who published them the next year in his vitriolic exposé entitled *Mormonism Unvailed.* Howe argued that Sidney Rigdon, while still a Reformed Baptist preacher, had come across the manuscript and had used it to help him write the Book of Mormon, which he then secretly conveyed to Joseph Smith, who published the book as his own production.

After Philastus Hurlbut gathered his affidavits, he found one manuscript among Solomon Spaulding's papers, but neither he nor Howe published it. About fifty years later, in 1884, L. L. Rice found this manuscript among papers he had inherited from Howe. He gave the manuscript to Oberlin College in Ohio, and it was published the next year.

The manuscript, entitled "Manuscript Story — Conneaut Creek," bears no relationship to the Book of Mormon in either style or content. It is written in modern English and is only about one-sixth the length of the Book of Mormon. The story commences with a group of Romans during the reign of Constantine who were blown off course on their way to Britain and landed in America. In this novel one of the Romans served as the narrator of what the group observed. Most of the chronicle is the description of two Indian nations who have the Ohio River as a common border. A romance between a prince of one nation and a princess of the other leads to a great war between the two groups, which is described in some detail.

Most writers who mention the subject, both nonmembers of the Church and members, either directly indicate or appear to assume that the Spaulding manuscript claimed the American Indians were the lost ten tribes of Israel or remnants of these tribes. This it does not do. In fact, the manuscript makes no attempt to explain the origins of the Indians.

The similarities between this manuscript and the Book of Mormon are general and superficial at best. In the introduction to his novel, Spaulding described finding the manuscript buried in the earth, but it was a parchment written in Latin, not metal plates with a Middle Eastern language. Spaulding developed his own unique nomenclature for his story, but not one of these names bears any resemblance to Book of Mormon names. The story has in it a transatlantic migration, although the group came from Rome, not Jerusalem. And there is a great war between two civilizations, both Indian, although neither succeeds in completely annihilating the other. Yet these vague similarities could have led Spaulding's neighbors, especially with prompting from Hurlbut, to believe the Book of Mormon was lifted from Spaulding's manuscript.

The affidavits that Hurlbut gathered are very similar in style and content, which suggests that if Hurlbut did not write them himself, he strongly influenced their composition. There is a similarity of syntax and phrasing and an amazing uniformity of details in the various statements. These eight witnesses had just read or were recently familiar with the Book of Mormon, but it had been twenty-plus years since they had heard excerpts from the Spaulding manuscript. With this time differential, these witnesses unconsciously could easily have transposed some details of the Book of Mormon, which was fresh in their minds, to the broad general story Spaulding wrote, which was distant and dim to them.

In his *Mormonism Unvailed,* Howe argued that Joseph Smith did not possess enough education or understanding of theology to have written the more religious parts of the Book of Mormon. He decided it must have been done by Sidney Rigdon, who had been a skilled

"*I* am the Son of Mormon . . .
And I am the same who
hideth up this sacred record
unto the Lord . . . for it shall
be brought out of the
darkness unto the light,
according to the word
of God . . ."

MORMON 8:12-16

VANCOUVER SECOND WARD
24 MAY 1992

SUNDAY SCHOOL

Opening Hymn	#140, Did You Think to Pray?
Invocation	Arleen Fulton
Practice Hymn	#195, How Great the Wisdom and the Love

****

SACRAMENT MEETING

Presiding	Bishop Jim Adamson
Conducting	Bishop Jim Adamson
Opening Hymn	#266, The Time Is Far Spent
Invocation	Kevin Ball
Ward Business	
Sacrament Hymn	#196, Jesus, Once of Humble Birth
Sacrament	
Youth Speaker	Ryan Wegner
Speakers	Susan Ball
	Jim Lackey
Ward Choir	"Master, the Tempest Is Raging"
Speakers	Kathy Lackey
	Jon Lackey
Closing Hymn	#84, Faith of Our Fathers
Benediction	Judi Georgeades
Greeters	Elders Phillips and Christiansen

****

BIRTHDAYS

24	Kristin Lowe	28	Nancy Van Renselaar
26	Craig Hogman	29	Francis Moore
27	Nathan Horrocks		Allen Rhyasen
	Roger Meline	30	Tom Layne
28	Mary Ann Ard		Ross Luke
	David Bischoff		Jim Whited
	Ethan Higley		

RELIEF SOCIETY

Today: Aging Is Part of God's Plan (p. 178)
Next Week: Conference Address, "The Tongue Can Be A Sharp
Sword", Elder Marvin J. Ashton, *Ensign*, May 1992, p.18.

****

ELDERS QUORUM

Today: Finding Forgiveness for Our Sins (p. 63)
Next Week: Teaching Your Family to Care for the Poor (p.55)

****

ANNOUNCEMENTS

May 28   Pack Meeting, 7 pm. Join our Indian Braves at the
         Akela's Council. Pow Wow will be in the Primary
         Room. Remember to call advancements in to Lora
         Stamm by Monday night.

May 29   Come enjoy a special evening with the Stake at the
         "Night of Classics" beginning at 7 pm in the chapel.
         If anyone is interested in displaying your beautiful
         artwork, please contact Debra Jones at 256-6978.

May 30   Pancake Breakfast, 9 am at the Stake Center multi-
         purpose room. For all single adults and their
         families. Pancakes and eggs will be served.

June 6   Visiting Teaching Convention, Saturday, June 6 from
         10 am to 12 noon. Join us for a great luncheon and
         program.

June
19-20   2nd Ward Annual Camp-Out at Beacon Rock State Park.
         Bring your tents and families and come enjoy an
         overnighter with the ward family. Bring your own
         dinner for Friday night. Breakfast will be provided
         and cooked for everyone Saturday morning. (No water
         balloons please!!)

****

TEMPLE ENDOWMENTS

     Please report your temple attendance to Bro. Stever for
attendance at any temple.

Name _____ Date _____

Number of temple units performed this week _____

Girl Names
1. Aurora?
2. Brier Rose
3. Wendy
4. Ariel
5. Cynthia
6. Annastatista
7. Christine

Boy Names
1. Peter
2. Matthew
3. Luke
4. Danny
5. Joe
6. Jordan
7. Kevin

Ariel

Wendy

Brier Rose

~~CYNTH~~

Cynthia

~~Anna~~ Christie

~~Ann~~

and influential Reformed Baptist, or Campbellite, preacher in north-eastern Ohio before joining with the Latter-day Saints. Howe claimed that Sidney Rigdon had come upon the Spaulding manu-script and had copied or stolen it and subsequently added the the-ology to it to produce the Book of Mormon. During all of this, Howe argued, Rigdon secretly communicated with Joseph Smith to palm the book off as Joseph's creation.

This part of the theory breaks down for several reasons. First of all, the style of the Book of Mormon is very different from the embellished rhetoric Sidney Rigdon exhibited in his sermons. Sec-ond, there is no proof to show that Sidney Rigdon ever came in contact with the Spaulding manuscript. And third, the attempts to show him secretly communicating with Joseph Smith are simply unfounded. During the writing and printing of the Book of Mormon, from 1827 to 1830, Sidney Rigdon was a popular preacher in north-eastern Ohio, and his whereabouts were known to a number of people. Yet none ever indicated that he was involved in such a conspiracy, and neither did any of Joseph's associates. Such a com-plicity would have been virtually impossible to carry out, especially since it would have involved either Joseph Smith or Sidney Rigdon periodically traveling about three hundred miles to see the other and consequently being gone from their areas of residence for long periods of time, taking into account the primitive modes of travel in those days.

Sidney Rigdon continued avidly to teach his Reformed Baptist faith until he heard the message of the Restoration from the first Latter-day Saint missionaries in his area, almost eight months after the publication of the Book of Mormon and the organization of the Church. This, of course, would have been extremely unlikely if he had really been the author of the book and thus the originator of much early Latter-day Saint theology. In fact, if Sidney Rigdon had written the Book of Mormon, it is improbable that a man of his prominence would have let Joseph Smith found the Church and be the leader and then later let Joseph publicly censure him several times when he opposed the Prophet's policies. Even when Rigdon was excommunicated in August 1844 because of his opposition to Brigham Young's leadership of the Church, he made no intimation that he was the author of the Book of Mormon. Late in his life, long after parting with Brigham Young and the body of the Latter-day Saints, Sidney Rigdon forcefully reiterated to his questioning son that he had had nothing to do with writing the Book of Mormon.

He added that he knew Joseph Smith was a prophet and that the Book of Mormon was true.

At the end of his book *Mormonism Unvailed,* Howe reported briefly that a Spaulding manuscript had been found; but since it was so different in language, style, and detail from the Book of Mormon, he conjectured that Spaulding had produced a revised version that was similar to the Book of Mormon before his death in 1816. Howe felt it must have been this purported revised manuscript from which Spaulding read extracts to some of his neighbors.

Those anti-Mormon writers who have bothered to read *Mormonism Unvailed* and the Spaulding manuscript found in 1884 have usually accepted Howe's belief in a still-lost, revised Spaulding manuscript. Solomon Spaulding wrote other stories, according to his widow and daughter and several acquaintances, but they never claimed there was a second version of the manuscript. Hurlbut himself believed there was only one manuscript, the one he obtained from Mrs. Spaulding, which was the one later published in 1885. He also believed it had served as the basis of the Book of Mormon, although, after examining it, Howe realized it had not, as noted above.

If there had been a revised second version of the manuscript, one would logically expect some of the fact, details, and incidents in it to be similar to the original version. Yet none of the affidavit witnesses recalled details from the extant Spaulding manuscript, only from the Book of Mormon. For example, the names they remember are Book of Mormon names; yet Spaulding had created a lexicon of his own names in his manuscript. If he had revised the story, certainly he would have kept some of the original names in the second edition, and surely several of the witnesses would have remembered at least one or two if their memories of events over twenty years previous really served them as well as they claimed.

Furthermore, since no writer can easily change his style, one could assume that the revised version of Spaulding's story, had there been a revised version, would be at least somewhat comparable in style to the first. And if the Book of Mormon had really been plagiarized, as claimed, from Spaulding's supposed second edition, then one might logically expect similarities in style between the extant manuscript and the Book of Mormon. But the Book of Mormon is much different in style from the flowery figures of speech and romantic rhetoric that Spaulding employed.

If there were a second version of the manuscript there would still be the problem of getting it to Sidney Rigdon and finally to Joseph Smith. As noted earlier, this is the weakest link in the conspiratorial chain of improbabilities and unlikely events that attempt to show the Spaulding manuscript as the basis for the Book of Mormon.

While Spaulding's manuscript said nothing about the origin of the American Indians, there were many people during Joseph Smith's lifetime and earlier in American history who believed that the Indians were the descendants of the lost ten tribes of Israel. A number of books had been written on the subject. As settlers from Europe came in contact with the Indians of North American, they were naturally curious about the origins of these people. Theologians especially looked to the Bible for answers, and some speculated that the lost tribes were the ancestors of the Indians. Joseph Smith might easily have been familiar with that theme.

Therefore, during the past thirty years some non-Mormon scholars, realizing the weakness of the Spaulding manuscript theory, have for the most part abandoned it and postulated that Joseph Smith might have gained some of the ideas for the Book of Mormon from a book by Ethan Smith entitled *View of the Hebrews,* first published in Vermont in 1823, with a revised, enlarged edition published in 1825. In this book Ethan Smith endeavored to show, on the basis of scientific research of the time, that the American Indians were the descendants of the lost ten tribes of Israel.

But though the Book of Mormon does report several migrations of small groups of Israelites to the western hemisphere, it does not say that the native peoples of America were of the lost ten tribes. Furthermore, there is no evidence that Joseph Smith ever saw a copy of *View of the Hebrews.* In 1842 the *Times and Seasons,* which Joseph Smith edited, quoted from an 1833 book that quoted from the *View of the Hebrews.* The passage apparently was published to show that at least some authorities believed ancient Hebrews had come to America. (*Times and Seasons,* June 1842, 3:813–14.) If the Prophet had originally used Ethan Smith's book to help him write the Book of Mormon, almost certainly he would not have later published a quotation from it to illustrate a point, since plagiarists normally keep their sources a secret.

Out of the multitude of ideas and events in the Book of Mormon and in the *View of the Hebrews* there are several broad similarities, but many more significant differences; and a correlation at some point between two things does not prove one caused the other; it may mean, for example, that both things were the result of an independent third factor.

Critics who have recognized that the Book of Mormon could not have been plagiarized from any single source claim that Joseph Smith was a skilled eclectic who borrowed ideas from all over his social and intellectual environment and thereby was able to create the potpourri called the Book of Mormon. This "environmentalist" approach is usually the most satisfying for scholars who in some measure conscientiously examine the question of the book's origins but cannot admit the possibility of divine intervention. But Dr. Hugh Nibley of Brigham Young University most successfully argued that there are ideas and material in the book different from the prevailing beliefs of Joseph Smith's era and different from any other source extant in the 1820s, including the Bible. It is, he argued, significant that since the publication of the Book of Mormon, there have been such things uncovered as ancient Middle Eastern sources that in no case contradict, but rather parallel, many Book of Mormon ideas and word usages. He concluded that guesswork on the part of the Prophet Joseph could not possibly account for all these parallels, which were unknown at the time of the Book of Mormon translation. (See *Lehi in the Desert, An Approach to the Book of Mormon,* and *Since Cumorah,* vols. 5, 6, and 7 in *The Collected Works of Hugh Nibley* [Salt Lake City: Deseret Book Co., 1988].)

In short, the simplest and most accurate assumption about the origin of the Book of Mormon is that it is exactly what Joseph Smith said it was, an ancient work translated "by the gift and power of God." (Testimony of the Three Witnesses.)

QA

What is B. H. Roberts's "Study of the Book of Mormon" and how have critics used it to discredit the Book of Mormon?

John W. Welch, professor of law and president of the Foundation for Ancient Research and Mormon Studies (FARMS), Brigham Young University

I first seriously encountered the writings of Elder B. H. Roberts of the First Council of the Seventy (1857–1933) when I was a college student. I was impressed by the stimulating analysis of Latter-day

Saint religious concepts in his *Seventy's Course in Theology* (1907–1919). I was caught up by the personally passionate historical prose in his *Missouri Persecutions* (1900), *The Rise and Fall of Nauvoo* (1900), and the *Comprehensive History of the Church* (1930). There was fire-power and electrifying conviction in his words. He called his faith "unshakeable."

Recently, that faith has been drawn into question in the minds of some people because of a set of papers about the Book of Mormon that B. H. Roberts wrote in 1922. In these papers, Roberts bluntly lists many Book of Mormon "problems" and raises many arguments that he contemplated could be made against the Book of Mormon. As I read these papers, it became apparent that many people would misunderstand. For those who may be interested, here are the questions I think some people may ask about Elder Roberts's Book of Mormon studies, and here are answers that recent research now provides.

Q. What kind of a person was B. H. Roberts?

A. He was fiercely loyal to The Church of Jesus Christ of Latter-day Saints. He had strong opinions and on most occasions was outspoken and bluntly forthright.[1]

All his life, B. H. Roberts sought after truth, spiritually and intellectually. For Brother Roberts, president of the Eastern States Mission from 1922 to 1927 and one of the seven Presidents of the Seventy from 1888 until his death in 1933, the search for truth was an all-consuming passion. He faced historical facts fearlessly, he confronted scientific theories confidently, and he squared off in debate spontaneously.

Q. Did B. H. Roberts think scientific evidence could prove or disprove the Book of Mormon?

A. No. He felt that scientific evidence was interesting and significant but not infallible or controlling. Elder Roberts uncompromisingly recognized and openly acknowledged the Holy Ghost as the teacher of all truth. He said in 1909:

"This [power of the Holy Ghost] must ever be the chief source of evidence for the truth of the Book of Mormon. All other evidence is secondary to this, the primary and infallible. No arrangement of evidence, however skilfully ordered; no argument, however adroitly made, can ever take its place; for this witness of the Holy Spirit to the soul of man for the truth of the Nephite volume of scripture, is God's evidence to the truth; and will ever be the chief reliance of those who accept the Book of Mormon, and expect to see its acceptance extended throughout the world."[2]

Thus, he was not afraid to ask questions about the Book of Mormon or anything else. "I am taking the position that our faith is not only unshaken but unshakeable in the Book of Mormon, and therefore we can look without fear upon all that can be said against it," Elder Roberts wrote upon completion of his Book of Mormon studies.

Q. Did B. H. Roberts think he had all the answers?

A. Brother Roberts knew that he had certain answers to many historical, scientific, and gospel questions. He also knew that he did not have them all. A rational person will not seek more truth if he thinks he already has it all. Elder Roberts continued exploring, reading, thinking, and writing books, articles, tracts, and pamphlets until he died in September 1933 at the age of seventy-six.

His knowledge of the Book of Mormon was no different. He was one of the first people ever to make a scholarly study of the Book of Mormon. His exploratory investigations found many things in the Book of Mormon that he considered "master strokes of philosophy" (as he wrote in 1928)[3] and sure signs of "divine origin" (as he spoke in 1932).[4] Still, he knew that there were questions for which he had no answers. Yet he "most humbly prayed" and "most anxiously" awaited the "further development of knowledge that will make it possible for us to give a reasonable answer to those who question us concerning [these] matters" (as he wrote in 1921).[5]

Q. How long have B. H. Roberts's papers on Book of Mormon "difficulties" been around?

A. The papers, most of which were never given by Elder Roberts to anyone, have been in the hands of his family. They were donated to the University of Utah in 1979 and 1981, since which time copies have been made available.[6]

Q. How have critics of the Church responded to these papers?

A. For critics of the Book of Mormon, Elder Roberts's notes have appeared to be a bonanza. Here is one of the most intellectual General Authorities of his day seeming to expose all the evidentiary weaknesses of his own case. It is like a military officer writing an intelligence report telling the enemy where his own troops are most vulnerable. In the study, Brother Roberts was blunt. He stated a case against the Book of Mormon in tough terms. It is clear that Elder Roberts recognized there may be no answers to some of his hard questions, but that did not deter him from asking the questions.

Q. Why did Elder Roberts write such things?

A. First, the project grew out of committee assignments Elder Roberts was given in 1921 by Elder James E. Talmage and President Heber J. Grant. The committee was asked to respond to several questions about Book of Mormon archaeology. B. H. Roberts pursued the assignment vigorously.

Second, Elder Roberts loved to debate. He knew how to argue a case toe-to-toe and believed that much good could emerge thereby. Even as a mission president, B. H. Roberts, who was an outspoken character all his life, would dress up in street clothes and go out to debate on the street corners of New York. When he saw unresolved problems, he would try to state those problems as clearly and as strongly as possible and then pursue the controversy.

Third, he was loyal. He wanted to help the Church wherever he could. He knew that future generations would probably face these issues, and he wanted them to be prepared. In 1927 he said of his study, "Such a question as that may possibly arise some day, and if it does, it would be greatly to the advantage of our future Defenders of the Faith, if they had in hand a thorough digest of the subject matter."[7] To have presented these issues any less forcefully or dramatically would have been uncharacteristic of Brother Roberts.

Q. What is Elder Roberts's Study of the Book of Mormon?

A. The "Study" is twenty typewritten chapters (each about fifteen pages long). The first fourteen chapters discuss similarities between the Book of Mormon and a book by Ethan Smith published in Vermont in 1823 (second edition in 1825) entitled *View of the Hebrews; or, The Tribes of Israel in America.* The last six chapters of the "Study" consider the proposition that the Book of Mormon is of human rather than divine origin.

The "Study" is sometimes confused with a shorter, 145–page paper entitled "Book of Mormon Difficulties," which is what B. H. Roberts first wrote by way of committee assignment from Elder James E. Talmage in 1921. In that paper, B. H. Roberts pointed out the difficulties he ran into as he was responding to five questions asked about the Book of Mormon by a Mr. Couch from Washington, D.C. Brother Roberts found in his research that the prevailing scientific theories about Indian origins and pre-Columbian fauna, flora, and technology differed from what he believed about such things.

Q. Do we know exactly when B. H. Roberts wrote the second work, "Study of the Book of Mormon"?

A. Yes. The first page of the original typescript says that the

"Study" was written thirteen years "to be exact" after the publication of *New Witnesses for God* (which appeared in 1909). Because of this and several other telltale changes Roberts made on the typescript,[8] we can date the typing of the "Study" to before he left to serve as mission president in New York on 29 May 1922. Most of his proofreading changes were made before that time as well. This means — contrary to assertions some people have made — that Elder Roberts did not write the "Study" during his mission presidency.

Q. Did Brother Roberts consider the "Study" a finished piece?

A. No. He never submitted it to Church authorities[9] and, uncharacteristically, proofread it only lightly.

Q. What did B. H. Roberts think of the "Study"?

A. In 1932 he called it an "awful" book. He said that he had not written it for publication.[10]

Q. Did Elder Roberts draw any conclusions from the "Study"?

A. No. He said in an unsent cover letter accompanying the "Study," "I do not say my conclusions, for they are undrawn. . . . What is herein set forth does not represent any conclusions of mine." Throughout the "Study" Elder Roberts asked questions. They are tough rhetorical questions, but still they are just questions, not assertions and not conclusions. They are questions he expected opponents to be asking. To these he puzzled: "What shall our answer be?" "What is to be our general standing before the enlightened opinion of mankind?" These problems he called "legitimate queries." He said they would be powerful weapons "in the hands of a skillful opponent," and he aimed to blunt them by paying attention to them.

Q. Did Elder Roberts worry that people would misunderstand his "Study"?

A. Yes. He wrote, "Let me say once for all, so as to avoid what might otherwise call for repeated explanation, that what is herein set forth does not represent any conclusions of mine."

Q. Why does Elder Roberts not suggest any answers to the problems he is raising in his study?

A. The "Study" is not an answer book. It is a question book. Many of the questions he had answered before, and others he would answer in the future. For example, he raised the objection that the small party of Nephites could not possibly have constructed a temple like the large and opulent temple of Solomon. Brother Roberts had already answered that question himself in 1909.[11]

As another example, he poses the question of whether Joseph

Smith's powers of imagination were sufficient to have written the Book of Mormon. Elder Roberts regularly preached in the 1930s that the "perfect" sacrament prayers in Moroni 4–5 are evidence that the Book of Mormon was not written by Joseph Smith.

Some of the questions require no answer, such as the bogus suggestion that Joseph Smith got the name *Ether* from the name *Ethan Smith*. Elder Roberts himself says in the "Study," "Do not take the idea too seriously."

Q. How careful was B. H. Roberts in this research?

A. Not very. This particular piece of research shows signs of haste and remained unfinished. In fact, the "Study" was written inside of a few months. Much of it consists of long quotations from other sources, given with little analysis. Even Elder Roberts's reading of the Book of Mormon was not always as careful as it could have been. Several of the problems he raised grew out of mistaken assumptions he had made about the Book of Mormon. For example, Brother Roberts assumed that the lands of the Book of Mormon were all relatively flat. He apparently overlooked many contrary statements, such as Alma 47:9, which speaks of a large mountain and valley.

Q. Would B. H. Roberts feel embarrassed to know that some of his research was incomplete or flawed?

A. Absolutely not. He wrote that "the generations who succeed us in unfolding in a larger way some of the yet unlearned truths of the Gospel, will find that we have had some misconceptions and made some wrong deductions in our day and time. The book of knowledge is never a sealed book. It is never completed and forever closed; rather it is an eternally open book, in which one may go on constantly discovering new truths and modifying our knowledge of old ones."[12] This observation pertains equally today to our continuing efforts to know the Book of Mormon better, both through study and also by faith.

Q. Did the "Study" change Elder Roberts's use of the Book of Mormon?

A. No. Before and after the "Study" he used the Book of Mormon as the focus of his missionary programs. He voluntarily chose to speak on Book of Mormon subjects again and again in conferences and in the media.[13] More than fifty-six major talks or statements were made by B. H. Roberts after the "Study" in which he affirmed his faith in the Book of Mormon.[14] After the "Study," Elder Roberts may have taken less interest in archaeology and placed more emphasis on the doctrinal and philosophical strengths of the Book of Mormon, but in no way did he ever doubt or reject the historicity of this "ancient American volume of scripture," as he called it on many occasions.

Q. Did Elder Roberts, perhaps knowing that his "Study" would be troublesome to people, affirm his testimony of the truthfulness of the Book of Mormon after he wrote the "Study"?

A. He wrote in May 1922 of "the tremendous truth" of the Book of Mormon. He said in 1924 that the Saints should build upon the Book of Mormon "wherein is no darkness or doubt." He spoke at general conference in April 1928 of the "hundred more such glorious things that have come to the world in that book to enlighten the children of men." He spoke repeatedly of the historicity of the book.[15]

Nevertheless, Brother Roberts knew that he had been abrasive and challenging at times during his many years of service to the Church. At October general conference, 1929, Elder Roberts may have had his Book of Mormon "Study" in mind when he remarked: "I happened to be reminded today that next April it will be fifty years since I commenced my public ministry in the Church. . . . I am mentioning some of these things in order that my profession of faith that I have made here today may be supported by the evidence of steady, persistent effort on my part to develop and to advocate and to establish this great work of God.

"But this is my object, and my object alone; that after bearing testimony to the fundamental things of this work, and my confidence in it, I hope that if anywhere along the line I have caused any of you to doubt my faith in this work, then let this testimony and my indicated life's work be a correction of it. I make reference to these personal things in fifty years of service so that you may know that my testimony has some sanctions for it in the life of service I have given to the cause."[16]

Q. Is it possible that B. H. Roberts had a faithful facade that he wore in public but in private was a skeptical doubter?

A. If Elder Roberts was anything, he was outspoken and honest. It is extremely difficult to believe that he was two-faced. In his April 1928 general conference talk, Elder Roberts emotionally spoke of the Book of Mormon and of the appearance of the resurrected Jesus Christ among the Nephites gathered at the temple in Bountiful. He said: "And now, O Lord Jesus, if thou couldst but come into the consciousness of our souls this day, as thou didst come into the vision of the ancient Nephites in the Land of Bountiful, we would join their great song of praise and worship, saying—Hosanna! Hosanna! Blessed be the name of the Most High God! And we, like them, would fall down at the feet of Jesus and worship him this Easter day! Amen." In powerful statements like this one, Elder Roberts revealed his deep-felt faith in the Book of Mormon.

Q. Did B. H. Roberts ever say anything after 1922 that could lead someone to think that he had lost faith in the Book of Mormon?

A. Yes, on one known occasion. Elder Roberts had a conversation with Wesley Lloyd, one of his former missionaries, in Salt Lake City on 7 August 1933, six weeks before his death. He began this conversation, as reported by Brother Lloyd, complaining that his unpublished manuscript "The Way, the Truth, the Life" had been subjected to "severe criticism" and rejected by the Brethren. He thought he had been personally attacked. He then took issue with a new Church policy of refraining from sending missionaries into the field without financial backing.[17] He next complained about Brigham Young. Finally, he turned to the Book of Mormon, complaining that back in 1922 a "crisis had arisen where revelation was necessary" but that no answer had been forthcoming.

No doubt, Brother Roberts voiced some complaints that day. The important thing is that he did not resign his Church position as he said he might do. He did not cease working on his missionary correspondence course. He did not give up on the Church. And he did not give up on the Book of Mormon. These complaints are not representative of his more fundamental attitudes and beliefs.

The Wesley Lloyd journal should not be misunderstood.[18] Brother Lloyd said that Roberts "shifted his base on the Book of Mormon." Shifting bases, however, does not mean abandoning. In reality, we know how Elder Roberts shifted: in his later years, B. H. Roberts found his doctrinal approach to the Book of Mormon's divinity more satisfying than his archaeological approach had been.[19] Brother Lloyd said that Elder Roberts thought that the Book of Mormon was in need of "the more bolstering." Needing "more" bolstering was always B. H. Roberts's position.

It may also be relevant that Elder Roberts, at age seventy-six, was in ill health. He had lost a foot, spent several months near death's door in hospitals, and suffered from the advanced stages of the diabetes that would kill him a few weeks later.[20] Undoubtedly, Elder Roberts also felt a great loss at the death of Elder James Talmage on 27 July 1933, about a week before this conversation with Lloyd.

These facts help place in context what the old fighter was feeling that day as he conversed with his young friend. After that conversation, Elder Roberts went to Chicago to represent the Church at a world conference of religious leaders. He also told Jack Christensen (another of his missionaries), sometime around 1 September 1933, "Ethan Smith played no part in the formation of the Book of Mormon. You accept Joseph Smith and all the scriptures!"[21]

Q. Is it necessary for members of the Church today to read B. H. Roberts's "Study" to be up to date on Book of Mormon studies?

A. No. In fact, the "Study" is now to a considerable extent out of date. Most of his questions have since found answers.

The "Study" marks a beginning stage in the history of Book of Mormon studies. With Elder Roberts, students of the Book of Mormon began to think more deeply about shallow and inadequate archaeological explanations or "proofs" of the Book of Mormon. With Elder Roberts, such scholars as Elder John A. Widtsoe, and a few years later Hugh Nibley[22] and Sidney Sperry, began to expand our approaches to the study of the Book of Mormon.

Q. What were Elder Roberts's main questions?

A. Elder Roberts raised questions in five areas.

1. He found that the prevailing theory in the 1920s about the origin of the American Indian was that they all came long ago over the Bering Strait, not across the sea.

2. He pointed out the apparent absence of a credible relationship of the Book of Mormon account to the archaeology of the 1920s.

On these first two matters, we, along with science, still await definitive answers. As President Anthony W. Ivins, a counselor to President Heber J. Grant, said in general conference, April 1929, "Where was the City of Zarahemla? . . . It does not make any difference to us. There has never been anything yet set forth that definitely settles that question. So the Church says we are just waiting until we discover the truth. All kinds of theories have been advanced."[23] Plausible answers, however, have recently been developed. One such scientific and scholarly theory recently advanced is John L. Sorenson's *An Ancient American Setting for the Book of Mormon*.[24] For example, in B. H. Roberts's day there was no evidence of pre-Columbian domesticated barley in the Americas; today there is.

3. Elder Roberts pointed out certain seemingly absurd or erroneous passages in the Book of Mormon.

4. He suggested similarities between Book of Mormon conversion stories and early nineteenth-century spiritual experiences.

Today, many of these alleged absurdities, on closer examination, turn out to be strengths rather than weaknesses. For example, Alma 46 says that Captain Moroni waved the "rent" of his coat in the air. This seems impossible in English, since one cannot wave the "tear." But in Hebrew the expression is a natural one.[25] The similarity between the Nephites falling down during King Benjamin's speech and Methodists falling down at revival meetings in Joseph Smith's day is superficial. More extensive are the similarities between King Benjamin's speech and ancient Israelite festival and coronation celebrations.[26]

5. B. H. Roberts displayed a list of twenty-six purported "parallels" between the Book of Mormon and a book written in 1823 (second edition 1825). That book, *View of the Hebrews*, argues that the American Indians were descendants of the lost ten tribes of Israel (a theory which Elder Roberts rightly wrote in 1932 is not the theory of the Book of Mormon). Since the alleged points of contact between *View of the Hebrews* and the Book of Mormon are scattered throughout *View of the Hebrews* and in some cases are supposedly quite specific, the hypothesis that Joseph Smith directly relied on *View of the Hebrews* becomes plausible only if one assumes that Joseph Smith knew *View of the Hebrews* quite well and accepted it as correct. If this were so, then he should have followed it—or at least not contradicted it—on its major points. But this does not turn out to be the case. Consider the following "unparallels":

a. *View of the Hebrews* begins with a chapter on the destruction of Jerusalem by the Romans. It has nothing to say, however, about the much earlier destruction of Jerusalem in Lehi's day by the Babylonians.

b. Chapter 3 composes most of *View of the Hebrews*. It produces numerous "distinguished Hebraisms" as "proof" that the American Indians are Israelites. But few of these points are found in the Book of Mormon, as one would expect if Joseph Smith had used *View of the Hebrews* in trying to make his book persuasive. For example: *View of the Hebrews* asserts repeatedly that the ten tribes came to America via the Bering Strait, which they crossed on "dry land." According to *View of the Hebrews*, this opinion is unquestionable, supported by all the authorities. From there *View of the Hebrews* documents that the Israelites spread from north to east and then to the south at a very late date. These are critical points for *View of the Hebrews*, in whose view Amos 8:11–12 prophesies that the tribes would go from the north to the east. Significant population migrations in the Book of Mormon, however, follow a crossing of the ocean and then always move from south to north.

c. *View of the Hebrews* reports that the Indians are Israelites because they use the word *Hallelujah*. Here is one of *View of the Hebrews's* favorite proofs, a dead giveaway that the Indians are Israelites. Yet this word is not used in the Book of Mormon. Furthermore, a table showing thirty-four Indian words or sentence fragments with claimed Hebrew equivalents appears in *View of the Hebrews* (2d ed., pp. 90–91). No reader of the book could have easily missed this chart. If Joseph Smith had wanted to make up names to use in the Book of Mormon that would substantiate his claim that he had found some authentic Western Hemisphere Hebrew words, he would have looked hard at such a ready-made list. Yet none of these thirty-four Hebrew/Indian words (*Keah, Lani, Uwoh, Phale, Kurbet,* etc.) resemble any of the 175 words that appear for the first time in the Book of Mormon.

d. *View of the Hebrews* says that the Indians are Israelites because they carry small boxes with them into battle. These are to protect them against injury. In *View of the Hebrews*, they are considered sure signs that the Indians' ancestors knew of the ark of the covenant. If Joseph Smith were depending on *View of the Hebrews*, he would likely not have passed up such a distinguished and oft-attested "Hebraism" as this. Yet in all Book of Mormon battle scenes, there is no such ark, box, or bag serving as a military fetish.

e. The Indians are Israelites because the Mohawk tribe, a tribe held in great reverence by all the others, was paid tribute. To *View of the Hebrews*, the conclusion was that the Mohawks are the vestiges of the tribe of Levi, Israel's tribe of priests. If Joseph Smith were relying on such a belief, one might think that he would have provided something about Levites in the Book of Mormon, but he did not.

f. *View of the Hebrews* claims that the righteous Indians quickly lost knowledge that they were all from the same family, were active "for a long time" well into recent times, and that their destruction occurred about A.D. 1400, as evidenced by tree ring counts near some of the fortifications of these people. The Book of Mormon rejects these notions, reporting that tribal affiliations were maintained for almost a thousand years and that the destruction of the Nephites occurred in the fourth century after Christ.

g. *View of the Hebrews* argues that the Indians are Israelites because they knew the legends of Quetzalcoatl. But the surprise here is that *View of the Hebrews* argues that Quetzalcoatl was none other than—not Jesus—but Moses! "Who could this be but *Moses*, the ancient legislator in Israel?" (*View of the Hebrews*, 2d ed., p. 206; emphasis in original.) He was white, gave laws, required penance (strict obedience), had a serpent with green plumage (brazen, fiery-flying serpent in the wilderness), appeased God's wrath (by sacrifices), was associated with a great famine (in Egypt), spoke from a volcano (Sinai), walked barefoot (removed his shoes), and opened a golden age (seven years of plenty in Egypt—which has nothing to do with Moses, by the way). If *View of the Hebrews* provided inspiration for the Book of Mormon, it did not provide much. In addition to the point that *View of the Hebrews* sees Quetzalcoatl as Moses, none of these hallmark details associated with Quetzalcoatl are incorporated into the account of Christ's visit to Bountiful in 3 Nephi.

The foregoing seven points can be multiplied literally twelve times over.[27] In the face of such differences, the few similarities pale. Both works speak of long migrations for religious reasons; both report wars; both say the people knew how to write and work with metals; and both praise generosity and denounce pride; *View of the Hebrews* speaks of Indian lore that they left a "lost book" back in Palestine and buried other records with their chiefs. B. H. Roberts asks the question: "Can such numerous and startling points of resemblance and suggestive contact be merely coincidence?" One can answer yes, for the differences outweigh the similarities and most of the similarities lose force upon examination. If Joseph Smith had given *View of the Hebrews* credence (assuming that he ever saw the book), he would not have contradicted and ignored it in so many ways.[28]

Q. Do we have all the answers to Book of Mormon questions?

A. No. We may never have all the answers to questions about the Book of Mormon. But in the sixty years since B. H. Roberts made his study, many things which he thought someone might say were weak or odd about the Book of Mormon have turned out to strengthen its credibility.

The Lord apparently does not intend the Book of Mormon to be an open-and-shut case intellectually, either pro or con. If he had intended that, he would have left more concrete evidences. Instead, the Lord has given us the opportunity to address the Book of Mormon as a matter of faith, as a modern-day miracle, a product of divine revelation. As such, it serves, through revelation, as a keystone of the Restoration and as a sacred testimony of Jesus Christ. As B. H. Roberts did, all readers of the Book of Mormon should take the Holy Ghost—not a list of preconceived, self-limiting issues—as their guide.

Few have sensed the will of the Lord in this regard more keenly than B. H. Roberts, who for many years was the "lightning rod" among the General Authorities to absorb the strikes against the Book of Mormon and supply answers whenever he could. Often he had good replies, but sometimes he had none. He never expected or claimed to have all the answers.

Today, while we have better answers, we still do not have all the answers; we should not expect or need to have. But that does not mean that we lose faith in the Book of Mormon.

Elder Roberts, in fact, is an inspiring example of one who kept the faith in the face of serious questions for which he did not have the answers. If in his works we find some things that on the surface seem confusing, we should remember his words in October 1929: "If anywhere along the line I have caused any of you to doubt my faith in this work, then let this testimony and my indicated life's work be a correction of it." So let it be.

Notes

1. See Truman G. Madsen, *Defender of the Faith: The B. H. Roberts Story* (Salt Lake City: Bookcraft, 1980).

2. B. H. Roberts, *New Witnesses for God,* 3 vols. (Salt Lake City: Deseret News, 1909), 2:vi–vii.

3. *Deseret News,* 16 June 1928.

4. Stake Conference Minutes, San Francisco Stake, 23–24 April 1932.

5. Roberts wrote this in 1921 in a paper entitled "Book of Mormon Difficulties," which he submitted to the First Presidency and the Quorum of the Twelve.

6. Most recently these papers have appeared in *Studies of the Book of Mormon,* ed. Brigham D. Madsen (Chicago: University of Illinois Press, 1985).

7. B. H. Roberts to Elder Richard R. Lyman, 24 October 1927.

8. Documentation dating the "Study" is presented in a report by John W. Welch and Truman G. Madsen, "Did B. H. Roberts Lose Faith in the Book of Mormon?" (FARMS Preliminary Report, 1985, P. O. Box 7113 University Station, Provo, UT 84602.)

9. This corrects, with Madsen's concurrence, his statement in the *Ensign,* December 1983, p. 15. See letter of B. H. Roberts to Elder Richard R. Lyman, 24 October 1927, stating that he had not yet decided to submit the "Study" to the First Presidency.

10. Truman G. Madsen, *Ensign,* Dec. 1983, p. 15.

11. Roberts, *New Witnesses for God,* 3:523.

12. Roberts, *New Witnesses for God,* 3:503–4.

13. See Truman G. Madsen, "B. H. Roberts and the Book of Mormon," *BYU Studies* 19 (Summer 1979), pp. 427–45.

14. These are all collected in "B. H. Roberts: His Final Decade — Statements about the Book of Mormon (1922–1933)," available as FARMS Reprint ROB-33.

15. For a lengthy listing of these statements, see Welch and Madsen, "Did B. H. Roberts Lose Faith in the Book of Mormon?"

16. In Conference Report, Oct. 1929, pp. 89–91.

17. This was in the middle of the Great Depression.

18. Brother Lloyd was a careful reporter, but still, inadvertent errors happen. Apparently Roberts was not precise in all respects when he spoke to Lloyd. The "Study" was done during 1922, not later, as Lloyd reported. Elder Lyman asked if the research would "increase our difficulties," not "help our prestige." The "Study" was 450 pages, not 400, and was never sent to President Grant. Lloyd said that Roberts, in the "Study," "swings to a psychological explanation of the Book of Mormon and shows that the plates were not objective but subjective with Joseph Smith." But there is no such "swinging" or "showing" in the "Study."

19. See letter of Mark Allen, one of Roberts's missionaries, written 20 July 1983, in possession of Truman G. Madsen.

20. Madsen, *Defender of the Faith,* p. 376.

21. Jack Christensen was interviewed by Truman Madsen, 25 April 1979.

22. For a discussion of Hugh Nibley's contributions to Book of Mormon studies, see *Ensign,* April 1985, p. 50.

23. In Conference Report, Apr. 1929, pp. 15–16.

24. Deseret Book Co., 1985. See also *Ensign,* Sept. 1984, pp. 26–37, and Oct. 1984, pp. 12–23.

25. See John A. Tvedtnes, "Hebraisms in the Book of Mormon: A Preliminary Survey," *BYU Studies* 11 (Autumn 1970), p. 51. Readers interested in an expanded treatment of Roberts's questions are referred to "Finding Answers to B. H. Roberts's Questions, and 'An Unparallel,' " (FARMS Preliminary Report, 1985).

26. This is demonstrated in a report entitled "King Benjamin's Speech in the Context of Ancient Israelite Festivals" (FARMS Preliminary Report, 1985).

27. I discuss eighty-four such distinctions in "Finding Answers to B. H. Roberts's Questions, and 'An Unparallel.' "

28. There is no evidence that Joseph Smith ever saw or knew anything about *View of the Hebrews,* and there was no library in Harmony, Penn-

sylvania, where Joseph lived while translating all of the Book of Mormon except for the final work done in June 1830 at the Whitmer farm. The theory that Oliver Cowdery introduced Joseph to *View of the Hebrews* and that Joseph, who then used it to formulate the basic storyline of the Book of Mormon, is impossible. Oliver and Joseph first met on 5 April 1829, long after the basic story of the Book of Mormon was known to Emma Smith, Martin Harris, the Hales family, the Smith family, and others, through the translation of the 116 pages that were lost in 1828.

Further discussions of dissimilarities between *View of the Hebrews* and the Book of Mormon are available in Spencer J. Palmer and William L. Knecht, "View of the Hebrews: Substitute for Inspiration?" *BYU Studies* 5 (Winter 1964), pp. 105–13; Hugh Nibley, "The Comparative Method," *Improvement Era,* Oct. 1959, pp. 744–59 and Nov. 1959, pp. 848, 854, 856; Hugh Nibley, *No Ma'am That's Not History* (Salt Lake City: Bookcraft, 1946); and Bruce Blumell, *Ensign,* Sept. 1976, pp. 84–87, each available as reprints from FARMS. See also Ariel L. Crowley, "Analysis of Ethan Smith's 'View of the Hebrews': A Comparison with the Book of Mormon," in *About the Book of Mormon* (Salt Lake City: Deseret News Press, 1961); William Riley, "A Comparison of Passages from Isaiah and Other Old Testament Prophets in Ethan Smith's *View of the Hebrews* and the Book of Mormon," Master's thesis, Brigham Young University, 1971.

DOCTRINE AND COVENANTS

QA

What are the features of the 1981 edition of the Doctrine and Covenants that can aid us in our scripture study?

Bill Applegarth, principal, Cottonwood Seminary, Salt Lake City, Utah

Seven major improvements were made in the 1981 edition of the Doctrine and Covenants:

1. Important text was added: sections 137 and 138, Official Declaration 2, and excerpts from three addresses by President Wilford Woodruff concerning Official Declaration 1.

2. A new Explanatory Introduction was written.

3. Many of the section headings were rewritten to give clear, concise historical background.

4. A synopsis of the verses was added at the beginning of each section.

5. The footnotes were expanded to include cross-references to all the standard works and to the Topical Guide in the Latter-day Saint edition of the King James Version of the Bible.

6. The index was expanded and combined with the indexes of the Book of Mormon and the Pearl of Great Price.

7. Maps of New England, New York-Ohio, and Missouri-Illinois were included, as well as a map of the United States in 1847.

Using these new features as we read and study the Doctrine and Covenants will increase our understanding of the principles taught in this book of modern-day revelations.

The *section headings* tell us the date the revelation was received, where it occurred and who was present, and other historical circumstances. This information can help us better understand what prompted the revelation or what questions the Lord was answering. For example, in the headnote to section 76, we are told that the Prophet Joseph Smith and Sidney Rigdon were working on the translation of the Bible and had just translated John 5:28–29: "Marvel not at this: for the hour is coming, in the which all that are in the graves shall hear his voice, and shall come forth; they that have done good, unto the resurrection of life; and they that have done evil, unto the resurrection of damnation." As Joseph Smith and

Sidney Rigdon were meditating on the passage, "the Lord touched the eyes of [their] understanding . . . and the glory of the Lord shone round about." (D&C 76:19.) Other revelations also become more meaningful when we see them in their proper historical perspective.

The *section synopsis,* immediately following the section heading, gives us a preview of the text before we read it, helping us understand what the section is about. The synopsis shows which verses the main ideas occur in, directing us quickly to specific ideas. For example, the synopsis at the beginning of section 76 tells us that information on "the glory and reward of exalted beings in the celestial kingdom" is found in verses 50 through 70. When we finish reading the section, we can review the synopsis to see if we have recognized and understood the main points of the revelation.

The *footnotes* cross-reference ideas and words in the Doctrine and Covenants to related concepts in all the standard works. The footnotes also list references in the Topical Guide in the Bible.

The *index* is a great tool when we study by topics. It can help us find answers to questions about doctrines and prepare talks and lessons. We can look up key words in the index, and find a list of specific scriptural references for each subject. For example, if we want information on baptism for the dead, the index will direct us to five scriptures in the Doctrine and Covenants that explain the Lord's instructions and Joseph Smith's teachings on the subject.

The four *maps* can help us better understand the geography of the United States during the time most of these revelations were received.

The study helps in the current edition of the Doctrine and Covenants have been developed so that we may better understand and apply the scriptures in our lives. It remains now for us to use them.

QA

Does Doctrine and Covenants 84:19–22 mean that a person has to have the Melchizedek Priesthood in order to see God? Joseph Smith didn't have the priesthood at the time of the First Vision.

Melvin J. Petersen, professor of Church history and doctrine, Brigham Young University

Several scriptures show that a person doesn't have to have the Melchizedek Priesthood or be a recipient of its ordinances in order to see either the Father or the Son.

In the New Testament, for example, we read that Saul of Tarsus, later known as Paul the Apostle, saw the resurrected Jesus on the road to Damascus. At the time of this experience, Saul held no true priesthood; he was, in fact, trying to destroy the Lord's disciples, whom he considered heretics. It wasn't until after the heavenly vision that he received any of the ordinances of the priesthood. (See Acts 9:3–18.)

In the Book of Mormon, Lamoni, a Lamanite king, saw the Lord before receiving the priesthood or its ordinances. He was overcome by the Spirit after hearing Ammon's missionary message, and in the process of his conversion he beheld the Redeemer. (See Alma 18:36–19:13.)

The Savior himself explained on one occasion, "Not that any man hath seen the Father, save he which is of God, he hath seen the Father." (John 6:46.) The apostle John wrote that one who does evil "hath not seen God." (3 John 1:11.)

At another time, the Lord said: "He that hath my commandments and keepeth them, he it is that loveth me: and he that loveth me shall be loved of my Father, and I will love him, and will manifest myself to him." (John 14:21.)

Does the same hold true for seeing God the Father? Apparently so. Jesus said that "if a man love me, he will keep my words; and my Father will love him, and we will come unto him, and make our abode with him." (John 14:23; see also D&C 130:3.)

Such visions are extremely rare, however. "No man hath seen God at any time," Jesus explained, *"except he hath borne record of the Son; for except it is through him no man can be saved."* (JST John 1:19; italics added.) This enlightening comment explains that when God the Father appears to a person, it is primarily to testify of His Son, which is exactly what happened when the Father and the Son appeared to Joseph Smith.

Joseph Smith held no priesthood, nor had he received any priesthood ordinances at the time of the First Vision. But he loved the Lord and wanted to know how to order his life. In response to his earnest prayer, he saw the Father and the Son, he heard what they said, he spoke and asked questions, and he received answers. (See Joseph Smith–History 1:15–20.)

"The Power of Godliness"

Although a person need not hold the priesthood to be visited by God, that does not mean priesthood power is absent during the experience. In many cases, those who have seen God report that they were overshadowed by divine power. Moses, for example, recorded that he was spiritually and physically changed—"transfigured"—during his visit with the Lord: "Mine own eyes have beheld God," he wrote, "but not my natural, but my spiritual eyes, for my natural eyes could not have beheld; for I should have withered and died in his presence; but his glory was upon me; and I beheld his face, for I was transfigured before him." (Moses 1:11.)

The process by which a mortal is changed from his natural condition to a transfigured state is further clarified by a revelation given to the Prophet Joseph Smith: "No man has seen God at any time in the flesh, except *quickened by the Spirit of God*. Neither can any natural man abide the presence of God, neither after the carnal mind." (D&C 67:11–12; italics added.)

Sidney Rigdon and Joseph Smith describe an experience in which "the Lord touched the eyes of our understandings and they were opened, and the glory of the Lord shone round about. And we beheld the glory of the Son, on the right hand of the Father, and received of his fulness." (D&C 76:20.) They then went on to see in vision the three degrees of glory.

This same experience, they declared, is available to all those who love God and purify themselves. But it comes only "through the power and manifestation of the Spirit," that "while in the flesh, they may be able to bear his presence in the world of glory." (D&C 76:118.)

That is evidently one aspect of the "power of godliness" mentioned in Doctrine and Covenants 84:22. And it is priesthood power. The Prophet Joseph Smith explained that the Melchizedek Priesthood "is the highest and holiest Priesthood, and is after the order of the Son of God. . . . It is the channel through which the Almighty commenced revealing His glory at the beginning of the creation of this earth, and through which He has continued to reveal Himself to the children of men to the present time." (*Teachings of the Prophet Joseph Smith*, sel. Joseph Fielding Smith [Salt Lake City: Deseret Book Co., 1938], p. 167.)

"A Fulness of Glory"

Apparently, then, the power God uses to quicken men and women spiritually so that they can see him is the priesthood, the Holy Priesthood, after the Order of the Son of God, usually called the Melchizedek Priesthood. (See D&C 107:1–4.) Some, including

Moses, have associated this power with "glory," or God's "Presence," or the Holy Spirit. (See D&C 94:8–9; 97:15–16; 1 Nephi 17:41–52.)

This spiritual quickening is usually a temporary state that withdraws when the visit is finished. But sanctified beings who enjoy the promise of eternal life are endowed with a fulness of this power of godliness. If they endure in this state, the Savior promises that they will enjoy a fulness of glory forever as exalted beings and "dwell in the presence of God and his Christ forever." (See D&C 76:50–70; 88:3–5.)

This, in fact, was the goal Moses sought when he brought the children of Israel to Mount Sinai. Jehovah had wanted to sanctify Israel and make them "a kingdom of priests, and an holy nation" through covenant with him. (See Exodus 19:5–6.) Their sanctification would have been accomplished as God has ordained—through obedience to the laws and ordinances of the gospel. By exercising faith in Christ unto repentance and covenanting to keep his commandments by being baptized, each of the children of Israel could have been sanctified by receiving the Holy Ghost. (See 2 Nephi 31:17–20; 3 Nephi 27:18–21.)

Thus sanctified by the Spirit and endowed with the gift of the Holy Ghost, Israel would have entered a heightened spiritual state in which, through the ordinances of the Melchizedek Priesthood now administered in God's holy temples, they could have had access to the "mysteries of the kingdom, even the key of the knowledge of God." With that key, they would, in effect, have had the key to eternal life. Eventually, they might have so risen in spiritual stature, going "from grace to grace, from exaltation to exaltation," that they could have entered into God's rest fully and forever to "dwell in everlasting burnings, and to sit in glory, as do those who sit enthroned in everlasting power." (See Smith, *Teachings of the Prophet Joseph Smith,* pp. 298–99, 346–47; see also D&C 93:11–20.) They would truly have come to *know* God, which the Savior said is eternal life. (See John 17:1–3.)

But they weren't ready. Although ancient Israel saw the cloud in which Jehovah descended upon Mount Sinai and heard his voice, they were not permitted to see him. If they had tried, they would have perished. (See Exodus 19:9, 16–21.) The Lord explained that they were "exceedingly sinful. And no sinful man hath at any time, neither shall there be any sinful man at any time, that shall see my face and live." (JST Exodus 33:20.) Israel "hardened their hearts and could not endure his presence." They turned instead to the worship of a golden calf. Angered by their actions, the Lord "swore that they should not enter into his rest while in the wilderness, which rest is the fulness of his glory." (D&C 84:24.)

Since they could not abide the Lord's presence, the priesthood and the ordinances that would have set them onto the path of eternal life were withheld. God "took Moses out of their midst, and the Holy Priesthood also; and the lesser priesthood continued." (See D&C 84:25–26; JST Exodus 34:1–2.)

"The Knowledge of God"

Commenting upon Doctrine and Covenants 84:19, President Joseph Fielding Smith said: "It is impossible for men to obtain the knowledge of the mysteries of the kingdom or the knowledge of God, without the authority of the priesthood. Secular learning, the study of the sciences, arts and history, will not reveal these vital truths to man. It is the Holy Priesthood that unlocks the door to heaven and reveals to man the mysteries of the Kingdom of God. It is this Divine Authority which makes known the knowledge of God! Is there any wonder that the world today is groping in gross darkness concerning God and the things of his kingdom? We should also remember that these great truths are not made known even to members of the Church unless they place their lives in harmony with the law on which these blessings are predicated." (*Church History and Modern Revelation,* 2 vols. [Salt Lake City: Deseret Book Co., 1953], 1:338.)

Seeing God is a wonderful but a rare thing. He comes to whomever he will, overshadowing them by his power so that they can endure his presence. But obtaining the knowledge of God, which obviously involves more than just seeing him, requires all the ordinances of the Melchizedek Priesthood. Secular sources or man's best efforts will not do.

"When we read things of this nature," said President Joseph Fielding Smith, referring to Doctrine and Covenants 84:19–22, "it ought to make every man among us who holds the priesthood rejoice to think that we have that great authority by which *we may know God.* Not only the men holding the priesthood know that great truth, but because of the priesthood and the *ordinances thereof,* every member of the Church, men and women alike, may know God." (*Doctrines of Salvation,* comp. Bruce R. McConkie, 3 vols. [Salt Lake City: Bookcraft, 1954–56], 3:142–43.)

QA

Why does Doctrine and Covenants 104:1 say that the united order is an everlasting order until the Lord comes, yet it is not practiced today?

Stephen K. Iba, Church Educational System Area Director, Salt Lake Valley North Area

Whenever a covenant or commandment is entered into between God and his children, it should be understood in terms of larger, eternal laws and principles. The Prophet Joseph Smith stated that "we are looked upon by God as though we were in eternity. God dwells in eternity, and does not view things as we do." (*Teachings of the Prophet Joseph Smith*, sel. Joseph Fielding Smith [Salt Lake City: Deseret Book Co., 1938], p. 356.) "For my thoughts are not your thoughts, neither are your ways my ways, saith the Lord. For as the heavens are higher than the earth, so are my ways higher than your ways, and my thoughts than your thoughts." (Isaiah 55:8–9.)

These statements suggest that God may have something else in mind when he uses such words as *everlasting, eternal, Endless,* or *forever.* "Endless torment" and "eternal damnation," for example, do not mean there is no end to punishment, only that such punishment is God's punishment. "The punishment which is given from my hand is endless punishment, for Endless is my name." (D&C 19:10.)

A number of scriptures in the Bible sustain this principle. For example, during the Mosaic dispensation, the Lord commanded Israel to celebrate Passover: "And this day shall be unto you for a memorial; and ye shall keep it a feast to the Lord throughout your generations; ye shall keep it a feast by an ordinance for ever." (Exodus 12:14.) Similarly, the Day of Atonement, where the high priest would execute a sacrificial offering for all the people yearly, was sanctioned and sealed by Jehovah as "an everlasting statute unto you." (Leviticus 16:34.)

Today, we celebrate neither the Passover nor the Day of Atonement. We understand that both were in similitude of the everlasting release of God's children from the bondage of sin and death through our great High Priest, Jesus Christ. (See Hebrews 6:20.) With the Savior's advent on earth, those ordinances were superseded by the ordinances of the gospel. (See Hebrews 8.)

That is also true of the "everlasting covenant" of circumcision revealed to Abraham. (See Genesis 17:9–14.) In the first century after Christ, this practice created problems when Gentiles were converted to Christianity. Consequently, an apostolic council pronounced that this "everlasting" rite ended when Christ restored the fulness of the gospel. (See Acts 15:6–31.)

Early in the Restoration, the Lord revealed the law of consecration and commanded the Saints to be united in *all* things—doctrinally, spiritually, socially, and economically. This law, they were told, would help them establish Zion upon the principles of the law of the celestial kingdom. The united order was instituted to help implement the principles of the law of consecration. Within three years, however, the Lord chastened the Church for transgression and withdrew the practice of the united order from the Saints. (See D&C 105:2–6, 9–13, 27–37.)

Although the united order was suspended, some aspects of the law of consecration remained. Those aspects that are active today were mentioned by President Marion G. Romney in general conference: "Full implementation of the united order must, according to the revelation, await the redemption of Zion. (See D&C 105:34.) In the meantime—while we are being more perfectly taught and are gaining experience—we should be strictly living the principles of the united order insofar as they are embodied in present Church requirements, such as tithing, fast offerings, welfare projects, storehouses, and other principles and practices. Through these programs we should, as individuals, implement in our own lives the bases of the united order." (In Conference Report, Apr. 1977, p. 120.)

Although the united order was placed in abeyance, it is part of the everlasting gospel of Jesus Christ. The principle is clear in the scriptures: the Lord is everlasting and eternal; hence, everything he commands is everlasting and eternal, although a particular commandment may not be practiced all the time, but only for the period the Lord wills. It is also important to understand that when the Lord commands, we are invited to obey to be blessed. Our obedience or disobedience to his law will have "everlasting" consequences. So it is with the united order. It will be lived in full when the Lord commands. It is his law, which is everlasting for all who receive it.

QA

More than a century and a half ago, the Prophet Joseph Smith learned from the Lord that tobacco is not good for us. Since then, medical science has determined the same thing. How has society responded to this information?

Dr. James Mason, director of the Centers for Disease Control, Atlanta, Georgia

The revelation known today as section 89 of the Doctrine and Covenants was received on 27 February 1833. Few revelations have come under more scrutiny than this "word of wisdom," and few have served as well to vindicate Joseph Smith's calling as a prophet. The counsel he received that day in 1833 has since received increasing support from scientific and medical research, much of it only in the past few decades. The Lord's admonition to refrain from tobacco is but one example.

For the past twenty-two years, the Surgeon General of the United States has identified cigarette smoking as the single most important cause of disease and premature death. Tobacco kills thirteen times as many Americans as hard drugs do, and eight times as many as automobile accidents. The worldwide cost in lives now approaches 2.5 million lives per year, with about 360,000 deaths annually in the United States. Over a billion people now consume almost a trillion cigarettes per year, an average of more than half a pack per day.

Lung cancer alone claims 129,000 lives per year; coronary heart disease kills another 170,000 annually. Some smokers contract cancer of the larynx, mouth, esophagus, bladder, and pancreas; some suffer with chronic bronchitis, pulmonary emphysema, peptic ulcer, allergies, thrombosis, reduced fertility, and peripheral vascular disease. Smokers can even be affected by the medicines they take to get well, because the desired pharmacological effects of some drugs can be altered by the chemical residue of tobacco in their bodies.

The United States Public Health Service calls Americans' addiction to tobacco "the most widespread example of drug dependence in our country." Nicotine is an addictive drug, and the American Lung Association and other agencies state that smoking meets all the criteria of addiction. The fact that nine out of every ten American smokers say they want to "kick the habit" provides additional evidence of the addictive qualities of tobacco.

The Lord has told us that "tobacco is not for the body, neither for the belly, and is not good for man." (D&C 89:8.) In spite of this and other warnings, the rate of smoking is increasing in many countries where the citizens can least afford tobacco products and smoking's adverse effect on their health. The people of these countries are already confronted with high infant and child mortality rates, short adult life span, and limited health care facilities. Family incomes are low and often do not cover basic requirements for food and clothing. Even so, smoking is on the increase in eastern bloc countries, Canada, and Egypt, where more young people than adults smoke. In some schools surveyed in Santiago, Chile, two-thirds of the children smoked.

Statistics in other countries, including the United States, Great Britain, Norway, and Sweden, are more positive and show a decrease in smoking, particularly in the age of starting to smoke and the incidence of smoking. An analysis of cigarette smoking in the United States from 1981 to 1983 showed gradual reductions in smoking. According to an American Cancer Society study, the number of men who smoke dropped from 48.4 percent in 1959 to 26.15 percent in 1982. The percentage of women smokers declined, too, from 27.2 to 21.1 during the same period. Nevertheless, women in general, and young Caucasian women in particular, compose a higher percentage of smokers than ever before because their consumption of tobacco is not falling as rapidly as in other groups. Women eighteen to twenty-two years old currently have a higher smoking rate than men—34.9 percent versus 34 percent. If present trends continue, smoking rates for men and women will be identical in the United States by 1990.

That trend alarms many researchers who have found that in the past few decades, women have taken up smoking almost with a vengeance. As a result, the average life expectancy advantage women have had over men is gradually being eroded. Over the past thirty-two years, there has been a 315 percent increase in the lung cancer death rate among women, and lung cancer is expected to surpass breast cancer as the leading cancer killer of American women. It has already done so in five states.

Smoking by mothers of unborn children is even more serious because it places their offspring at risk. Nicotine, numerous toxic chemicals, and radioactive polonium all interfere with fetal development, because the fetus can receive these substances through the mother's blood. Twice as many underweight babies are born to smokers as are born to other women. And because birth weight is a key factor in infant mortality, tobacco use by a mother can threaten her baby's life. Furthermore, Americans pay more than $152 million a year for intensive care services to underweight babies of smoking mothers. To add to these grim statistics, birth defects, including mental retardation, abnormal facial features, and heart defects may occur in infants of women who smoke two or more packs of cigarettes per day during pregnancy. Each year more than 3 million babies are born thus afflicted, and the number is growing as more women become smokers.

The tragic and needless deaths, disease, and untoward effects on the unborn that occur as a result of tobacco witness to the truth of the Word of Wisdom.

Even those who don't smoke are at risk in a smoking environment. For example, children of smoking parents experience much higher rates of respiratory illness, including colds, pneumonia, and bronchitis. They can also suffer lifelong effects; evidence shows that passive smoking in childhood (inhaling the smoke of others' tobacco products) delays physical and intellectual development.

Passive smokers are about three times more likely to die of lung cancer than are those not exposed. More than ten studies have linked lung cancer in nonsmoking men and women to their smoking spouses. In fact, passive smoking is estimated to cause more cancer deaths in the United States than all regulated industrial air pollutants combined. This may affect five thousand nonsmokers per year, or one-third of the cases of lung cancer not directly attributed to smoking.

Smoking is not only a deadly habit but a costly one. The price Americans paid in 1985 for lost productivity and health care was approximately 65 billion dollars. And this figure does not include the cost of the tobacco itself—another $30 billion!—nor the loss of food and other beneficial products the land could have been used to produce.

In response to tobacco's terrible cost in lives and health, many governmental and private agencies have launched campaigns attacking smoking. One result is that television stations now no longer carry advertising for cigarettes and cigars. The year 1982 marked the first decrease in the sale of cigarettes since 1969, and sales declined even further in 1983.

But as sales fall, the advertising budgets of cigarette manufacturers rise. The more than $2.7 billion spent on cigarette advertising in 1983 was mostly to convince young people to smoke. The Lord was aware of these temptations when he warned, "In consequence of evils and designs which do and will exist in the hearts of conspiring men in the last days, I have warned you, and forewarn you, by giving unto you this word of wisdom by revelation." (D&C 89:4.)

One ironic result of campaigns to reduce smoking has been the marked increase in the use of "smokeless" tobacco. As the sales of cigarettes decline in the wake of negative health publicity, sales of smokeless tobacco are dramatically increasing. The use of "chew" or "snuff" in the United States has increased more than 40 percent in the last two decades, and as many as 22 million Americans may now be users.

There are three kinds of smokeless tobacco: chewing tobacco, dry snuff (usually inhaled), and moist snuff (tucked between the gum and lip). Youth are becoming heavily involved in this form of tobacco use. A study of one thousand high school students in Colorado noted that 22 percent of the male students chewed tobacco or dipped snuff, with 10 percent using it on a regular or daily basis. Even young children are becoming involved; a 1983 study in Louisiana showed that 21 percent of ten-year-olds dipped snuff!

The health hazards of smokeless tobacco have long been known. As early as 1761, John Hill, a British physician and botanist, blamed a cancerous lesion in a patient's nose on the patient's "immoderate" use of snuff. Two hundred and twenty-five years later, the Massachusetts Department of Public Health ordered that snuff carry warning labels about its cancer-causing properties. The United States Congress has recently mandated tough warning labels on all smokeless tobacco products and advertising.

Physical symptoms of disease caused by smokeless tobacco include receding gums, disintegration of bone where the wad of tobacco is held in the mouth, and formation on the gums of white patches called leukoplakia. A significant percentage of these leukoplakia patches become cancerous. Researchers in the United States, Canada, Sweden, Great Britain, India, and Denmark have concluded that smokeless tobacco is linked to oral, pharyngeal, and laryngeal cancer. A study in the southern United States showed that short-time snuff users had a fourfold increase in cancer; long-time users had a rate fifty times higher!

The smokeless tobacco industry is gearing up to fight any hint that its products are not good for health. Manufacturers are resisting warning labels. One manufacturer with a $30 million budget promoted its product in conjunction with the 1984 Summer Olympics with the slogan, "Take a pouch instead of a puff," falsely implying that smokeless tobaccos are a safe alternative to cigarette smoking.

Users who think smokeless tobacco is nonaddictive are wrong; there is just as much addiction with smokeless tobacco as with cigarettes. The only difference is that instead of being inhaled, the poisonous alkaloid is readily absorbed through the lining of the mouth.

There is some good news in all this: we have no reason to believe that addiction to tobacco cannot be overcome. More than 33 million Americans have heeded the warnings and given up smoking since 1964 when the first Surgeon General's report on the consequences of smoking was issued. No one is so addicted that he or she cannot stop smoking. The Word of Wisdom was "given for a principle with promise, adapted to the capacity of the weak and the weakest of all saints, who are or can be called saints." (D&C 89:3.)

It is good news that smokers of all ages can experience substantial health benefits from giving up tobacco. Even those who have smoked for as long as fifty years have a great deal to gain by giving up their habit. They feel noticeably better within a year, and they also reduce their chances of having a stroke or a heart attack.

The Lord finished his revelation on the Word of Wisdom with a promise to the Saints: "And all saints who remember to keep and do these sayings, walking in obedience to the commandments, shall receive health in their navel and marrow to their bones; and shall find wisdom and great treasures of knowledge, even hidden treasures; and shall run and not be weary, and shall walk and not faint." (D&C 89:18–20.)

NEW
TESTAMENT

QA

How do we reconcile the passage "God is a spirit" with God's being a personage of flesh and bones?

William O. Nelson, director, Melchizedek Priesthood Department

Latter-day Saints are sometimes accused of having an antibiblical theology because they believe that God is a glorified being of flesh and bones, not just a spirit essence. Some who write anti-Mormon pamphlets insist that the Latter-day Saint concept of Deity is contrary to what is recognized as traditional Christian doctrine. In this they are quite correct. The traditional view of the Trinity is well over a thousand years old, and time has a way of hallowing ideas, whether or not they are true.

One of the most demonstrable truths from the Bible is the physical, bodily resurrection of Jesus Christ. When Jesus came forth from the tomb, he showed himself to his apostles. Even they thought him to be a spirit, but he said: "Behold my hands and my feet, that it is I myself: handle me, and see; for a spirit hath not flesh and bones, as ye see me have." Then he showed them his hands and feet, and when they were still skeptical, he asked for meat and honeycomb and ate before them. (Luke 24:36–43.) Then they saw he was no apparition.

Thomas was not present at Jesus' first appearance to the Twelve, so he remained skeptical. He told the others: "Except I shall see in his hands the print of the nails, and put my finger into the print of the nails, and thrust my hand into his side, I will not believe." (John 20:24–25.) One week later, Jesus again appeared to the disciples. This time, Thomas was among them. The Lord greeted them, then spoke to Thomas: "Reach hither thy finger, and behold my hands; and reach hither thy hand, and thrust it into my side: and be not faithless, but believing." Thomas could only exclaim, "My Lord and my God." (John 20:26–28.) That day he became a special witness of the Lord's literal resurrection.

After Jesus was resurrected, more than five hundred also saw him and testified of his physical resurrection. (See 1 Corinthians 15:5–8.) The apostles, too, were witnesses of his ascension into heaven when two angels told them that Jesus would return in like manner as he had ascended. (See Acts 1:9–11.)

We also know that at his second coming Christ will appear with a physical body. John testified that "every eye shall see him." (Revelation 1:7.) Zechariah prophesied that "his *feet* shall stand in that day upon the mount of Olives" (Zechariah 14:4; italics added), and the beleaguered Israelites "shall look upon [him] whom they have pierced, and they shall mourn for him." (Zechariah 12:10.) And then "one shall say unto him, What are these wounds in thine *hands*? Then he shall answer, Those with which I was wounded in the house of my friends." (Zechariah 13:6; italics added.)

With such an abundance of biblical testimony from the ancient apostles and prophets, how did traditional Christianity come to the idea that somehow Jesus' bodily identity was dissolved into spirit essence? How did the Christian sects come to accept the idea that though three personages compose the Godhead, they are one immaterial spirit? Certainly the ideas are not apostolic in origin.

The early apostles took the gospel into a Greco-Roman world that espoused Neoplatonism, a philosophy derived from Plato's teachings on idealism. One Neoplatonic idea was that matter is essentially evil.[1] As long as apostles led the Church, they opposed such philosophies. Paul's first letter to the Corinthians is an example of this opposition. Apparently, some who held to the belief that matter was evil were baptized but had difficulty accepting the physical resurrection of Jesus. They reasoned that since Jesus was perfectly good, he could not have a material body. In his letter, Paul addressed the Greek belief in the body's corruptibility by bearing testimony that a resurrected body, like Christ's, is incorruptible. (See 1 Corinthians 15:3–8, 12–20, 35–42.) Likewise the apostle John asserted in his gospel and epistles that Jesus was a divine being of flesh in mortality to counteract the heresy that he was not or could not have been flesh because matter was evil. (See John 1:14; 1 John 1:1–3; 4:3.)

The dilemma of the church after the first century was how to sustain a unified church without a body of general authorities. By the early second century, the church had gone through three major persecutions by the Roman emperors Nero (A.D. 54–68), Domitian (A.D. 81–96), and Trajan (A.D. 98–117), and apostasy and heresy were rampant. The apostles were gone—all martyred except for John—and church leaders who had known the apostles but did not have their apostolic keys—such men as Papias, Clement of Rome, and Polycarp—were dead.

The defenders of the church in the late second and third century were Christian apologists and scholars, many of whom were trained in Greek philosophy and in rhetoric and logic. They brought the classical culture of Greece into the church for two reasons: first, to rhetorically and logically "prove" the Christian gospel to a world steeped in Greek culture; second, to make Christianity intellectually respectable. Their efforts were an understandable human reaction to counteract the persecution that the church had suffered for two centuries. But it made the church compatible with the very culture the church had once disdained.

The synthesis of Greek philosophy and the Christian gospel is well documented. H. I. Marrou described how Origen and others caused the church to embrace Hellenistic culture and ideas.[2] In his definitive work, Edwin Hatch wrote that the early Christians' study of Greek philosophy created a certain "habit of mind":

"When Christianity came into contact with the society in which that habit of mind existed, it modified, it reformed, it elevated, the ideas which it contained and the motives which stimulated it to action; but in its turn it was itself profoundly modified by the habit of mind of those who accepted it. It was impossible for Greeks, . . . with an education which penetrated their whole nature, to receive or to retain Christianity in its primitive simplicity."[3]

As the church entered the third century, many ridiculed Christianity because they regarded it as polytheistic—that is, it had a theology of three Gods: the Father, the Son, and the Holy Ghost. By this time the more sophisticated had rejected polytheistic pagan deities and had become monotheistic, accepting but one God. So the issue for the church was how to make Christian theology accord with respectable opinion.

Tertullian, a lawyer, offered this solution: the true God was composed of immaterial spiritual substance, and though the three personages that composed the Godhead were distinct, this was only a material manifestation of an invisible God. As for how three persons could be one, it was explained that the persons were legally conceived entities, "just as a corporation is composed of various people though it is not the people."[4]

Fusing the ideas of church theologians, such as Irenaeus, Origen, Tertullian, and Athanasius, the Trinitarian formula of three spirits in one was finally accepted as official doctrine by the council of Nicea in A.D. 325. (Lyon, pp. 144–53; Barker, pp. 249–71.)

The key issue through these early centuries was whether Christians would accept a God who was corporeal and material or one who was pure spirit. Here Greek philosophy prevailed, with its antipathy to materialism, opposition to polytheism, and revulsion to the idea that God had a body.

The unsurpassed intellectual in Christian history was Augustine. He thoroughly fused the theology of the New Testament with Neoplatonism. In examining Christian doctrine, Augustine confessed to a strong preconception — a repugnance to the idea that God had a body.[5] He acknowledged that he had labored on the thesis of the Trinity for fifteen years without "ever reaching a satisfactory conclusion."[6] Finally he rationalized that if one accepts the Platonic idea that spirit essence is the purest manifestation of reality and that matter is the most corrupt, God must therefore be an immaterial being. He was then able to accept the doctrine of the Trinity.[7] As Plato had done before him, Augustine decided that since God is the ultimate good, he cannot be associated with anything material.

Augustine's personal theology became that of the Roman Empire and remains an influence in historic Christianity to this day. Such is the basis for traditional Christianity's teaching on the Trinity, a belief described by modern clerics as a mystery.

In view of biblical teachings on the nature of God and the historic development of the concept of the Trinity, we might ask, Which view is biblically more defensible?

As a child reared in a Protestant home and educated in a parochial grammar school, I vividly recall many occasions when teachers would vainly attempt to explain the mystery of the Trinity. We were told that there were three persons but not three Gods. The three persons were one spiritual substance, so there could not be three separate beings.

One explanation likened the Trinity to water, steam, and ice, which are different formations of the same element. Another likened the Trinity to writing a book. The author starts with an *idea,* then the idea becomes incarnate when the writer converts the idea to *words.* Then when others read the words of the book, it has an *effect* on the reader. The Idea is the Father, the Word is the Son, and the Effect is the Holy Ghost.

It was hard to fathom a Deity of this nature, let alone love him. But even more significant, the great teaching of Paul that we are

God's literal offspring (see Acts 17:28–29) is not even taught in traditional Christian theology. Unfortunately, because of this misunderstanding of God's true nature, millions of our Heavenly Father's children have failed to understand their true identity.

In contrast to the preponderance of scriptural support for the physical body of the Lord, there is meager evidence in the Bible to support belief in a God who is a spirit essence. The most frequently cited passage is a conversation between Jesus and a Samaritan woman. The Samaritans had a corrupted form of Jewish and heathen worship. The Savior said:

"Ye worship ye know not what: we know what we worship. . . .

"But the hour cometh, and now is, when the true worshippers shall worship the Father in spirit and in truth: for the Father seeketh such to worship him.

"*God is a Spirit:* and they that worship him must worship him in spirit and in truth." (John 4:22–24; italics added.)

By revelation, the Prophet Joseph Smith translated verse 24 to read: "For unto such hath God promised his Spirit. And they who worship him, must worship in spirit and in truth." (JST John 4:26.)

The Prophet's interpretation not only harmonizes with the other passages and episodes in the scriptural records but also demonstrates how taking one isolated passage out of context creates false theology. Even without Joseph Smith's changes, the passage makes sense. It can be said that God is a spirit, just as it can be said, "Man is spirit." (D&C 93:33.) President Gordon B. Hinckley explained: "God is a spirit, and so are you, in the combination of spirit and body that makes of you a living being. . . .

"Each of us is a dual being of spiritual entity and physical entity. All know of the reality of death when the body dies, and each of us also knows that the spirit lives on as an individual entity and that at some time, under the divine plan made possible by the sacrifice of the Son of God, there will be a reunion of spirit and body. Jesus' declaration that God is a spirit no more denies that he has a body than does the statement that I am a spirit while also having a body." (*Ensign,* Nov. 1986, p. 49.)

An important point to remember with regard to doctrinal teachings is that the Lord's church functions on the basis of two fundamental principles: (1) the testimony of apostolic witnesses, who know by personal experience the reality and truth of the Lord and his teachings; and (2) the testimony of each member, based upon knowledge, faith, and the witness of the Holy Ghost.

A modern prophet, Joseph Smith, Jr., provided the world with an eyewitness testimony of God's true nature. Concerning a glorious visitation by the Father and the Son, Joseph testified, "I saw two Personages, whose brightness and glory defy all description, standing above me in the air. One of them spake unto me, calling me by name and said, pointing to the other — *This is my Beloved Son. Hear Him!*" (Joseph Smith–History 1:17.)

Joseph Smith saw a confirmation of what Jesus had impressed upon Philip long ago: "Have I been so long time with you, and yet hast thou not known me, Philip? he that hath seen me hath seen the Father; and how sayest thou then, Shew us the Father?" (John 14:9.) Jesus was apparently informing his disciples that he and his Father were alike in attributes, in power, and in bodily appearance.

How different from the prevailing beliefs that were propounded from the pulpits at the time of Joseph Smith! The resurrected Jesus declared to the Prophet that those creeds were "abominable," for so strongly were they riveted to the hearts of men that their hearts were drawn away from their Heavenly Father. (Joseph Smith–History 1:19; D&C 123:7.)

The greatest contribution of the Prophet Joseph Smith to this modern era is the Book of Mormon, which contains a testimony of the resurrected Christ and his ministry to the people of the Western Hemisphere *after* his resurrection in Jerusalem. The Book of Mormon records that twenty-five hundred people saw and heard the Savior and testified of his bodily resurrection of flesh and bones.

Compare with the idea of an all-powerful yet immaterial three-in-one spiritual essence these two sentences from Joseph Smith, who was speaking as revelation dictated:

"The Father has a body of flesh and bones as tangible as man's; the Son also; but the Holy Ghost has not a body of flesh and bones, but is a personage of Spirit." (D&C 130:22.)

"There is no such thing as immaterial matter. All spirit is matter, but it is more fine or pure." (D&C 131:7.)

Living prophets and apostles today continue to teach of God's true nature. They testify that Jesus Christ is a living, resurrected being with a body of flesh and bones. How do they know? Like apostles of old, they are his special witnesses.

Each individual may receive confirmation of spiritual truths by the power of the Holy Ghost. As Moroni in the Book of Mormon urged us to do: "Ask God, the Eternal Father, in the name of Christ, if these things are not true; and if ye shall ask with a sincere heart, with real intent, having faith in Christ, he will manifest the truth of it unto you, by the power of the Holy Ghost." (Moroni 10:4.)

With confirmation by the Holy Ghost, we can know that the nature of God the Father, his Son Jesus Christ, and the Holy Ghost, as taught by the Bible and as revealed to the Prophet Joseph Smith, is true. Those who have received their understanding about God from errant traditional Christianity need no longer struggle with that confused and confusing doctrine. The Prophet's inspired declarations about the Godhead are in total agreement with the biblical evidence that Jesus and the Father have distinct, material bodies.

Notes

1. See James L. Barker, *Apostasy from the Divine Church* (Salt Lake City: Bookcraft, 1960), pp. 229–35.

2. *A History of Education in Antiquity*, trans. George Lamb (New York: Mentor Books, 1956), pp. 424–29.

3. *The Influence of Greek Ideas on Christianity* (New York: Harper & Row, 1957), p. 49.

4. T. Edgar Lyon, *Apostasy to Restoration* (Salt Lake City: The Church of Jesus Christ of Latter-day Saints, 1960), p. 113.

5. *The Confessions*, 5.10.19–20; 7.1.1, in *Great Books of the Western World* (Chicago: Encyclopedia Britannica, 1952), 8:32, 43.

6. D. Thomasius, as quoted in Hugh Nibley, *The World and the Prophets*, vol. 3 of *The Collected Works of Hugh Nibley* (Salt Lake City: Deseret Book Co., 1987), p. 95.

7. *Confessions*, 4.16.29, 31; 5.10.19–20; 6.3.4–4.5; *The City of God*, 7.5–6; in *Great Books*, 18:26, 32, 36, 267–69.

QA

How do we support the position that Christ organized a church with various officers, particularly in view of Matthew 18:19–20 and 1 Corinthians 12:12–14?

Robert J. Woodford, instructor, LDS Institute of Religion, University of Utah, Salt Lake City, Utah

At first glance, these two passages of scripture might seem to show that an organized church and its ordinances are unnecessary. Many people, interpreting these passages out of context, have concluded that it is necessary only to accept Christ as the Savior and that all who do so—regardless of their church membership—belong to a "church of believers." This, they reason, is the one true church spoken of in the scriptures. These people believe that an organized church of Christ, with ordinances and authorized officers, is optional. But a closer look at the context in which these passages of scripture were given actually confirms that the Savior did organize a church with authorized leaders and essential ordinances.

Consider first Matthew 18:19–20:

"Again I say unto you, That if two of you shall agree on earth as touching any thing that they shall ask, it shall be done for them of my Father which is in heaven.

"For where two or three are gathered together in my name, there am I in the midst of them."

The Savior spoke these words to his apostles—to those he had already called to lead his church. Shortly after the Transfiguration (see Matthew 17:1–13), the Apostles had asked the Savior who was greatest in the kingdom of heaven. This passage is part of his response. The Savior had called to their attention that they had the power to seal and loose, both on earth and in heaven. (See Matthew 18:18.) Now he told them that whatever two of them agreed on concerning anything, and it was right, it would be done for them by the Father. (See v. 19.) He also gave them the promise that he would be with his disciples whenever they met in his name. (See v. 20.) This last promise seems to be meant for all disciples, not just the twelve apostles. In either case, it clearly applies to those who have already entered Christ's church, not to just anyone who might meet in the Savior's name.

The second scripture, 1 Corinthians 12:12–14, reads as follows:

"For as the body is one, and hath many members, and all the members of that one body, being many, are one body: so also is Christ.

"For by one Spirit are we all baptized into one body, whether we be Jews or Gentiles, whether we be bond or free; and have been all made to drink into one Spirit.

"For the body is not one member, but many."

Paul had learned that the Saints at Corinth were contending over points of doctrine, each faction aligning itself behind the church leader they supposed taught the views they espoused. Paul opened his letter by reproving them:

"Now this I say, that every one of you saith, I am of Paul; and I of Apollos; and I of Cephas; and I of Christ.

"Is Christ divided?" (1 Corinthians 1:12–13.)

He then taught them the truth concerning some of the disputed doctrines and urged them to unite with all the leaders God had set in the Church. (See chapter 12.) Specifically, he mentioned apostles, prophets, and teachers (see 12:28), but this obviously was not intended to be a complete listing. Paul used the figure of the human body to illustrate the relationship the Saints have with the Church leaders and the Savior. He said that just as no part of the body can claim that it has no need of another part, so no member of the Church can claim not to need any other part of the Church, whether it be another member, Church leader, or the Savior.

Paul used this same figure in his letter to the Ephesians to teach them the same principle:

"And he gave some, apostles; and some, prophets; and some, evangelists; and some, pastors and teachers;

"For the perfecting of the saints, for the work of the ministry, for the edifying of the body of Christ:

"Till we all come in the unity of the faith, and of the knowledge of the Son of God, unto a perfect man, unto the measure of the stature of the fulness of Christ:

"That we henceforth be no more children, tossed to and fro, and carried about with every wind of doctrine, by the sleight of men, and cunning craftiness, whereby they lie in wait to deceive;

"But speaking the truth in love, may grow up unto him in all things, which is the head, even Christ:

"From whom the whole body fitly joined together and compacted by that which every joint supplieth, according to the effectual working in the measure of every part, maketh increase of the body unto the edifying of itself in love." (Ephesians 4:11–16.)

Paul had already explained this relationship to the Ephesian Saints using a different figure. In language both beautiful and expressive, he likened the Church to the household of God:

"Now therefore ye are no more strangers and foreigners, but fellowcitizens with the saints, and of the household of God;

"And are built upon the foundation of the apostles and prophets, Jesus Christ himself being the chief corner stone;

"In whom all the building fitly framed together groweth unto an holy temple in the Lord:

"In whom ye also are builded together for an habitation of God through the Spirit." (Ephesians 2:19–22.)

Wherever Paul labored as a missionary he organized branches of the Church and ordained elders to preside. (See Acts 14:23.) Thus, we have in the epistles of Paul many scriptures concerning Church leaders and their duties. For example, Paul instructed Titus to ordain elders in every city in Crete where there were members. (See Titus 1:5.) He taught Timothy about the qualifications of bishops and deacons (see 1 Timothy 3:1–13), and he referred to high priests in the letter to the Hebrews (see Hebrews 5:1; 8:3).

The Savior himself initiated the formal organization of the church when he ordained the twelve apostles. (See Mark 3:14.) He also appointed seventy men to assist the apostles in their work. (See Luke 10:1.) Shortly after his death, the apostles perpetuated the number in their quorum by choosing Matthias to replace the fallen Judas. (See Acts 1:23–26.) They also enlarged the organization of the Church when they chose seven men to aid in the temporal affairs of the Church. (See Acts 6:1–7.)

The Bible does not record all of the officers in the Church and their specific duties at the time of the Savior, nor does it provide much detail on how that organization developed as the Church grew and spread. But we see ample evidence from these scriptures that there was a formal organization of men authorized to perform specific duties within the Church.

As Latter-day Saints, we "believe in the same organization that existed in the Primitive Church, namely, apostles, prophets, pastors, teachers, evangelists, and so forth." (Articles of Faith 1:6.) The duties of these officers in the Church today are given to us through our Latter-day scriptures and the words of our living prophets. We also believe that those who act in an official capacity within that organization "must be called of God, by prophecy, and by the laying on of hands." (Articles of Faith 1:5.) We also believe that The Church of Jesus Christ of Latter-day Saints is the same church that was organized by the Savior, restored in these latter days. And finally, we believe that after making the commitment to follow the Savior, a person must be baptized by one who has authority in order to obtain a remission of sins and to be admitted into the Lord's church. (See Articles of Faith 1:4.) Then he must labor in the church and kingdom of God, serving both God and his fellowmen even as did the Savior. (See 2 Nephi 31:13–21.)

QA

How do we interpret scriptures in the New Testament that seem to condemn genealogy?

George H. Fudge, former managing director of the Genealogical Department

The Apostle Paul referred to "genealogies" in letters to Timothy and Titus. To Timothy he said, "Neither give heed to fables and endless genealogies, which minister [present] questions, rather than godly edifying which is in faith: so do." (1 Timothy 1:4.)

To Titus he said, "But avoid foolish questions, and genealogies, and contentions, and strivings about the law; for they are unprofitable and vain." (Titus 3:9.)

These passages, taken out of context, could cause misunderstanding. Paul was not condemning genealogy work itself. The importance of genealogy had been well established from the time of Adam down to Paul's day. The respected Bible scholar Dr. Adam Clarke told us that "the Jews had scrupulously preserved their genealogical tables till the advent of Christ; and the evangelists had recourse to them, and appealed to them in reference to our Lord's descent from the house of David; Matthew taking this genealogy in the descending, Luke in the ascending, line. And whatever difficulties we may now find in these genealogies, they were certainly clear to the Jews; nor did the most determined enemies of the Gospel attempt to raise one objection to it from the appeal which the evangelists had made to their own public and accredited tables."[1]

Paul himself was aware of the necessity for ordinances for the dead (see 1 Corinthians 15:29) and understood the accompanying necessity of genealogical work in this activity. Why, then, would Paul make those remarks about genealogy to Timothy and Titus?

Paul was living in a time of conflict and confusion. False teachers abounded, preaching false doctrines and fables. Two specific problems existed relating to genealogies:

First, some apostate teachers recited their genealogies to give credence to their claims as coming with authority. Many Jews had become arrogant because of their illustrious ancestors. Some even flaunted their lineage when opposing the Savior himself: "We be Abraham's seed" (John 8:33), they said, as if to indicate that they were thereby natural inheritors of the truth.

Second, some of the apostate Jewish teachers were guilty of

manufacturing their own genealogies—creating them in hopes of giving the added weight of authority to their teachings.

Such practices understandably caused a great deal of contention among the Jews, as well as between Jews and Gentiles. No wonder Paul condemned them as "fables and endless genealogies," "contentions, and strivings about the law," and "unprofitable and vain."

Bible commentators agree upon this interpretation. The statement to Timothy, said one authority, "seems to refer to legends and fictitious genealogies of OT [Old Testament] personages."[2] Adam Clarke wrote that these fables were "idle fancies; things of no moment; doctrines and opinions unauthenticated; silly legends, of which no people ever possessed a greater stock than the Jews."[3]

Regarding "endless genealogies," Paul meant "those genealogies which were uncertain—that never could be made out, either in the ascending or descending line. . . . We are told that Herod destroyed the public registers; he, being an Idumean, was jealous of the noble origin of the Jews; and, that none might be able to reproach him with his descent, he ordered the genealogical tables, which were kept among the archives in the temple, to be burnt. . . . From this time the Jews could refer to their genealogies only from memory, or from those imperfect tables which had been preserved in private hands; and to make out any regular line from these must have been *endless* and uncertain. It is probably to this that the apostle refers; I mean the endless and useless labour which the attempts to make out these genealogies must produce, the authentic tables being destroyed."[4]

It is clear from these commentaries that the apostle Paul had no intention of condemning genealogy or the need for maintaining genealogical records. Rather, he was referring to genealogies that caused endless dispute, some of which were fraudulent and not to be accepted.

As an apostle and a student of the scriptures, Paul was undoubtedly aware of the important role legitimate genealogy had played from the beginning:

The Lord commanded Adam to keep a "book of remembrance" and a genealogy, known as "the book of the generations of Adam." (Moses 6:5, 8.) Genealogical records were handed down by the fathers from generation to generation to Abraham, who said, "I shall endeavor, hereafter, to delineate the chronology running back from myself to the beginning of the creation, for the records have come into my hands, which I hold unto this present time." (Abraham 1:28.)

Genealogical records were indispensable to the ancient Israelites. "All Israel were reckoned by genealogies; and, behold, they were written in the book of the kings of Israel and Judah." (1 Chronicles 9:1.) Local genealogical records were also kept, reckoning people "by their genealogy in their villages." (1 Chronicles 9:22.) Through such records, the Israelites were able to establish lineage, and the Levites were able to prove their right to the priesthood.

Genealogies are listed in several places in both the Old and the New Testament. We are all familiar with the long lists of "begats" that record parentage and lineage. For example, Genesis lists the generations following Adam. Later, in the first chapter of 1 Chronicles, we find the genealogy from Adam to Abraham; then in succeeding chapters, the generations following Abraham are given. The Savior's own genealogy is recorded twice in the New Testament, once in Matthew 1:1–17 and again in Luke 3:23–38.

The Book of Mormon also shows the diligence of the prophets to keep genealogical records. The Lord commanded Lehi to obtain the brass plates, which contained not only a record of the Jews but also "a genealogy of his fathers." When he received the plates, he rejoiced, finding them "of great worth unto us." (See 1 Nephi 5:14, 21.) Later prophets were commanded to preserve the plates "that our genealogy may be kept." (Jarom 1:1; see also Omni 1:1.)

Obviously, the acts of recording and preserving genealogies are not condemned either by the Lord or by his servants; however, genealogy is not to be used in a self-righteous or self-aggrandizing way. To members of the Church, genealogy should be a means to a very worthy end: by seeking out and preserving our genealogy, we identify our kinsmen, enabling us to perform ordinances of salvation in their behalf.

Notes

1. Adam Clarke, *The New Testament . . . with a Commentary and Critical Notes,* 2 vols. [New York: Abingdon Press, 1973], 2:583–84.

2. Raymond E. Brown, Joseph A. Fitzmyer, and Roland E. Murphy, eds., *The Jerome Biblical Commentary* [Englewood Cliffs, New Jersey: Prentice-Hall, 1968], p. 353.

3. Clarke, 2:583.

4. Clarke, 2:583–84.

QA

Does the practice of baptism for the dead (see 1 Corinthians 15:29) refer to a non-Christian practice, or was it a practice of the gospel of Jesus Christ?

Robert L. Millet, associate professor and chairman of the department of ancient scripture, Brigham Young University

Baptism for the dead was indeed a practice of the Church of Jesus Christ in the meridian of time. We know that it was practiced among the first-century Christians and that it was restored in our own dispensation through the Prophet Joseph Smith.

"Else What Shall They Do . . . ?"

The apostle Paul refers to the practice of baptism for the dead in 1 Corinthians. Probably written about A.D. 56 or 57, this book is a masterpiece of religious literature and a remarkable testimony of the Savior and his gospel.

Chapter 15, perhaps the most potent chapter doctrinally in the epistle, testifies of the resurrection of the Lord. In it Paul presented the core of that message known to us as the gospel, or the "glad tidings" that Christ atoned for our sins, died, rose again the third day, and ascended into heaven. Joseph Smith called these events "the fundamental principles of our religion," to which all other doctrines are but appendages.[1]

Paul showed the necessity for the Savior's rising from the tomb and explained that the physical evidence of the divine Sonship of Christ is the Resurrection. If Christ had not risen from the dead, Paul asserted, the preaching of the apostles and the faith of the Saints would be in vain. "If in this life only we have hope in Christ," he said, "we are of all men most miserable." (1 Corinthians 15:19.)

After establishing that the Lord has conquered all enemies, including death, Paul added: "And when all things shall be subdued unto him, then shall the Son also himself be subject unto him [the Father] that put all things under him, that God may be all in all. *Else what shall they do which are baptized for the dead, if the dead rise not at all? why are they then baptized for the dead?*" (1 Corinthians 15:28–29; italics added.)

Interpretations of Paul's Words

Verse 29 has spawned a host of interpretations by biblical scholars of various faiths. Many consider the original meaning of the passage to be at best "difficult" or "unclear." One commentator stated that Paul "alludes to a practice of the Corinthian community as evidence for Christian faith in the resurrection of the dead. It seems that in Corinth some Christians would undergo baptism in the name of their deceased non-Christian relatives and friends, hoping that this vicarious baptism might assure them a share in the redemption of Christ."[2]

Some recent translations of the Bible have attempted to clarify this passage. The New English Bible, for example, translates 1 Corinthians 15:29: "Again, there are those who receive baptism on behalf of the dead. Why should they do this? If the dead are not raised at all, what do they mean by being baptized on their behalf?"

Many non–Latter-day Saint scholars believe that in 1 Corinthians Paul was denouncing or condemning the practice of baptism for the dead as heretical. That is a strange conclusion, however, since he uses the practice of baptism for the dead to support the doctrine of the Resurrection. In essence, he says, "Why are we performing baptisms in behalf of our dead, if, as some propose, there will be no resurrection of the dead? If there is to be no resurrection, would not such baptisms be a waste of time?"

On the subject of baptism for the dead, one Latter-day Saint writer observed, "Paul was most sensitive to blasphemy and false ceremonialism—of all people he would not have argued for the foundation truth of the Resurrection with a questionable example. He obviously did not feel that the principle was disharmonious with the gospel."[3]

Other Early Christian Allusions

A surprising amount of evidence suggests that the doctrine of salvation for the dead was known and understood by ancient Christian communities. Early commentary on the Pauline statement in Hebrews that "they without us should not be made perfect" (see Hebrews 11:40) holds that the passage referred to the Old Testament Saints who were trapped in Hades awaiting the help of their New Testament counterparts and that Christ held the keys that would "open the doors of the Underworld to the faithful souls there."[4] It is significant that in his book, *Dialogue with Trypho*, Justin Martyr, the early Christian apologist, cites an apocryphon which he charges had been deleted from the book of Jeremiah, but was still to be found in some synagogue copies of the text: "The Lord God remembered His dead people of Israel who lay in the graves; and He descended to preach to them His own salvation."[5] Irenaeus also taught: "The Lord descended to the parts under the earth, announcing to them also the good news of his coming, there being remission of sins for such as believe on him."[6]

One of the early Christian documents linking the writings of Peter on Christ's ministry in the spirit world (see 1 Peter 3:18–20; 4:6) with those of Paul on baptism for the dead is the "Shepherd of Hermas," which states that "these apostles and teachers who preached the name of the Son of God, having fallen asleep in the power and faith of the Son of God, preached also to those who had fallen asleep before them, and themselves gave to them the seal of the preaching. *They went down therefore with them into the water and came up again,* but the latter went down alive and came up alive, while the former, who had fallen asleep before, went down dead but came up alive. *Through them, therefore, they were made alive, and received the knowledge of the name of the Son of God.*" (Italics added.)[7]

The Doctrine of Salvation for the Dead

The doctrine that no man or woman will ultimately be denied a blessing he or she did not have the opportunity to receive is set forth in beauty and plainness in the Book of Mormon. (See 2 Nephi 9:25; Mosiah 3:11; 15:24; Alma 41:3; Moroni 8:22.) Further, in our own dispensation, the Prophet Joseph Smith received yet another revelation on the subject of salvation for the dead, the vision of the celestial kingdom. (See D&C 137.)

The words of the Lord to Joseph Smith in 1836 were emphatic and comforting: "All who have died without a knowledge of this gospel, *who would have received it if they had been permitted to tarry,* shall be heirs of the celestial kingdom of God;

"Also all that shall die henceforth without a knowledge of it, *who would have received it with all their hearts,* shall be heirs of that kingdom;

"For I, the Lord, will judge all men according to their works, *according to the desire of their hearts.*" (D&C 137:7–9; italics added.)

Though the vision of the celestial kingdom did not reveal the particulars of how the dead could receive the ordinances of the gospel, such truths were soon forthcoming. On 15 August 1840, some four and a half years after he received the vision of the celestial kingdom, Joseph Smith delivered his first public discourse on baptism for the dead at the funeral of Seymour Brunson, a member of the Nauvoo High Council. In that address, the Prophet quoted from

1 Corinthians. According to one account, he said that "the Apostle [Paul] was talking to a people who understood baptism for the dead, for it was practiced among them. He went on to say that people could now act for their friends who had departed this life, and that the plan of salvation was calculated to save all who were willing to obey the requirements of the law of God."[8]

Salvation and Baptism for the Dead

Two months later, on 19 October 1840, Joseph Smith wrote: "The Saints have the privilege of being baptized for those of their relatives who are dead [note his tie of this doctrine to the vision of the celestial kingdom] *whom they believe would have embraced the Gospel, if they had been privileged with hearing it,* and who have received the Gospel in the spirit, through the instrumentality of those who have been commissioned to preach to them while in prison." (Italics added.)[9]

The doctrine of salvation for the dead became a major emphasis of the Prophet Joseph, who later wrote, "The greatest responsibility in this world that God has laid upon us is to seek after our dead,"[10] and "This doctrine was the burden of the scriptures. Those Saints who neglect it in behalf of their deceased relatives, do it at the peril of their own salvation."[11] The leaders of the Church in Nauvoo were told that "these are principles in relation to the dead and the living that cannot be lightly passed over, as pertaining to our salvation. For their salvation is necessary and essential to our salvation." (D&C 128:15.)

Thus, both the doctrine of salvation for the dead and the ordinance of baptism for the dead, of which we have but an allusion in Paul's letter to the former-day Saints, have been revealed and restored in our own dispensation. We live in a day long anticipated by the prophets of ages past, a day when God has begun to "gather together in one all things in Christ, both which are in heaven, and which are on earth; even in him." (Ephesians 1:10.)

Notes

1. *Teachings of the Prophet Joseph Smith,* sel. Joseph Fielding Smith (Salt Lake City: Deseret Book Co., 1938), p. 121.

2. Richard Kugelman, "The First Letter to the Corinthians," in *The Jerome Biblical Commentary,* 2 vols., ed. Raymond E. Brown, Joseph A. Fitzmyer, and Roland E. Murphy (Englewood Cliffs, N.J.: Prentice-Hall, 1968), 2:273.

3. Richard Lloyd Anderson, *Understanding Paul* (Salt Lake City: Deseret Book Co., 1983), p. 405.

4. J. A. MacCulloch, *The Harrowing of Hell* (Edinburgh, Scotland: T. & T. Clark, 1930), pp. 48–49.

5. Ibid., pp. 84–85; also in *The Ante-Nicene Fathers,* 10 vols. (Grand Rapids, Mich.: Wm. B. Eerdmans Publishing Co., 1951), 1:235.

6. Irenaeus, *Against Heresies* 4.27.1, in J. B. Lightfoot, *The Apostolic Fathers* (Grand Rapids, Mich.: Baker Book House, 1962), pp. 277–78.

7. *The Shepherd of Hermas,* similitude 9.16.2–4 (Loeb Classical Library, Kirsopp Lake trans.); cited in Anderson, *Understanding Paul,* pp. 407–8.

8. A report of Simon Baker in Journal History of the Church, under date of 15 August 1840, in Archives of The Church of Jesus Christ of Latter-day Saints, Salt Lake City, Utah; cited in *The Words of Joseph Smith,* comp. Andrew F. Ehat and Lyndon W. Cook (Provo, Utah: Brigham Young University Religious Studies Center, 1980), p. 49.

9. *Teachings of the Prophet Joseph Smith,* pp. 179–80.

10. Ibid., p. 356.

11. Ibid., p. 193.

QA

Were the blessings of the temple available to the Saints of Jesus' time, or did they become available after his death?

Robert J. Matthews, dean, Religious Education, Brigham Young University

Since the nature of man has not changed since the fall of Adam,[1] it requires the same ordinances and powers of the gospel to save mankind at one time as at another. Therefore, the gospel of Jesus Christ has been the same in every age of the world. The gospel with its ordinances was first revealed to Adam and was taught and practiced by the ancient Saints at various times from Adam to the time of Christ. Since the plan of salvation is older than this earth, there has been no difficulty in the Lord revealing the same ordinances and principles in every dispensation.[2]

The gospel that was taught to the ancients contained certain fundamental elements of the temple endowment, as is verified by the explanation to Figure 3, Facsimile No. 2, of the Book of Abraham. We are also told that the Lord has "always commanded" his people to build special houses for the administration of sacred ordinances.

(See D&C 124:39–40.) Thus, ordinances that are now performed in the temple have been available to men and women living upon the earth whenever the gospel was preached and received among them. We understand, however, that no ordinances were performed for the dead until after Jesus died and inaugurated the preaching of the gospel in the world of departed spirits.[3] Thereafter, the Church in the meridian of time was privileged to perform the ordinances of the gospel not only for the living, as had been done in earlier dispensations, but also for the dead. This is partially evidenced by Paul's reference to baptism for the dead. (See 1 Corinthians 15:29.)

The temple ceremony pertains to exaltation and eternal life, and references in the New Testament show that the members of the Church at that time knew that. For example, Peter reminded the Saints that they had been given "all things that pertain unto life and godliness, . . . whereby are given unto us exceeding great and precious promises: that by these ye might be partakers of the divine nature." (2 Peter 1:3–4.) Paul spoke of obtaining a "crown of righteousness" (2 Timothy 4:8) and of the Saints becoming "heirs of God and joint-heirs with Christ" (Romans 8:17). And John wrote of the faithful becoming "kings and priests unto God" to "reign on the earth." (Revelation 1:6; 5:10.) In the Church we recognize these as matters pertaining to the higher ordinances of the gospel that are administered in the temple.

That such things are mentioned repeatedly in the New Testament epistles is significant, because these epistles were not written for nonmembers but were of a regulatory nature, directed to the branches of the Church. The manner in which these items are presented in the epistles, without explanation, indicates that the persons to whom the epistles were written were already familiar with the doctrines. Consequently, those in the Church today who are familiar with temple ordinances can understand from these epistles that the Saints in New Testament times had the same temple blessings and ordinances.

President Heber C. Kimball taught that the temple endowment used in the Church in this dispensation is the same in principle as the endowment in the ancient Church. He further noted that Jesus "was the one that inducted his Apostles into these ordinances."[4] President Joseph Fielding Smith stated that it was his belief that Peter, James, and John received the endowment on the Mount of Transfiguration.[5] Since they were instructed not to tell of the occurrences on the Mount until after Jesus was "risen again from the dead" (Matthew 17:9), it appears that similar blessings were not given to the other members of the Twelve, or to the Church, until after the Savior's resurrection. Furthermore, there is a strong suggestion from apocryphal sources that the forty-day post-resurrection ministry of Jesus consisted, in part, of the establishment of a sacred ritual among the disciples.[6] The scriptures are silent concerning the details of this, but Luke identified it as a time in which Jesus was "speaking of the things pertaining to the kingdom of God." (Acts 1:3.)

Although today we refer to these sacred things as "temple" ordinances, they could be administered in other locations under certain circumstances if no temple were available. This principle is alluded to in Doctrine and Covenants 124:28–31. High mountains and other places have served as holy sites until a temple could be constructed.[7] As a consequence, at one period of time baptisms for the dead were performed in the Mississippi River at Nauvoo,[8] and endowments were given on Ensign Peak at the north edge of the Salt Lake Valley.[9] Likewise an endowment house was erected in the northwest corner of Temple Square and was used until the Salt Lake Temple was built.[10] Since the temple in Jerusalem was in the hands of the apostate Jewish rulers, it is certain that these special ordinances were performed in other places by the Church in New Testament times.

Notes

1. Joseph Smith, *Teachings of the Prophet Joseph Smith,* sel. Joseph Fielding Smith (Salt Lake City, Deseret Book Co., 1938), p. 60.

2. Ibid., pp. 168, 308.

3. Joseph Fielding Smith, *Doctrines of Salvation,* 3 vols. (Salt Lake City: Bookcraft, 1955), 164–65.

4. In *Journal of Discourses,* 26 vols. (London: Latter-day Saints' Book Depot, 1854–86), 10:240–41.

5. Joseph Fielding Smith, *Doctrines of Salvation,* 2:165, 170.

6. See Hugh Nibley, *When the Lights Went Out* (Salt Lake City: Deseret Book Co., 1970), pp. 32–88.

7. Joseph Fielding Smith, *Doctrines of Salvation,* 2:170, 231–34. See also explanation by Brigham Young, *Journal of Discourses,* 10:252.

8. Smith, *Doctrines of Salvation,* 2:169.

9. Smith, *Doctrines of Salvation,* 2:165.

10. Smith, *Doctrines of Salvation,* 2:245.

QA

Inasmuch as Latter-day Saints believe in marriage for eternity, how do we explain Jesus' teachings in Matthew 22:29–30?

David H. Yarn, Jr., professor emeritus of philosophy and religion, Brigham Young University

Matthew 22:29–30 is part of a larger context that commences with verse 23, as follows:

"The same day came to him the Sadducees, which say that there is no resurrection, and asked him,

"Saying, master, Moses said, If a man die, having no children, his brother shall marry his wife, and raise up seed unto his brother.

"Now there were with us seven brethren: and the first, when he had married a wife, deceased, and, having no issue, left his wife unto his brother:

"Likewise the second also, and the third, unto the seventh.

"And last of all the woman died also.

"Therefore in the resurrection whose wife shall she be of the seven? for they all had her.

"Jesus answered and said unto them, Ye do err, not knowing the scriptures, nor the power of God.

"For in the resurrection they neither marry, nor are given in marriage, but are as the angels of God in heaven." (Vv. 23–30.)

To understand these verses, we need to understand the context in which the Sadducees asked their question and the context in which Jesus answered it.

First, it should be emphasized that this is a hypothetical situation presented to the Lord by the Sadducees, who, as the scripture itself asserts, did not even believe in the resurrection. They were simply doing what both they and the Pharisees so often did—asking the Lord questions simply to bait him, to see if they could catch him contradicting what Moses, the great Lawgiver, had said.

The question itself was based upon the teachings of Moses: "If a man die, having no children, his brother shall marry his wife, and raise up seed unto his brother." (Matthew 22:24; see also Deuteronomy 25:5–10.) In the hypothetical case suggested by the Sadducees, in which seven brothers each had been married to the same woman, in turn, the question was, "In the resurrection whose wife shall she be of the seven?"

113

According to J. R. Dummelow's *A Commentary on The Holy Bible,* "The point raised by the Sadducees was often debated by the Jewish doctors, who decided that a 'woman who married two husbands in this world is restored to the first in the next.' " (New York: Macmillan, 1927, p. 698.) Most Jews at the time believed in a material resurrection, and so the question had some importance to them.

On the other hand, although the Sadducees didn't believe in the resurrection, they were more than happy to use it to try to "bring Jesus into contempt and ridicule with the multitude by asking Him a question which they thought He could not answer." (Ibid., p. 697.)

But Jesus did answer them, and he began with a mild rebuke: "Ye do err," he said, "not knowing the scriptures, nor the power of God." Consider the handicap the Sadducees had placed upon themselves. They did not really understand the scriptures and probably had no wish to do so on this point. They were steeped in false doctrine and without the gift of the Holy Ghost had no access to the revelatory power of the Spirit. The Savior's answer, therefore, was not a full doctrinal explanation of the doctrine of eternal marriage. Instead, he quickly defused their argument and then testified of the resurrection using the scriptures that the Sadducees held most sacred.

First, the Savior effectively dismissed their question on marriage by stating that "in the resurrection they neither marry, nor are given in marriage, but are as the angels of God in heaven." In that way, the Savior turned to the more fundamental issue of the Sadducees' disbelief in resurrection. Then the Savior bore certain testimony of the resurrection:

"But as touching the resurrection of the dead, have ye not read that which was spoken unto you by God, saying,

"I am the God of Abraham, and the God of Isaac, and the God of Jacob? God is not the God of the dead, but of the living." (Vv. 31–32.)

At this point, the Sadducees were silenced. In Mark's account of the episode, the Lord adds, "Ye therefore do greatly err." (Mark 12:27.) The Savior had made their error painfully clear by referring to the Law—Exodus 6:3—for support. The Law was considered by all Jews, Sadducees included, as the highest authority in the canon of scripture. They couldn't very well argue with the scriptures they held in highest esteem.

What, then, do we make of the Savior's statement that "in the resurrection they neither marry, nor are given in marriage?"

First, we see that it was made in response to an attempt by the Sadducees to trap the Lord. Consequently, it would not have been the Lord's final word on the subject. Why should the Lord scatter pearls before them that they would only trample underfoot? (See Matthew 7:6.) They were no more prepared to listen to a discourse on eternal marriage than they were prepared to accept the reality of the resurrection.

Second, the Lord *did not* say there would be no people in the married state in the resurrection but that there would be *no marriages made* in the resurrection.

Third, we must be clear about the "they" who are neither marrying nor being given in marriage. The context of the scriptures just cited suggests a generic rather than a specific meaning. Simply put, that means no marriages are made in the resurrection. The Lord was warning the Sadducees. They were Jews of the day who had rejected him and therefore had no access to the higher ordinances of the Melchizedek Priesthood. How could these men, whom Jesus had called a "generation of vipers" (Matthew 3:7), qualify for the highest blessings of the celestial kingdom?

What the Savior declared of the Sadducees who would later have part in his death is hardly applicable to his Saints who, through the ordinances of the priesthood and their righteousness, qualify for exaltation in the celestial kingdom, which the Lord equates with eternal marriage. (See D&C 132:19–24.)

The Savior made statements on other occasions that support the idea of eternal marriage. To the Pharisees, who at least believed in the resurrection, he said: "Have ye not read, that he which made them at the beginning made them male and female,

"And said, For this cause shall a man leave father and mother, and shall cleave to his wife: and they twain shall be one flesh?

"Wherefore they are no more twain, but one flesh. *What therefore God hath joined together, let not man put asunder.*" (Matthew 19:4–6; italics added.)

The marriage of Adam and Eve, performed prior to the Fall, was certainly done in an eternal context (see Genesis 2:18–24), and the authority to bind on earth *and in heaven* was given to Peter and the other apostles (see Matthew 16:19; 18:18).

Although this authority was lost with the priesthood through apostasy, it has been restored in our day. The Lord's promise is that those marriages performed by his authority and "sealed unto them by the Holy Spirit of promise, by him who is anointed, unto whom

I have appointed this power and the keys of this priesthood" shall endure forever. (D&C 132:19.)

QA

I get the impression from reading 1 Corinthians 7:7–9 that Paul was not married and was against marriage in general. How can his views be reconciled with the revealed truths of eternal marriage?

C. Wilfred Griggs, university professor of ancient scripture, Brigham Young University

Many people believe that Paul was antagonistic toward marriage because of the passage, "For I would that all men were even as I myself. But every man hath his proper gift of God, one after this manner, and another after that.

"I say therefore to the unmarried and widows, It is good for them if they abide even as I.

"But if they cannot contain, let them marry: for it is better to marry than to burn." (1 Corinthians 7:7–9.)

But this belief does not account for all the other statements that Paul made concerning marriage. Paul's teachings, as recorded in letters that were sent to churches and Saints in various stages of spiritual progression, reflect the character and experience of a man who understands family relationships and can speak with authority on the subject.

In the first place, Paul himself was likely to have been married because of his Judaic background. In his defense before the Jewish crowd outside the Roman barracks of the Antonian tower, Paul stated that he was taught according to the perfect manner of the law of the fathers and was zealous in living that law. (See Acts 22:3.) Again, in his defense before the Pharisees and Sadducees, Paul claimed that he was a Pharisee, the son of a Pharisee. (See Acts 23:6.) To the Galatians, Paul had written that he was more zealous in fulfilling the requirements of his religion than were others of his time. (See Galatians 1:14.) The emphasis that the Jews put on marriage as part of their law and tradition would certainly have been used against Paul in view of such statements if he had not been married.[1]

116

Further evidence that Paul was married is found in the likelihood that Paul was a member of the Sanhedrin. One of the qualifications for becoming a member of that body was that a man must be married and the father of children,[2] which was thought to make him more merciful in dispensing justice in the courts. Paul (Saul) was one of the official witnesses of the stoning of Stephen (see Acts 7:58), an action ordered by the Sanhedrin. He also gave his vote with the Sanhedrin against the Christians prior to his conversion. (See Acts 26:10.)[3] Further evidence of Paul's position is found in Acts 9:1–2 where Paul went before the high priest and requested letters authorizing his "official" persecution in bringing Christians to trial and imprisonment. In view of these evidences, most non–Latter-day Saint scholars do not argue that Paul had never been married but that he was either divorced or was a widower by the time he wrote to the Corinthian church.

But let us take a closer look at 1 Corinthians 7 to see if the evidence supports this last conjecture. At the outset, Paul referred to a letter the Corinthians wrote to him: "Now concerning the things whereof ye wrote unto me: It is good for a man not to touch a woman." Although the King James Version does not make it clear who makes the statement "it is good for a man not to touch a woman," the Greek text and the Inspired Version both make this a statement of the Corinthians. We do not know the context of this statement, because we do not have the Corinthian epistle to Paul. The only context we can supply is Paul's answer and, fortunately, that does give us some clue to their problem. In 1 Corinthians 7:7 Paul wished that all men were as he was. But what is that? Could it be that he wished all men were divorced or that all had lost their companions in death, or did he simply wish that men would be so dedicated to the work of the Lord that they be as though they were single?

Evidence of the latter possibility can be found later in the chapter. In verses 10 and 11, Paul did not tell the married Saints to become separated, but if they were separated, he suggested either that they remain that way rather than marry someone else or that they become reconciled. Paul even enjoined against separation in part-member families if the husband and wife were compatible (see vv. 12–14), because the member might someday be able to help save his spouse (see v. 16). Some scholars conjecture that Paul was divorced as a result of a "mixed" marriage, but the Corinthians would have thrown this advice right back to him if such had been the case.

117

One reason Paul wrote to the Corinthians concerning these matters is found in verse 29, where he stated, "this I say, brethren, the time is short: it remaineth, that . . . they that have wives be as though they had none." He further stated that the unmarried Saints (and those who are as though unmarried) care for the things of the Lord, but too often a married person puts other things before the work of the Lord. (See vv. 32–33.) Paul was simply reminding those who have been called to God's work to put that calling first, even before earthly matters.

In the Joseph Smith Translation, the Prophet made an important addition to 1 Corinthians 7:29 that supports this interpretation: "But I speak unto you who are called unto the ministry. For this I say, brethren, the time that remaineth is but short, that ye shall be sent forth unto the ministry. Even they who have wives, shall be as though they had none; for ye are called and chosen to do the Lord's work." Contrary to generally accepted interpretations, Paul is not condemning marriage in this chapter but is evidently replying to a problem regarding missionaries who desire to become married. His advice is that while they are on their missions (and he declared that the time for missionary work is short) they should be concerned with the work of the Lord and not with family or personal matters.

Concerning the importance of marriage for a member of the Church and the relationships of family members toward each other and the Lord, Paul exhorted the Saints to be followers of *himself,* especially in the ordinances of the Church. (See 1 Corinthians 11:1–2.) He taught that the husband is to honor the Lord as his head and the wife is to honor the husband as her head, and that "neither is the man without the woman, neither the woman without the man, in the Lord." (1 Corinthians 11:11.)

What sense would these statements make if they came from an unmarried man? In view of all that Paul said on marriage in 1 Corinthians, it is quite unlikely that the Corinthians would have accepted his epistle and his arguments if he had been divorced or separated from a wife. The message of 2 Corinthians 7, however, is that the first epistle was accepted and many Saints repented.

It is evident from the frequency of Paul's counsel on marriage and family that he placed great importance on the subject. Paul exhorted the women in the Ephesian branch of the church to submit themselves to their own husbands (literally, become subject to or obedient to), as they would to the Lord, comparing the husband and the family to Christ and the Church. (See Ephesians 5.) But he also charged the husbands to love their wives (see Ephesians 5:25) as their Savior loved the Church, so that they might sanctify and perfect their families through love. Paraphrasing one of the great commandments — to love one's neighbor as oneself — Paul said, "So ought men to love their wives as their own bodies. He that loveth his wife loveth himself." (V. 28.) A husband is not to rule as a tyrant over his wife but is to preside in love. (See v. 33.)

Paul's letter to Philippi deserves special consideration in pursuing this subject. Philippi was the first European city in which Paul preached and was one of the most righteous branches of the Church at that time of which we have record: "Wherefore, my beloved, as ye have always obeyed, not as in my presence only, but now much more in my absence." (Philippians 2:12.) During Paul's missionary travels and while he was in prison at Rome, the Philippian church was the only one to remain in constant communication with him by courier, sending gifts and necessities to their beloved apostle. (See Philippians 4:15–18.) In his letter to this faithful group, Paul addressed some of the sisters: "I beseech Euodias, and beseech Syntyche, that they be of the same mind in the Lord. And I intreat thee also, *true yokefellow,* help those women who laboured with me in the gospel, with Clement also, and with other my fellow-labourers." (Philippians 4:2–3; italics added.) *Gnèsie syzuge,* the words translated "true yokefellow," are here taken as feminine and are a noun that means "wife." Ancient commentators believed that Paul was addressing his wife (see, for example, Clement of Alex., *Strom.* 3:53:1, and Origen, *Comm. in Ep. ad. Romans* 1:1), and this is the most sensible translation of the Greek in this context. If he were married at the time, one would expect Paul to leave his wife with a faithful group of Saints, where she would suffer least from want and lack of support during his absence. Both her presence at Philippi and the love of the members there for Paul would account for the constant communication with the apostle, and, if this interpretation is true, it is natural that Paul would ask his wife to assist some of the women who had done so much on his behalf.

Finally, in Paul's last epistles, which were written to Timothy and Titus, he placed further emphasis on the desirability of marriage. In listing the qualities necessary for a bishop, Paul included being married (see 1 Timothy 3:2) and being a good leader over his house: "For if a man know not how to rule his own house, how shall he take care of the church of God?" (1 Timothy 3:5; see also Titus 1:5–9.) Even those called "deacons" in that day (the Greek literally means "one who serves" or a "helper") were to be married and have orderly households. (See 1 Timothy 3:10–13.)

The evidence of Paul's writings leads to the conclusion that he not only tolerated marriage among the Saints but encouraged and exhorted them to marry and have children. He indicated that marriage is an essential part of the gospel framework and asserted that one of the signs of the apostasy in the last days would be teachings against marriage. (See 1 Timothy 4:1–3.) Certainly Jesus was foremost in importance to Paul, just as he should be in our hearts today, and on occasion Paul had to remind men called to the ministry to be fully dedicated to the Lord's work. Nevertheless, Paul understood and taught that in the presence of the Lord, the man will not be without the woman, neither the woman without the man.

Notes

1. Mishnah, Aboth 5:21, trans. H. Danby, p. 458. "At five years old (one is fit) for the scripture, at ten years for the Mishnah, at thirteen for (the fulfilling of) the commandments, at fifteen for the Talmud, at eighteen for the bridechamber, at twenty for pursuing (a calling), at thirty for authority, at forty for discernment, at fifty for counsel, at sixty to be an elder, at seventy for grey hairs, at eighty for special strength." See also David Smith, *Life and Letters of St. Paul*, p. 30f.

2. Sanhedrin 36:2.

3. Conybeare and Howson, *Life and Epistles of St. Paul*, pp. 59, 64. The Greek of Acts 26:10 is technical terminology and literally means: "I cast my vote against them," meaning that Paul voted for condemnation of the Saints. Such language has reference to a formal court, and Paul would have to have been a member of the Sanhedrin before he could cast his vote in a judicial proceeding.

QA

Will you explain these references in the Bible in view of the Latter-day Saint doctrine that works are necessary for salvation: Ephesians 2:8–9, Titus 3:5, and Romans 4:5?

Robert E. Parsons, associate professor of ancient scripture, Brigham Young University

We need to understand that what Paul referred to as "works" is different from what we mean by "works." To Latter-day Saints, "works" mean basically two things:

1. Accepting and complying with the principles and ordinances of the gospel of Christ that admit us to membership in his church and qualify us as candidates for the kingdom of God.

2. Enduring to the end of our probationary period by striving to live the commandments that Christ has given us. When our lives fall short of this goal, we repent and again endeavor to keep his commandments. As we do so, going from "grace to grace," receiving "grace for grace," the Savior sanctifies us through the ministrations of the Holy Spirit. (See D&C 93:11–20; 2 Thessalonians 2:13–17; Titus 2:11–14.)

The scriptures are very explicit on the need for the ordinances of the gospel and for obedience to God's commandments. The Lord himself said, "Verily, verily, I say unto thee, Except a man be born of water and of the Spirit, he cannot enter into the kingdom of God." (John 3:5.) And "Not every one that saith unto me, Lord, Lord, shall enter into the kingdom of heaven; but he that doeth the will of my Father which is in heaven." (Matthew 7:21.)

Those who quote such scriptures as Ephesians 2:8–9, Titus 3:5, and Romans 4:5 usually do so to argue that faith alone is sufficient to save us. All we need do, they explain, is to confess verbally or mentally that we accept Christ as our Savior. Since Paul is the principal writer they use to support this idea, let's look at some other statements Paul makes that teach that salvation depends on more than confession of faith. Consider the following statements by Paul.

On the Nature of Faith

"Without faith it is impossible to please [God]: for he that cometh to God must believe that he is, and that he is a rewarder of them that diligently seek him." (Hebrews 11:6.)

"Let us lay aside every weight, and the sin which doth so easily beset us, and let us run with patience the race that is set before us,

"Looking unto Jesus the author and finisher of our faith." (Hebrews 12:1–2; see also vv. 5–17.)

On the Necessity for Repentance and Baptism by Water and by the Holy Ghost

"Why tarriest thou? [Ananias told Paul after Paul's vision of the Savior on the Road to Damascus] arise, and be baptized, and wash away thy sins, calling on the name of the Lord." (Acts 22:16.)

To those Ephesians who had been baptized "unto John's baptism" but had not been given the gift of the Holy Ghost, Paul said:

"John verily baptized with the baptism of repentance, saying unto the people, that they should believe on him which should come after him, that is, on Christ Jesus.

"When they heard this, they were baptized in the name of the Lord Jesus.

"And when Paul had laid his hands upon them, the Holy Ghost came on them." (Acts 19:4–6; see also vv. 1–3; 1 Corinthians 6:9–12.)

On the Need for Righteous Activity Following Faith in Christ

"Be not deceived; God is not mocked: for whatsoever a man soweth, that shall he also reap.

"For he that soweth to his flesh shall of the flesh reap corruption; but he that soweth to the Spirit shall of the Spirit reap life everlasting.

"And let us not be weary in well doing: for in due season we shall reap, if we faint not." (Galatians 6:7–9.)

"[God] will render to every man according to his deeds:

"To them who by patient continuance in well doing seek for glory and honour and immortality, eternal life:

"But unto them that are contentious, and do not obey the truth, but obey unrighteousness, indignation and wrath." (Romans 2:6–8.)

When discussing a gospel concept, we must read all that is written about the subject and not just quote an isolated verse or concept. Isolating verses this way has led to the multiplicity of doctrines taught by the numerous Christian denominations in the world today.

The confusion over Paul's writings about whether works are necessary for salvation stems from a widespread misunderstanding of his use of the word *works*. Throughout Paul's ministry, he waged a constant fight against false doctrine. In the early years of his ministry, most members of the Church were Jews; hence the false doctrine he had to contend with was largely Jewish. Predominant among these doctrines was the idea that even though Christ had come, obedience to the "works" of the Law of Moses was still necessary for salvation. These works involved the outward performances of the Law, such as circumcision and animal sacrifice.

A similar idea involved the Jewish notion that salvation depends on the treasure of good and bad works one lays up for himself during his life. If there are more good works than bad in your store, you are considered righteous; but if you have more bad works on the ledger than good, you are condemned. Furthermore, your good works could be supplemented by the surplus of good works performed by the patriarchs in their lives; this "credit" of works could then be transferred to you in order to tip the balance in your favor. "It was taught that the whole transaction was a matter of contract, God owing a debt to man for goodness." (*Dictionary of the Bible,* ed. James Hastings [New York: Charles Scribner's Sons, 1944], p. 693.)

The controversy stemming from these false notions about works and the Law of Moses raged for years, even though it had been officially settled by a council of the apostles in Jerusalem in A.D. 50. The great challenge Paul had was to convince the Jewish converts that they were not saved by the dead works of the Law of Moses, nor that salvation was payment owed them by God because of their good works. Salvation, he taught, was a gift made possible only through the atonement of Jesus Christ.

Later in his ministry, as more and more Gentiles joined the Church, Paul also had to contend with pagan—mostly Greek—philosophies and religious ideas. As the Cambridge Bible dictionary points out, the Greeks were "gifted by race with a keen sense of the joys of physical existence, with a passion for freedom and a genius for rhetoric and logic, but reared in the midst of the grossest moral corruption, undisciplined and self-conceited." (LDS edition of the King James Version of the Bible, p. 744.) In New Testament times, most of the world was steeped in Greek culture and practices.

Although Gentile converts became deeply conscious of their sins when exposed to the gospel, Greek philosophy often led them into errors similar to the ones the Jewish converts struggled with. One error was the belief that one could "attain moral perfection by mechanical means, the careful observance of external ordinances and ascetic restrictions, coupled with special devotion to a host of angelic mediators." (Ibid., p. 746.)

It was in this context that Paul wrote his letters. They were written to solve local Church problems and were not intended to present a detailed picture of the plan of salvation. His letters were sent to members of the Church, Saints of God who had already been introduced to the gospel and the doctrines of salvation, many of whom were struggling with false doctrines and traditions. In countering those doctrines that centered on the outward works of the Law of Moses or on the belief that a person can save himself through his own works, Paul used the doctrine of faith in Christ as a focal point in his explanations.

With this background, then, let's look at the three scriptures in question—Ephesians 2:8–9, Titus 3:5, and Romans 4:5.

1. "For by grace are ye saved through faith; and that not of yourselves: it is the gift of God: not of works, lest any man should boast." (Ephesians 2:8–9.)

These verses were written to the Saints at Ephesus, which was heavily influenced by Greek culture. A Jewish element there also emphasized the necessity of keeping the Law of Moses. The Greek culture and Jewish teachings combined to create problems for the Church, including the tendency to glory in one's abilities and to trust in the Law of Moses for salvation. These verses were apparently written to counter the idea that we can save ourselves by our works independent of Christ. As Elder Bruce R. McConkie wrote: "No man has power to save himself anymore than he has power to resurrect himself. . . .

"No matter how righteous a man might be, no matter how great and extensive his good works, he could not save himself. Salvation is in Christ and comes through his atonement. God through Christ reconciles man to himself. But building on the atonement man must perform the works of righteousness to merit salvation, as verse 10 and the whole passage testify." (*Doctrinal New Testament Commentary,* 3 vols. [Salt Lake City: Bookcraft, 1965–73], 2:500.)

2. "Not by works of righteousness which we have done, but according to his mercy he saved us, by the washing of regeneration, and renewing of the Holy Ghost." (Titus 3:5.)

Rather than supporting the idea of salvation by faith alone, this scripture actually stresses the necessity for the ordinances of the gospel. To Titus, a former missionary companion, Paul mentioned again that it is Christ who saves us, not our works. Then he described how Christ's mercy is made operable in our behalf—through "the washing of regeneration" and by the "renewing of the Holy Ghost." J. R. Dummelow's commentary referred to the former as baptism and says that "the baptism to be efficient must be both by water and by the Spirit. It is not a mere outward act." (*A Commentary on the Holy Bible* [New York: Macmillan Co., 1936], p. 1008.) That's familiar doctrine to Latter-day Saints.

3. "But to him that worketh not, but believeth on him that justifieth the ungodly, his faith is counted for righteousness." (Romans 4:5.)

This verse is part of a long letter Paul wrote to the members of the Church in Rome, a city that was truly a melting pot of nations and beliefs. To the members there, mostly Gentiles but some Jews as well, both familiar with Jewish law and history (see Dummelow, *Commentary*, pp. 855–56), Paul explained that God's love and justice are extended to all men, Jew and Gentile alike, and that it is not the Law of Moses that saves us, but our faith in Christ, which moves us to righteous works. (Ibid., pp. 858–60.) As an example, he referred to Abraham, who found favor with God by his faith, not by his observance of any outward ordinance:

"For if Abraham were justified by works, he hath whereof to glory; but not before God.

"For what saith the scripture? Abraham believed God, and it was counted unto him for righteousness.

"Now to him that worketh is the reward not reckoned of grace, but of debt.

"But to him that worketh not, but believeth on him that justifieth the ungodly, his faith is counted for righteousness.

"Even as David also describeth the blessedness of the man, unto whom God imputeth righteousness without works,

"Saying, Blessed are they whose iniquities are forgiven, and whose sins are covered." (Romans 4:2–7.)

Verse 4 probably refers to the old Jewish belief that a person's storehouse of good works exacts payment from God in the form of salvation as if God owed the person a debt. If that were so, as Paul said in verse 2, Abraham would have something to boast about. But the truth is, "*all* have sinned, and come short of the glory of God." (Romans 3:23; italics added.) We are all "ungodly," therefore, and must rely on the mercy of God to justify us, to be forgiven of our iniquities. As we have already discussed, this great gift comes to us as we exercise faith in Christ, repent of our sins, submit to the ordinances of the gospel, and thereafter endure to the end in living a Christlike life.

Those who teach that faith or confession is sufficient for salvation usually teach that those who die without hearing of Christ and having an opportunity to confess faith in his name are consigned to an eternal hell. Justice and the whisperings of the Spirit manifest that such doctrine cannot be true, or God could not be a God of mercy and love. Likewise, the whisperings of the Spirit manifest that mere confession without the fruits of righteous living cannot save a person, or God could not be a God of justice.

The Book of Mormon teaches the doctrine clearly:

"Unless a man shall endure to the end, in following the example of the Son of the living God, he cannot be saved.

"Wherefore, do the things which I have told you I have seen that your Lord and your Redeemer should do; for, for this cause have they been shown unto me, that ye might know the gate by which ye should enter. For the gate by which ye should enter is repentance and baptism by water; and then cometh a remission of your sins by fire and by the Holy Ghost.

"And then are ye in this strait and narrow path which leads to eternal life. . . .

"And now, my beloved brethren, after ye have gotten into this strait and narrow path, I would ask if all is done? Behold, I say unto you, Nay. . . .

"Wherefore, ye must press forward with a steadfastness in Christ. . . . Wherefore, if ye shall press forward, feasting upon the word of Christ, and endure to the end, behold, thus saith the Father: Ye shall have eternal life." (2 Nephi 31:16–20.)

"For we labor diligently to write, to persuade our children, and also our brethren, to believe in Christ, and to be reconciled to God; for we know that it is by grace that we are saved, after all we can do." (2 Nephi 25:23.)

OLD
TESTAMENT

QA

Did Ezekiel's prophecy about two "sticks" foretell the coming forth of the Book of Mormon, or have Latter-day Saints misinterpreted Ezekiel 37:15–20?

Keith Meservy, associate professor of ancient scripture, Brigham Young University

Ezekiel's ancient prophecy of the two "sticks," or books, does more than foresee the Bible and Book of Mormon. It marks the coming of the Book of Mormon as the beginning of the great latter-day gathering.

Many critics have long frowned upon the Latter-day Saint interpretation of "sticks" in Ezekiel's prophecy (Ezekiel 37:15–20) as two books of scripture, the Bible and the Book of Mormon. They insist that sticks, either scrolls or tallies, do not make scriptures, and that even if they do, Latter-day Saints are taking the prophecy out of context: chapter 37 as a whole discusses the gathering of Israel, not books of scripture. They suggest that *stick* really represents a *scepter,* a tribe or one of the divided kingdoms of Judah or Israel. Nevertheless, new light shed on ancient scribal practices by a Mesopotamian archaeological discovery sends us back to this fascinating prophecy for a closer look.

The Translation of *Stick*

A correct interpretation of Ezekiel's prophecy depends primarily on the meaning of the Hebrew word *'ets,* translated *stick* in the King James Version of the Bible. Hebrew words, like words in any language, tend to have a general meaning as well as a variety of specialized meanings, depending on their use. In English, for instance, "Fire!" shouted on a rifle range means something different from "Fire!" shouted in a hotel. Idiomatic usage also affects meaning: "Have a heart," "won her heart," and "never lose heart" all use *heart* in different senses. In each instance, the context determines how the word is used and provides its meaning.

The general meaning of *'ets* is *wood,* as Jewish translators of the

Greek Septuagint showed in 259 translations out of 300 uses of *'ets*. *Stick* is merely one specific meaning used by King James translators; others include *tree, timber, helve, plank, stalk, staff, stock, gallows*. A tree isn't a plank, a plank isn't a gallows, and a gallows isn't a stick; but tree, plank, gallows, and stick are all wood. Context in each instance determines the way *'ets* is translated.

It makes no difference how Ezekiel used *'ets* elsewhere or how other writers in the Bible used it. We must look at Ezekiel's use of his wood (*'ets*) in chapter 37 to determine its meaning.

Ezekiel *wrote* on his wood. (This writing on wood should not be confused with the writing on a *rod* in Numbers 17. The tribal leaders in that passage wrote on rods or tribal staves, but the word *matteh* instead of *'ets* is used.) Since archaeologists know now that ancient Babylonians wrote on wood, this knowledge provides a valuable context within which to interpret the meaning of Ezekiel's action.

Babylonian Wax Writing Boards

At one time, Babylonian scribes were thought to write cuneiform texts only on soft clay tablets with a stylus. Their own tablets, however, tell us that sometimes they copied their texts from a *wooden tablet* (*is leu*). Since no archaeologist had ever found any of those wooden tablets, scholars wondered how cuneiform could have been written on them. Did scribes paint the characters on?

In 1948, as he read two ancient Babylonian texts, San Nicolo discovered that scribes were filling their tablets with wax. He remembered that Greeks and Romans filled writing boards with wax and then wrote on their surfaces. Since Babylonians were filling boards with wax, he theorized that they must also have been using wax writing boards.[1]

Five years later, archaeologist Max Mallowan discovered a set of sixteen hinged wax writing boards in Assyria that looked strikingly like Greek and Roman writing boards. The cuneiform inscription on the cover board identified it as an *is leu* (*wooden tablet*).

Having this tangible example, scholars recognized many examples of writing boards in use on the bas-relief sculpture of Assyrian palaces.[2] It became abundantly clear that a previously unknown method of making records was commonly used in ancient Mesopotamia.

Did Ezekiel Write on Wax Writing Boards?

From this evidence it is also clear that Ezekiel and his fellow Jewish captives lived in a world where scribes typically wrote on wax writing boards. Since he told us in chapter 37 that the Lord commanded him to take wood, or a board, and write upon it, we must ask, Did Ezekiel write on wax writing boards rather than on "sticks"?

When asking this question, we must remember that the primary meaning of 'ets as wood is not subject to question, as third-century B.C. Jewish translators show; however, wood might be the tree or the woods growing on the hill, or the wood for building or burning, or the wood for making things like staves and staffs. Had Ezekiel used his 'ets (wood) to build a house, a translator could have called his wood building boards, beams, planks, siding, or roofing. If he had planted, pruned, or burned his wood, a translator might have translated it as trees, wood, sticks. In fact, Ezekiel used 'ets in a number of ways—in Ezekiel 15:1–5 as wood for burning and in Ezekiel 31:3–18 as growing trees.

By Ezekiel's action of writing on wood, however, a translator could translate the term as (writing) board. Even so, the evidence that writing boards were regularly used in Ezekiel's day is insufficient to show that writing board was exactly what Ezekiel was referring to. So we must look for corroboratory evidence.

Part of this evidence is found in verse 17 of Ezekiel 37, which tells us that, having written on his boards, Ezekiel joined "them one to another into one stick [board]" and they became one in his hand. This joining action was typical of scribes who wrote on boards. The delicate inner surfaces had to be protected from marring or scarring. By joining two boards together by thongs or metal hinges, a scribe could fold them together—and lo, two boards became one in his hand.

Corroborating evidence is also found in the statement that Ezekiel identified the owner of each board by writing a cover inscription on it. Once again, he was doing what scribes normally did to their boards. Sargon, for example, put an inscription on the cover of his sixteen-board set to show that it belonged to him, what its contents were, and that it was placed in his palace at Dur-Sharrukin.[3]

Ezekiel's inscriptions identified Judah and Joseph as the owners of each of the two boards. The Hebrew preposition le [to/for] in front of the names Judah and Joseph shows to whom each of these boards belonged. Thus, we might better translate the inscriptions to show this possession by putting the words "(belonging) to" before each name: "(Belonging) to Judah, and (belonging) to the children of Israel his companions," and "(Belonging) to Joseph, the [board] of Ephraim, and (belonging) to all the house of Israel his companions." (Ezekiel 37:16.)

Ezekiel's *use* of the wood, therefore, helps define the meaning of *wood* in this context. He was told to write on wood, join the two boards into one, and inscribe the names of the owners on the covers. These three simple but specific actions were typical of scribal procedures; in fact, all of them were peculiar to scribes who wrote on boards. Since Ezekiel's use of *wood* is the key to the word's specific meaning, and since what he was doing typified the technical actions of scribes who wrote on wax writing boards, Ezekiel most likely was writing on wax writing boards.

If the King James translators had known that Ezekiel lived among scribes who wrote on wood, they might have translated the "stick" passage differently. Here is how one modern translation, the New English Bible, translates Ezekiel 37:15–19:

"These were the words of the Lord to me: Man, *take one leaf of a wooden tablet* and write on it, 'Judah and his associates of Israel.' Then take another leaf and write on it, 'Joseph, the leaf of Ephraim and all of his associates of Israel.' Now bring the two together to form one tablet; then they will be a folding tablet in your hand."

At this point, Ezekiel emphasized the ownership of the two tablets: "These are the words of the Lord God: I am taking the leaf of Joseph, *which belongs to* Ephraim and his associate tribes of Israel, and joining it to the leaf *of* Judah. Thus I shall make them one tablet." (Italics added.)

Could Ezekiel Have Used Wax Tablets?

We might ask, Could Hebrew or Aramaic characters be written efficiently upon wax surfaces? The question is perhaps irrelevant because Ezekiel seems to have made models, or visual aids, instead of authentic books. But even then, scholars agree that countless Aramaic documents must have been composed on wax tablets. (Aramaic was the language used by the Jews in Babylon.)

Leo Oppenheim, an Accadian scholar, suggested that "it is likely that Aramaic was written in this way before the Accadian scribes began to use it for cuneiform and that with the loss of these fragile books an entire literature in Aramaic may have perished in Mesopotamia."[4]

Max Mallowan concluded that wax writing boards became popular in Mesopotamia because they were "conveniently portable and [could] contain long texts easily available for consultation. Moreover, deletions or additions could be made without difficulty." Clay tablets, on the other hand, were durable but took a great amount of storage space in proportion to what was written upon them, and they allowed no alterations once they had dried.[5]

Have any Aramaic or Hebrew tablets been found? No. But two known examples of wooden tablets in the Assyrian language have survived—one made of wood and the other made of ivory. Furthermore, many cuneiform records refer to wooden tablets, and several bas-relief sculptures show that they were used extensively in Mesopotamia, in Hittite country, and in Zingirli, an Aramaic-speaking country.

This type of record-keeping was also widespread in Greece from the time of Homer and Herodotus and in Rome up to the time of medieval Europe. Such extensive use through hundreds of years of time among so many different nationalities and in so many different languages shows what a practical and popular method of writing it was.

Bar Rekub, a king of Zingirli about 740 B.C., shows us that Aramaic-speaking people were writing upon wax boards. We must assume that Jews in Babylonia regularly used writing boards, as their contemporaries did, to record transactions, historical events, and the like. We would be amazed if they didn't. Indeed, Luke mentioned that Zacharias "asked for a writing table, and wrote, saying, His name is John." (Luke 1:63.) The writing table (Greek, *pinakidion*) was a wax writing board. Furthermore, in the pseudepigraphical work of Ezra IV, Ezra was commanded to prepare for himself "many writing-tablets" so he could record the books God would reveal to him (14:24), and Jewish children anciently learned to read by using wax tablets because parchment was too expensive.[6] Jews borrowed the Greek word for a wax tablet—*pinakis*—and transliterated it into Hebrew as *pinqes*—"a board, tablet, especially, the folded writing tablets."[7] Ancient Jewish writers used wax tablets regularly.

If wax boards were used so extensively, why don't we have more examples? Simply because they were made of perishable organic material.

The set found in Assyria was preserved in the sludge at the bottom of an ancient well. Its conservation seemed to its discoverer a "little short of a miracle. . . . This singular good fortune has enabled us to rescue from oblivion a class of document which, though it must once have existed in a hundred other cities of Western Asia, has only survived in one. Here we have the earliest known material evidence of what must then have been a familiar form of scribal record."[8]

This discovery, Mallowan suggested, may explain "the extraordinary paucity of business documents of the ninth century in Assyria."[9]

Why, for example, are there no accounts from the prosperous reign of Assur-nasir-pal and Shalmaneser III? Mallowan concluded that "this hiatus may be accounted for by an extensive use at the time of wood, wax, and perhaps other equally perishable materials to record the normal business transactions of the day."[10]

But, we still might object, if Ezekiel were writing on wax boards, why didn't he call them *wax boards*? If he had, he would have done something even the Mesopotamian scribes didn't do.

They didn't call their tablets *"writing boards"* but used instead the nondescript phrase *wooden tablet (is leu)*. This usage was so firmly fixed in Mesopotamia that even when such boards were made of ivory, they were still called *wooden* tablets! For example, Sargon's sixteen-board set was called *is leu shin piri*, i.e., a *wooden* tablet of elephant *ivory*. Clearly, "wooden tablet" (*is leu*) had become the technical name for a writing board, regardless of the material from which it was made and regardless of how many boards made up one set.

Since Babylonians used a nondescript phrase to identify the wax writing board, we shouldn't require more of Ezekiel. We might suggest other words he could have used, like *sepher, megillah, gillayon,* but imprecise terms often work their way into popular usage without anyone's conscious effort.

Among the scholars who find it possible to read *'ets* in Ezekiel 37 as wax writing boards[11] is R. J. Williams, who agreed that *'etsim* in Ezekiel 37 were wax writing boards because they were joined together. He also noted that wooden tablets were referred to in several places in the Bible: *luach*—"tablet" in Isaiah 30:8 and "tables" in Habakkuk 2:2—most likely means a wooden tablet, although in the former passage it may have been of metal. The term *gillayon,* translated "roll" in Isaiah 8:1, "almost certainly designates a wooden tablet, since it is to be inscribed with a *heret,* used for carving in Exod. 32:4."[12]

Judah's and Joseph's Records

Sargon's sixteen-board set, with thirty writing surfaces, contained enough text — 7500 lines — that Max Mallowan claimed to have discovered at Nimrud "the earliest known form of ancient book, complete with binding, the inscribed ivory leaf being the top cover to the whole."[13]

Ezekiel's writing boards were labeled "(Belonging) to Judah," that is, "Judah's," and "(Belonging) to Joseph," that is, "Joseph's." His hearers, of course, knew that one tablet for Judah was much too short to contain all of Judah's records, which spanned hundreds of years. Rather, Ezekiel's one board with Judah's name on it symbolized Judah's records, as the one board with Joseph's name on it symbolized all of Joseph's records.

Because of the complex interrelationships of the tribes, any record of Judah would, of necessity, have been a record of various tribal companions residing in Judah's borders: Manasseh, Ephraim, Benjamin, Levi, and various others. (See 2 Chronicles 11:13–14; 15:9–10.) Likewise, within the Nephite branch of Joseph's tribe, there were members of Ephraim, Manasseh, Judah, and perhaps other tribes, depending upon the lineage of Zoram and the companions of Mulek. (See Alma 10:3; Helaman 8:21; 2 Nephi 1:30–31; Mosiah 25:2; *Journal of Discourses,* 26 vols. [London: Latter-day Saints' Book Depot, 1854–86], 23:184.)

Thus, Ezekiel's symbolism consisted of identifying two writing boards with Judah's and Joseph's records, which, in the context of the gathering of Israel, are joined together. He could hardly have found a simpler, more vivid symbol of the gathering of Israel than unification of separate tribal records.

His message indicates that in the day of gathering (the last days), Judah and Joseph would each have a record and that their records would be joined as one. In these last days, do Judah and Joseph have such records? No one, of course, asks the Jews, the "People of the Book," if Judah has records. And Latter-day Saints readily identify the Book of Mormon as representative of Joseph's record in Ephraim's hands. Judah's and Joseph's records do exist.

Not only did Ezekiel (representing Judah) know that each of these tribes would keep records, but Joseph of old also knew that he and Judah would be keepers of special records. The Lord had told him that "the fruit of thy loins shall write; and the fruit of the loins of Judah shall write; and that which shall be written . . . shall grow together." (2 Nephi 3:12.) Lehi reported this to his children, so the Nephites knew that they would keep records that would be joined with Judah's records. Similarly, Ezekiel taught the Jews that God would join those records together to carry out his work. Thus, the Lord clearly told the two tribes the fate and importance of the records they were keeping.

The Resurrection and the Gathering of Scattered Israel

Ezekiel often acted out his message, using tiles to portray the siege of Jerusalem (see Ezekiel 4:1-3), lying on his side to indicate the fate of Israel and Judah (see Ezekiel 4:4–17), and shaving his head to indicate the fate of the inhabitants of Jerusalem (see Ezekiel 5:1–4). His actions were part of his message. Quite naturally, his people would want to know what message he intended by joining together Judah's and Joseph's writing boards while speaking of the gathering.

From the beginning of his ministry, Ezekiel had evoked harsh images of destruction and scattering to induce his people to repent. But with the destruction of Jerusalem (see Ezekiel 33:21) and the arrival of more and more Jews in captivity, he turned to themes of gathering and hope. He used two vivid examples of God's power, the resurrection of the dead and the unification of separated records, to give scattered Israelites hope of return.

In Ezekiel's vision, the dry bones of the scattered remnants of Israel were heard to say: "Our bones are dried, and our hope is lost: we are cut off for our parts." (Ezekiel 37:11.) But those scattered, hopeless bones were assured that when divine power called them forth they would be covered with sinews, flesh, and skin and would be filled with breath. (See Ezekiel 37:5–6.) Israel could look forward to *individual* redemption from the grave.

With the destruction of their nation and the scattering to Babylonia and the four corners of the earth, the Israelites must have felt that *national* revival was also hopeless. But Ezekiel prophesied that the power of God would not only bring scattered bones together again but also would bring scattered peoples back to their land: "Behold, O my people, I will open your graves, and cause you to come up out of your graves, and *bring you into the land of Israel.*" (Ezekiel 37:12; italics added.)

By this revelation, Ezekiel assured not only contemporary Israelites, whose graves were far from home, but later readers who might die in Rome, or in Russia, or in America, or in Germany that by means of the resurrection God would bring them back to their land. (See Matthew 5:5; JST Genesis 15:9–12; Daniel 12:8–13; D&C 38:19–20; 45:11–14.)

God's gatherings, however, are not only *spatial* — from the four corners of the earth — and *temporal* — from the various epochs of time — but also *spiritual*. This last part of the gathering is the most crucial of all. When his people are gathered fully back to him, the Lord will be their God and they will be his people. (See Ezekiel 37:27.) The unification of Judah's and Joseph's records would be crucial in this spiritual gathering to God.

So when Ezekiel put the two records together and the people asked him what that action meant, he gave them the Lord's answer:

"I will take the children of Israel from among the [nations], whither they be gone, and will gather them on every side, and bring them into their own land: and I will make them one nation in the land upon the mountains of Israel; and one king shall be king to them all: and they shall be no more two nations, . . . but I will save them out of all their dwelling places, wherein they have sinned, and will cleanse them: so shall they be my people, and I will be their God." (Ezekiel 37:21–23.) His people would become a holy, converted people.

The Lord made this same point again when he said that the appearance in the last days of Joseph's record would be a sign of the gathering:

"I give unto you a sign, that ye may know the time when these things shall be about to take place — that I shall gather in, from their long dispersion, my people, O house of Israel, and shall establish again among them my Zion. . . . when these things which I declare unto you . . . shall be made known unto the Gentiles . . . it shall be a sign unto them, that . . . the work of the Father hath already commenced unto the fulfilling of the covenant which he hath made unto the people who are of the house of Israel." (3 Nephi 21:1–7.)

When Christ's words were published in the Book of Mormon in 1830, the things that he had declared to the Nephites were made known to the Gentiles. Thus, the appearance of Joseph's record — which made possible the joining of that record with Judah's — was a sign that the gathering had commenced.

Mormon, the editor of Joseph's records, also saw the latter-day appearance of his abridgment as a sign of the gathering of Israel: "*When* the Lord shall see fit, in his wisdom, that these sayings shall come unto the Gentiles . . . *then ye may know* that the covenant which the Father hath made with the children of Israel, concerning their restoration to the lands of their inheritance, is already beginning to be fulfilled." (3 Nephi 29:1; italics added.) His "when-then" prophecy is as clear as the 3 Nephi 21:1–7 prophecy by Jesus just mentioned: the publication of the Book of Mormon will signal the beginning of the gathering.

Indeed, Mormon's "when-then" prophecy is as clear as Ezekiel's. *When* Ezekiel put Judah's and Joseph's records together, *then* he promised that the Lord will take "the children of Israel . . . and will gather them . . . and bring them into their own land; and . . . make them one nation in the land upon the mountains of Israel . . . and they shall be no more two nations. . . . and [the Lord] will cleanse them" so they will be his people and he will be their God. (Ezekiel 37:20–27.) His actions are the *when* of the inspired communication, and his prophetic words are the timing for the *then* of the gathering.

Ezekiel demonstrated that the joining of two records, one for Judah and one for Joseph, would be a sign that Israel would be spiritually and physically gathered in from their long dispersion to become one nation led by God. The appearance of the Book of Mormon was crucial to the gathering. That record and the Bible would need to work together to bring about the spiritual gathering.

The Bible Alone Is Inadequate to Effect the Gathering

To understand the need for the joining and how it fits with the crucial spiritual gathering, we must know something about the conditions of latter-day Israel.

As effective as the Bible is in leading people back to God, it needs divine confirmation. Learned men and spiritual guides, having only the Bible, debate which words are divine, what authority biblical words have for modern man, and what a person must do to walk the strait and narrow way to God. They contend over the nature of God, the characteristics of his plan, and the purpose of earth life. Consequently, while they need decisive answers to their questions, they are divided over what the Bible says.

The source of this difficulty began, as explained in Joseph's book, when many plain and precious parts of the gospel were deliberately taken from the Bible to "pervert the right ways of the Lord" and to "blind the eyes and harden the hearts of the children of men." (1 Nephi 13:27.) This corruption has led to contention over the simplest aspects of faith.

Judah, in the person of Jeremiah, knew that perverse men in his own day were already manipulating the law of the Lord: "How can you say, 'We are wise, we have the law of the Lord,' when scribes with their lying pens have falsified it?" (New English Bible, Jeremiah 8:8.)[14] Consequently, as Nephi predicted, "an exceedingly great many do stumble, yea, insomuch that Satan hath great power over them." (1 Nephi 13:29.)

Plain and simple doctrine is necessary to fully bring people back to God, but the plain and simple doctrine in the Bible had been compromised. God therefore promised to establish the truth of his gospel by uniting Joseph's testimony with Judah's: "I will manifest myself unto thy seed, that they shall write many things which I shall minister unto them, which shall be plain and precious; . . . these things shall be hid up, to come forth unto the Gentiles . . . and in them shall be written my gospel." (1 Nephi 13:35–36.)

These and other writings mentioned in verse 39 "shall establish the truth of the first, which are of the twelve apostles of the Lamb, and shall make known the plain and precious things which have been taken away from them; and shall make known . . . that the Lamb of God is the Son of the Eternal Father, and the Savior of the world; and that all men must come unto him, or they cannot be saved.

"And they must come according to the words which shall be established by the mouth of the Lamb; and the words of the Lamb shall be made known in the records of thy seed, as well as in the records of the twelve apostles of the Lamb; wherefore they both shall be established in one; for there is one God and one Shepherd over all the earth." (1 Nephi 13:40–41.) Clearly the point is that divine truth will be established by two divine witnesses—the two records that are to come together in the hand of God to establish his truth.

The Lord asserted the crucial role of the Book of Mormon in the spiritual gathering when he commanded Nephi to write his sayings, that those "who shall be scattered . . . because of their unbelief, may be brought . . . to a knowledge of me, their Redeemer.

"And then will I gather them in from the four quarters of the earth; and then will I fulfil the covenant which the Father hath made unto all the people of the house of Israel." (3 Nephi 16:4–5.)

Complex movements have complex origins, and God had to do many things to make gathering possible. Two independent witnesses had to combine to convince truth-seekers that God is the same today as yesterday, that there is only one Messiah, that his plan of salvation is the same, that he saves all of his children, and that he keeps his covenants with his children. To this end, priesthood keys and organization, temples, and missionary work all had to be restored. But all of these came when the "keystone" to the gospel arch was put in place so that a person could learn true doctrine and get closer to God. By being joined together, Joseph's and Judah's testimonies would confound false doctrines, lay down contentions, establish peace, and remind readers of God's covenants with their fathers. All this would occur when God began to restore his people. (See 2 Nephi 3:12–13.)

The testimony of the Book of Mormon and the Bible together will accomplish what the Bible cannot do alone. The Lord explained to Nephi: "Know ye not that the testimony of two nations is a witness unto you that I am God? . . . And when the two nations shall run together the testimony of the two nations shall run together also.

"And I do this that I may prove unto many that I am the same yesterday, today, and forever. . . .

"My people, which are of the house of Israel, shall be gathered home unto the lands of their possessions; and my word also shall be gathered in one. And I will show . . . that I covenanted with Abraham that I would remember his seed forever." (2 Nephi 29:8–9, 14.)

The Lord's gathering is to be more than a gathering of bones back to their bodies and of live bodies back to their land. His gathering requires that souls be gathered to him and his word. Only such souls, who would choose him to be their God, could become his people.

The coming forth of the Book of Mormon signals the beginning of a special outpouring of God's power to gather his people in the latter days.

The Gathering Is Part of God's Restoration

That there are in the twentieth century two books, one belonging to Judah and his tribal companions and one belonging to Joseph and his tribal companions, is a miracle of major significance; they are marvelous works and wonders. That these two books have been united for the first time in history to aid in the gathering work, at the time when God has set about to make one fold having one shepherd, is another miracle. No uninspired man could have given a signal to the world in the early 1800s that God's long-awaited gathering was about to begin. But God gave that signal through Joseph Smith.

Ephraim is being identified and gathered — those scattered among the Gentiles as well as those in the western hemisphere descended from Joseph; and the vanguard of Judah has reestablished itself. Much more gathering lies in the future before all Israelites are gathered to the land of their inheritance and united under one king. Much of this will occur when Christ comes (see D&C 133:25–35) and when the resurrection takes place, as Ezekiel testified.

After Ezekiel had acted out the unification of records, uniting Judah's writing board with Joseph's, he prophesied that the Lord "will take the children of Israel from among the [Gentiles], . . . and will gather them on every side, and bring them into their own land. . . . So shall they be my people, and I will be their God." (Ezekiel 37:16, 21, 23.) No wonder, then, that when the time came for the gathering to take place, Moroni, the keyholder "of the record of the stick of Ephraim" (D&C 27:5) appeared to Joseph Smith. He introduced himself as "an angel of God, sent to bring joyful tidings that the covenant which God made with ancient Israel was at hand to be fulfilled." (*History of the Church,* 7 vols., 2d ed. rev., ed B. H. Roberts [Salt Lake City, Utah: The Church of Jesus Christ of Latter-day Saints, 1932–51], 4:537.) No wonder that, within one twenty-four hour period, Moroni had quoted and explained to Joseph Smith four different times how God was about to "set his hand again the second time to recover the remnant of his people" from the various nations where they were scattered and how he should "set up an ensign for the nations, and . . . assemble the outcasts of Israel, and gather together the dispersed of Judah from the corners of the earth." (Isaiah 11:11–12; see Joseph Smith–History 1:40.) What a message for a mere lad, who would soon learn, from the same angel, about the record of Joseph that would make all this possible!

The Bible and the Book of Mormon are divine instruments prepared by the Lord to help effect his gathering work. Both records testify that Jesus is the Christ, the Savior of the world, and that all people must come to him to be saved. God's purposes cannot be fulfilled merely by bringing people back to their land; he has to bring them back to himself. The fulness of the gospel message, made clear by the joining of these two sacred testaments, touches the honest in heart and gathers them to God.

Is it any wonder, then, that when Joseph's record had come from the ground (see Isaiah 29:4–5) and the book had been delivered to him who was not learned—the young Joseph Smith (see Isaiah 29:12)—the Lord could unite Joseph's record with Judah's and do his marvelous work? Then, said he, shall the "deaf hear the words of the book, and the eyes of the blind shall see out of obscurity, . . . and Jacob shall not now be ashamed, neither shall his face now wax pale. But when he seeth his children, the work of mine hands, in the midst of him, they shall sanctify my name, and sanctify the Holy One of Jacob, and shall fear the God of Israel." (Isaiah 29:18, 22–23.)

The Book of Mormon is the anciently prophesied book that joins with the Bible to unite mankind to the truth in latter days as part of the preparatory gathering work prior to the second coming of the Lord.

Notes

1. M. San Nicolo, "Haben die Babylonier Wachstafeln als Shrifttraeger gekannt?" *Orientalia* 17 (1948), pp. 59-70.

2. D. J. Wiseman, "Assyrian Writing-Boards," *Iraq* 17 (1955), p. 7.

3. Ibid.

4. A. Leo Oppenheim, *Ancient Mesopotamia* (Chicago: University of Chicago, 1964), p. 242.

5. M. E. L. Mallowan, *Nimrud and Its Remains* (London: Collins, 1966), 1:161.

6. Samuel Krauss, *Talmudische Archaeologic III* (Hildesheim: George Olms Verlagsbuchhandlung, 1966), p. 144.

7. Marcus Jastrow, *A Dictionary of the Targumim, the Talmud Babli and Jerushalmi, and the Midrashic Literature II* (Brooklyn, N.Y.: B. Shalom Publishers, 1967), p. 1165.

8. M. E. L. Mallowan, "Excavations at Nimrud: 1953," *Iraq* 16 (1956), p. 102.

9. Ibid.

10. Ibid.

11. See Herbert G. May's commentary on Ezekiel 37 in *Interpreter's Bible*, 4:270.

12. R. J. Williams, "Writing," *Interpreter's Dictionary of the Bible*, 4:917. See also Kurt Galling, "Tafel, Buch und Blatt," *Near Eastern Studies in Honor of William Foxwell Albright*, ed. Hans Goedicke (Baltimore: The Johns Hopkins Press, 1971), pp. 207–23.

13. Mallowan, "Excavations," p. 99.

14. See also the translations of the verse in the Revised Standard Version, Jerusalem Bible, and New International Version.

QA

How much emphasis is found in the writings of the Old Testament prophets on the subjects of the Restoration and the last days?

Brent Bulloch, instructor, LDS Institute of Religion, Arizona State University, Tempe, Arizona

A great deal of emphasis is found in the writings of the Old Testament prophets about the Restoration and the last days. In fact, the Old Testament is the only scriptural source for a number of latter-day prophecies.

As might be expected, most of these prophecies are found in what are commonly called the prophetic books — Isaiah through Malachi. More than half of the 250 chapters in these books deal in some way with the last days. For example, more than 80 percent of the chapters in the book of Isaiah contain material about the latter days. The last fourteen chapters of Ezekiel, nearly all of the book of Joel, much of Daniel, a large part of the book of Zechariah, and parts of Hosea, Micah, and Zephaniah each deal with the last days.

Some of the prophecies are readily identifiable. Others, however, are more obscure, symbolic, or have applications in more than one time period, making a good background of gospel knowledge and a sensitivity to the promptings of the Spirit essential to recognizing and understanding them. A knowledge of history, language, and customs is also helpful.

Entire books could be written to synthesize these prophecies, but the following is a brief summary of major themes. They are not listed chronologically; some events are simultaneous or interrelated rather than sequential.

The Restoration of the Gospel

1. The gospel will be restored and the everlasting covenant will be reestablished. (See Isaiah 29:13–14, 24; Daniel 2:28, 44–45; Jeremiah 31:31–34; Ezekiel 37:26.)

2. New scriptures will come forth out of the earth to stand with the Bible as a witness of God and his work. (See Psalm 85:11; Isaiah 29:4, 11–12, 18, 24; see also Ezekiel 37:15–20.)

3. The Lord's messenger will prepare the way for his coming. (See Malachi 3:1.) This is an example of a prophecy with more than one fulfillment, including John the Baptist in the meridian of time and in the last days, as well as Joseph Smith and other latter-day servants who prepare for the Lord's second advent. (See Matthew 11:10; Joseph Smith–History 1:36; D&C 35:4; Joseph Fielding Smith, *Doctrines of Salvation,* comp. Bruce R. McConkie, 3 vols. [Salt Lake City: Bookcraft, 1954–56], 3:10–12; Mark E. Petersen, *The Great Prologue* [Salt Lake City: Deseret Book Co., 1975], p. 98.) The everlasting covenant is also "a messenger . . . to prepare the way before [the Lord]." (D&C 45:9.)

4. Elijah will return before the Second Coming. (See Malachi 4:5–6.) Elijah appeared in the Kirtland Temple on 3 April 1836 and restored the keys of priesthood sealing powers. (See D&C 110:13–16; also see related sermon by Joseph Smith, *Teachings of the Prophet Joseph Smith,* sel. Joseph Fielding Smith [Salt Lake City: Deseret Book, 1938], pp. 330, 335–38.)

The Latter-day Gathering of Israel

1. An ensign raised as a standard to the nations will bring about the gathering. (See Isaiah 5:26–29; 10:20–23; 11:10, 12; 43:5–7; 49:22–23; Jeremiah 3:12–15; 16:16; 31:6–9; Ezekiel 34:11–13.) This ensign is the gospel of salvation and The Church of Jesus Christ of Latter-day Saints, which carries the gospel to the world. The Book of Mormon is also an ensign to the nations.

2. The house of Judah will be gathered to the land of their inheritance, the land of Jerusalem. (See Deuteronomy 30:1–5; Psalms 147:2–3; Isaiah 11:12; Jeremiah 3:18; 12:14–15; 30:3; Zechariah 2:12; see also Smith, *Teachings of the Prophet Joseph Smith,* p. 286.)

3. The other tribes will also return to the lands of their inheritance. (See Psalm 50:1–5; 107:1–7; Isaiah 11:11, 16; 43:6; Jeremiah 3:12, 18; 16:14–15; 23:3, 7–8; 30:3; Ezekiel 48.) They will return from the "north countries" to "be crowned with glory" under the hands of the "children of Ephraim" in Zion (see D&C 133:26–34) and will eventually go back to inhabit the lands of their original inheritance in Israel.

4. Many Gentiles will be gathered and numbered with the house

of Israel. (See Isaiah 11:10; 55:5; 56:6–8; 60:1–11; Malachi 1:11.) Those who are not naturally of the lineage of Israel are received into the house of Israel by adoption when they accept the gospel. They are then counted the same as if they had been born as literal seed of Israel. (See Abraham 2:8–11.)

5. When the tribes of Israel and Judah are gathered to their own lands, they will unite as one kingdom again and will no longer be two nations. In that condition they will enjoy great prosperity. (See Isaiah 11:13; Jeremiah 3:18; Ezekiel 28:24–26; 37:21–22; Amos 9:14–15.)

6. Israel will be given "a new heart," and the Lord will reestablish his covenant with them. This promise will not be fulfilled totally until after the Lord's return. (See Isaiah 12.1–6; Jeremiah 31:31–34; Ezekiel 11:17–20; 37:21–28; 39:23–29; Hosea 2:14–23; 3:4–5.)

7. Christ will reign as King over Israel, being from the loins of the ancient King David. (See Isaiah 55:3–4; Jeremiah 23:5–6; 30:3, 9; 33:15–17; Ezekiel 34:23–24; 37:21–25.)

Events Related Specifically to the House of Judah

1. Judah will return to Jerusalem and to the lands of their inheritance. (See Jeremiah 32:36–44; JST Zechariah 8:7–8; see also item 2 under "The Latter-day Gathering of Israel.")

2. The lands of Israel will be built up and become fruitful. (See Isaiah 29:17; 35:1–2, 6–7; 43:18–21; 60:6, 9, 13–14; Ezekiel 34:26–27; 36:33–36.)

3. A temple will be built in Jerusalem before the Second Coming. (See Isaiah 2:1–5; Ezekiel 40–48; Micah 4:1–2.) Ezekiel gives a very detailed description of the temple and many of the services to be performed there.

4. Water will come from under the Jewish temple and flow to the Dead Sea, causing it to become healed—sweetened, or made fresh. (See Ezekiel 47:1–12; Joel 3:18; Zechariah 14:8.) Joseph Smith said this event would take place before the Second Coming. (See *Teachings of the Prophet Joseph Smith,* p. 286.)

5. Two prophets will be raised up unto (not necessarily from) the Jewish nation after the gathering. (See Isaiah 51:17–20; Zechariah 4:11–14.) More is given on the mission of these two prophets in Revelation 11:1–14.

6. "All nations" will come in battle against Jerusalem. (See Ezekiel 38:1–17; Joel 2:1–11; 3:1–14; Zechariah 12:2–3; 14:1–2.)

7. The Lord will come to fight for Judah. He will stand upon the Mount of Olives and by a great earthquake will preserve the Jews from destruction and overthrow the opposing armies. (See Ezekiel 38:18–23; 39:1–7; Joel 2:32; 3:9–17; Zechariah 12:9; 14:2–9.)

8. The Jews will come to know their Savior and be converted. (See Zechariah 12:10–13; 13:6–9.)

9. The beasts of the field will participate in the "supper of the great God" (Revelation 19:17–18) and devour the carcasses of those slain by the Lord when he comes to preserve Judah (see Ezekiel 39:4, 8–22).

10. The city of Jerusalem will be built up as a holy city never to be thrown down again. Many will see the Lord there. (See Isaiah 60:13–14; 62:1–12; 65:18–19; Jeremiah 3:17; 33:10–11; Joel 3:18–21; Zechariah 8:1–23; 14:16–21.)

Gentile Nations

1. The gentile nations will come to know the Lord's power. He will fight against those who oppose his people. (See Isaiah 14:1–4; 17:9–14; 49:24–26; 54:15, 17; Zechariah 12:8–9; 14:3, 17–19.)

2. The nations of the world will be cast down. (See Daniel 2:44; 7:9–14; Jeremiah 46:28.) Many examples in the Old Testament of judgments and destructions being heaped upon wicked nations anciently may also be considered as types, or foreshadowings, of the destruction of wicked nations in the last days. (See Isaiah 13:1–22; Jeremiah 25:15–38; Nahum 2:1–13; Zephaniah 1:1–18.)

The Lord's Coming

1. An appearance at Adam-ondi-Ahman will precede the Lord's coming in glory. (See Daniel 7:9–14, 21–22, 26–27.) This appearance will be at a great priesthood meeting at which the Lord's leaders from all ages of the world will be assembled. An accounting will be made for stewardships and keys will be turned back to Christ prior to his assuming his rightful position as Lord over the whole earth. (See Joseph Fielding Smith, *The Way to Perfection* [Salt Lake City: Genealogical Society of Utah, 1946], pp. 287–91; Smith, *Teachings of the Prophet Joseph Smith,* pp. 122, 157–61, 167–68.)

2. The Lord will come suddenly to his temple. (See Haggai 2:6–9; Malachi 3:1.) This prophecy probably has a multiple fulfillment. The Lord already has come to his temple in this dispensation. (See D&C 110:1–10.) He will also appear in a temple in Jerusalem (see

Haggai 2:6–9) and the New Jerusalem in America (see D&C 42:35–36.)

3. The Lord will appear as deliverer to the Jews before his appearance to the world. (See references under "Events related specifically to the house of Judah"; D&C 45:48–53.)

4. The Lord will descend in majesty and power as king over the earth. (See JST Psalm 24:7–10; Isaiah 40:4–5, 10; 63:1–6; 66:15–16.) This is the great appearance in which all the world will see him together.

5. The wicked will be destroyed at the Lord's coming. (See Isaiah 2:10–22; 11:4; Zephaniah 1:14–18; Malachi 3:5; 4:1–3).

6. There will be great physical changes upon the earth in the last days associated with the Second Coming. (See Psalm 18.6–9, Isaiah 2:10, 19–21; 10:17–19; 13:9–13; 24:1–4, 6, 18–23; 40:4; 64:1–3; Joel 2:30–31; 3:15–16; Micah 1:3–4, 6; Haggai 2:6.) At that time the earth will be made ready for the millennial reign.

7. Christ will bring to pass the resurrection of the dead. (See Job 19:25–26; Isaiah 25:8; 26:19; Ezekiel 37:1–14; Daniel 12:2; Hosea 13:14.) At the time of Christ's coming, celestial souls will come forth. Afterward others will be resurrected in their proper order. (The reference to *resurrection* in Ezekiel 37 may properly be interpreted to have application to the literal resurrection of the body as well as to the resurrection or renewal of Israel as the Lord's people.)

Zion in the Last Days

1. Latter-day Ephraim will be blessed, stakes of Zion will be established, and the borders of Zion will be increased. (See Isaiah 54:2–5; Jeremiah 31:6–14; Zechariah 10:7–9.)

2. Work for both the living and the dead will contribute to the building up of Zion. (See Isaiah 42:6–7; 61:1; Obadiah 1:21; Malachi 4:5–6.) Joseph Smith taught that baptisms for the dead fulfilled the words of Obadiah wherein he referred to saviors on Mount Zion. (See *Teachings of the Prophet Joseph Smith*, p. 223.)

3. Zion will be established in the earth, and the world's affairs will be administered from two great world capitals: Jerusalem in the land of Israel and the New Jerusalem in America. (See Isaiah 2:2–3; 52:7–10; Micah 4:1–3; see also Smith, *Doctrines of Salvation*, 3:66–71.)

4. When Zion is established upon the earth, the Saints will possess it. (See Isaiah 34:8, 17; 35:1–2; see also Daniel 7:18, 22, 27.)

5. Christ will reign over all the earth. (See Psalm 22:27–31; 66:3–4; Isaiah 9:6–7; 32:1; Jeremiah 23:5–6; Daniel 7:13–14; Micah 4:6–7; Zephaniah 3:15; Zechariah 14:9.)

6. The earth will be cleansed and renewed. (See Isaiah 35:1–2; 65:17; 66:15; Malachi 4:1.)

7. During the Millennium, the Lord's Spirit will be poured out. Righteousness will prevail. Enmity, sorrow, and death will cease. The earth will be full of the knowledge of God, and all nations will bow before God and worship him. (See Isaiah 2:4; 11:5–9; 12; 65:17–25; Jeremiah 31:34; Hosea 2:18; Joel 2:28–29; Micah 4:3–5; Habakkuk 2:14; Zephaniah 3:9.)

Many other specific items about the last days can be learned by prayerfully studying the Lord's word. President Harold B. Lee indicated that we do not need to go to any source other than the scriptures to be properly informed concerning the last days. (See *Ensign,* Jan. 1973, p. 106.)

CHURCH

QA

What is an appropriate way to respond to unfriendly questions about the Church?

Steve F. Gilliland, director, LDS Institute of Religion, California State University–Long Beach, Long Beach, California

It is quite a responsibility to represent the Church to other people. What if you say the wrong thing? What if you offend them? And there's always the possibility that they might embarrass or offend *you.*

As an institute director and a bishop, I've been invited many times to answer questions about the Church in university classes and at other churches. My presentation emphasizes the positive aspects of the Church. It's easy to talk about the fruits of the gospel of Jesus Christ and all that we are trying to do to implement his teachings in this challenging world.

But I always worry about the questions; I cannot predict what direction they will come from. What if someone is hostile? Fortunately, the scriptures give insights that can help us in these situations. As I have studied the scriptures, particularly Alma 30, I've discovered some valuable principles that have guided me time and again when facing either friendly or antagonistic inquisitors.

Listen and Clarify

It's hard to hear clearly what is being said when you're under attack. I've become involved in unnecessary arguments because I was anxious and misperceived what the person was saying. At times we were in full agreement on the issue, but I thought he was saying something he was not.

Make sure you know what the person is saying. Ask clarifying questions, or repeat the question as you understand it, followed by "Is this what you are asking?" Let him know you understand his position, and give him a chance to clarify if necessary.

If a person "smites you on one cheek," he may expect retaliation — and it may disarm him if you turn your other cheek and listen.

151

He may be more likely to listen to what you have to say if you've listened to him first. (See Matthew 7:12.)

Suggest Corrections to Misunderstandings

It may be a temptation to accuse or attack an antagonist, to try to embarrass him or put him down, especially if you feel he is purposely distorting the facts. But your challenge is to love him and to avoid putting him on the defensive.

Explain the facts clearly, as Alma did to Korihor (see Alma 30:32–33), speaking as calmly and firmly as possible. If he berates you with quotations from books not accepted as official Church doctrine, inform him that Latter-day Saints have always been free to speculate but that the speculations of individuals do not constitute the official position of the Church. I would say at this point, "If you are interested in what the Church teaches, I'll be glad to explain it to you. I don't feel responsible for the speculations of others. Besides, without the individual available to explain, neither you nor I can understand fully what he meant. Do you want to know what the Church teaches?"

Most of the time the person is innocently repeating misinformation. A gentle reply setting the record straight may avoid putting him on the defensive. "A soft answer turneth away wrath: but grievous words stir up anger." (Proverbs 15:1.) The First Presidency has counseled us "to meet the criticisms and attacks upon the Church without resentment and without malice." (Letter dated 1 Dec. 1983.)

Focus on the Basics of the Gospel

Throwing a person into deep water doesn't help him learn to swim; it may even give him an aversion to going near the water. Similarly, without a proper foundation in the basic truths of the gospel, a person usually isn't ready for heavier doctrines. That's why the Lord counsels us to give people milk before giving them meat. (See D&C 19:22; 1 Corinthians 3:2.)

In their efforts to turn people away from the Church, some antagonists focus on doctrinal half-truths, distorting some of our richest and most precious doctrines that people aren't ready to understand. It is important that we return the discussion to the basics — the simple yet beautiful truths of the gospel.

Alma demonstrated this principle well. In control of himself and the situation, he moved the discussion with Korihor to the basic belief in God. "Believest thou that there is a God?" he asked. (Alma 30:37.)

Another basic gospel teaching is our belief in modern revelation and living prophets. Almost any question can be returned to that issue: "The real question here is not _____, but whether or not there is modern revelation in the Church today. The scriptures clearly teach the principle of living prophets. [See Amos 3:7; Acts 1:2; Ephesians 2:20.] I bear testimony that the Lord does direct the Church today through living prophets and that you can come to know this also. Would you like to know how you can come to know these things?" Another approach may be: "Time will not permit me to give you an answer to that question. Related to it, though, is the more basic question: _____."

Bear Testimony

Nothing is more basic to the gospel than our personal testimonies. Alma bore a simple, forthright witness to Korihor: "I know there is a God, and also that Christ shall come." (Alma 30:39.) If the person is receptive to the truth, the Holy Ghost is able to bear witness to him. The testimony of the Spirit will be the most powerful influence in his conversion. If a person is not receptive to the Spirit, however, all the reasoning in the world won't touch him.

Many people aren't ready for conversion but are curious about what the Church teaches. They deserve to hear the basic truths of the gospel and to have their misconceptions cleared up. But in the process they may challenge you to give some physical or logical proof of the gospel. Although the gospel can be explained logically, it's not our responsibility to try to prove it or to convince the other person. The only real proof is the witness of the Spirit.

Explain Your Attitude toward the Discussion

Explain that you are interested not in debating or arguing but in sharing your point of view and listening to his.

Alma didn't get pulled into the trap of trying to prove the gospel. In fact, he turned the tables on Korihor. "What evidence have ye that there is no God . . . ? Ye have none, save it be your word only." (Alma 30:40.) If the person is very contentious, a fair question to ask is "Do you just want to argue, or do you want to understand what I believe?"

Challenge the Person to Action

When Korihor persisted in demanding proof, Alma placed the burden of proof where it belonged—back on Korihor's shoulders. If he *really* wanted to know, he had "the testimony of all these thy brethren, and also all the holy prophets[.] The scriptures are laid before thee." (Alma 30:44.) Our promise to the world is the one Jesus gave: "If any man will do his [God's] will, he shall know of the doctrine, whether it be of God. . . . If ye continue in my word . . . ye shall know the truth." (John 7:17; 8:31–32.) If a person will *live* the gospel—obey the commandments, study the scriptures, pray—he will have spiritual experiences that will confirm the truthfulness of our message; he will not need to ask for proof.

What if you can't answer a question you're asked? Again, Alma demonstrated a proper course of action: "Now these mysteries are not yet fully made known unto me; therefore I shall forebear." (Alma 37:11.) Say "I don't know." People will respect you for your honesty. When I think there is an answer available, I usually tell them I'll try to find out what it is.

What if you confuse or offend them? Remember that the Holy Ghost has the power to reach beyond our sometimes clumsy efforts into the heart of anyone who is sincerely seeking the truth.

We are promised that as we study the scripture prayerfully, the inspiration we need "shall be given . . . in the very hour." (D&C 84:85.) As we become familiar with the Topical Guide in the Latter-day Saint edition of the King James Version of the Bible, we will discover at our fingertips a gold mine of scriptural references to use in sharing the gospel. And our church classes, such as Sunday School, priesthood meeting, seminary, and institute, can also help us become better prepared.

I take comfort in reading a statement of the First Presidency on this issue:

"We remind you that among the blessings of membership in the Church is the gift of the Holy Ghost, which is conferred upon each individual at the time of confirmation. This gift will be present with members, as well as leaders, who faithfully live the principles of the gospel of Jesus Christ.

"We have confidence that if you will respond with prayer, and in a spirit of humility, then inspiration will attend you." (Letter dated 1 Dec. 1983.)

154

QA

When nonmembers say we're not Christians, what is the best way to respond?

Jack Weyland, member of the Rapid City South Dakota Stake Mission presidency

Just recently a friend of mine, a member of the Church, was told by another that since he was a Mormon, he was not a Christian. I also have faced this situation a number of times. And every time it happens I'm astonished. I usually respond by saying, "But the name of the Church is The Church of Jesus Christ of Latter-day Saints. Every prayer we utter is offered in his name. Every ordinance we perform we do in his name. We believe all the Bible says about him, and we have additional scripture about the Savior—the Book of Mormon—that serves as a second witness of Jesus Christ, telling about his appearance to people in the New World immediately following his resurrection."

Sometimes this is what the other person needs to hear in order to understand that we really are Christians. But sometimes it is not enough. After listening to this explanation, one nonmember acquaintance responded with, "But you're still not Christian." I was stumped, so I simply asked, "Why do you say that?" What took place at that point was most interesting as we tried to communicate our definitions of Christianity and thus of what a Christian is.

No definitive statement of what constitutes Christianity is to be found in the Bible. If there were, there wouldn't be so many churches, some believing baptism to be essential, others saying it's not, some saying worship must be done on Saturdays, others on Sunday, for example. What it boils down to is that many nonmembers exclude us from Christianity because we don't believe exactly what they believe.

The problem in this instance is the assumption they base their definition on. By their definition, we aren't Christian; conversely, we could say *they* aren't Christian because they don't believe exactly what we do. There is no way to convince such people we are Christians without attacking their basic beliefs, and that usually results only in antagonism. Consequently, I simply bear my testimony and hope the Spirit will soften their hearts and open their minds.

Occasionally such an approach bears fruit and the person expresses a sincere interest in resolving our differences. If this happens, I try to help him gain a correct understanding of our beliefs in regard to his own as I am prompted by the Spirit to do so.

The doctrine of grace as set forth in a few selected passages from Paul's writings is a good example. Many Christians say we aren't Christians because we don't subscribe to their notions of the doctrine of grace. We believe that it is Christ's atonement that saves us but that we must endure to the end in doing good works if his atonement is to take effect on our behalf. Those who criticize this doctrine say that Christ's grace alone is sufficient, that once we have confessed our faith in him we need do nothing else to be saved.

The Apostle Paul, in writing to the Ephesians, said, "For by grace are ye saved through faith; and that not of yourselves: it is the gift of God. Not of works, lest any man should boast." (Ephesians 2:8–9.) We, of course, believe this to be true. We also believe that Paul was not telling us that works were unimportant; in verse 8 his purpose was simply to teach the importance of grace and its place in our salvation. I explain that King Benjamin said much the same thing in the Book of Mormon in his remarkable address to his people: "If ye should serve him who has created you from the beginning, and is preserving you from day to day, by lending you breath, that ye may live and move and do according to your own will, and even supporting you from one moment to another—I say, if ye should serve him with all your whole souls yet ye would be unprofitable servants." (Mosiah 2:21.)

When a member of another Christian religion argues that accepting Christ as our Savior is all that is necessary for us to do to be saved, I refer to what Nephi told us in the Book of Mormon: "For we labor diligently to write, to persuade our children, and also our brethren, to believe in Christ, and to be reconciled to God; for we know that it is by grace that we are saved, *after all we can do.*" (2 Nephi 25:23; italics added.)

That one last phrase, *after all we can do,* is extremely significant. It is by the atonement of Christ that we are saved, but it is necessary that we keep the commandments and obey the ordinances God has given us—in other words, do all we can to take advantage of the terms of Christ's atonement.

I also explain that we accept the Bible in its entirety regarding what it says on grace, faith, and works, and not just a few selected passages that are often misinterpreted. Because of this, we believe that works are also important. I point out that James wrote:

"What doth it profit, my brethren, though a man say he hath faith, and have not works? can faith save him?

"If a brother or sister be naked, and destitute of daily food,

"And one of you say to them, Depart in peace, be ye warmed and filled; notwithstanding ye give them not those things which are needful to the body; what doth it profit?

"Even so faith, if it hath not works, is dead, being alone.

"Yea, a man may say, Thou hast faith, and I have works: shew me thy faith without thy works, and I will shew thee my faith by my works. . . .

"Wilt thou know, O vain man, that faith without works is dead? . . .

"For as the body without the spirit is dead, so faith without works is dead also." (James 2:14–18, 20, 26.)

It is unfortunate that nonmembers do not have the Book of Mormon's definition of the gospel of Jesus Christ, a definition given by the Savior himself in 3 Nephi 27. Here the Savior described what constitutes true Christianity:

"Behold I have given unto you my gospel, and this is the gospel which I have given unto you—that I came into the world to do the will of my Father, because my Father sent me.

"And my Father sent me that I might be lifted up upon the cross; and after that I had been lifted up upon the cross, that I might draw all men unto me, that as I have been lifted up by men even so should men be lifted up by the Father, to stand before me, *to be judged of their works,* whether they be good or whether they be evil—

"And for this cause have I been lifted up; therefore, according to the power of the Father I will draw all men unto me, that they may be *judged according to their works.*

"And it shall come to pass, that whoso repenteth and is baptized in my name shall be filled; and if he endureth to the end, behold, him will I hold guiltless before my Father at that day when I shall stand to judge the world. . . .

"And no unclean thing can enter into his kingdom; therefore nothing entereth into his rest save it be those who have washed their garments in my blood, because of their faith, and the repentance of all their sins, and their faithfulness unto the end.

"Now this is the commandment: Repent, all ye ends of the earth, and come unto me and be baptized in my name, that ye may be sanctified by the reception of the Holy Ghost, that ye may stand spotless before me at the last day.

157

"Verily, verily, I say unto you, this is my gospel; and *ye know the things that ye must do in my church; for the works which ye have seen me do that shall ye also do;* for that which ye have seen me do even that shall ye do. . . .

" . . . Therefore what manner of men ought ye to be? Verily I say unto you, even as I am." (Vv. 13–16, 19–21, 27; italics added.)

It is clear, then, that we have much work to do as followers of Jesus Christ, works that require more than just acceptance of him as the Savior and Redeemer. And it is also clear that we can do this work because of the grace of God and because of our faith. The Book of Mormon contains a major statement concerning what this work is: our responsibilities and opportunities as Christians after we have accepted Jesus Christ as our Savior:

"And it came to pass after many days there were a goodly number gathered together at the place of Mormon, to hear the words of Alma. Yea, all were gathered together that believed on his word, to hear him. And he did teach them, and did preach unto them repentance, and redemption, and faith on the Lord.

"And it came to pass that he said unto them: Behold, here are the waters of Mormon . . . and now, as ye are desirous to come into the fold of God, and to be called his people, and are willing to bear one another's burdens, that they may be light.

"Yea, and are willing *to mourn with those that mourn;* yea, and *comfort those that stand in need of comfort,* and *to stand as witnesses of God* at all times and in all things, and in all places that ye may be in, even until death, that ye may be redeemed of God, and be numbered with those of the first resurrection, that ye may have eternal life —

"Now I say unto you, if this be the desire of your hearts, what have you against being baptized in the name of the Lord, *as a witness before him that ye have entered into a covenant with him, that ye will serve him and keep his commandments,* that he may pour out his Spirit more abundantly upon you?" (Mosiah 18:7–10; italics added.)

And when Alma baptized one of them, he said, "Helam, I baptize thee, having authority from the Almighty God, *as a testimony that ye have entered into a covenant to serve him until you are dead as to the mortal body;* and may the Spirit of the Lord be poured out upon you; and may he grant unto you eternal life, through the redemption of Christ, whom he has prepared from the foundation of the world." (Mosiah 18:13; italics added.)

It is clear that if we really accept the Savior, we covenant with

158

him to help him carry out his work—to bear each other's burdens, for example, to comfort each other, to testify of Christ, to keep his commandments.

After I have explained this, my acquaintance or friend might have further questions concerning other beliefs or differing points of doctrines. For each major point of difference in our definitions of what a Christian is, I try to do the same sort of thing that I do with the discussion on grace, faith, and works, as the Spirit guides, and if I am prepared to do so. (For those who argue that we worship the Prophet Joseph Smith—another common misconception—see Elder Robert E. Wells's discussion in the *Ensign,* Nov. 1982, p. 69.) If I am not prepared to discuss a point of difference, I accept the question as a challenge to get prepared to do so—for there will more than likely be another opportunity, with someone else if not with him.

This is indeed the gospel of Jesus Christ. We are taught how to be, in the truest sense of the word, *Christians.* We belong to the Church of Jesus Christ, restored to the earth to help prepare the way for the second coming of the Savior. He is at the head of this church, and he speaks to our prophet.

QA

How can I explain the Church's attitude toward the Bible? A friend of mine objects to the fact that we have additional scriptures and that we believe in the Bible only "as far as it is translated correctly."

Robert J. Matthews, dean, Religious Education, Brigham Young University

We esteem four books as scripture: the Bible, the Book of Mormon, the Doctrine and Covenants, and the Pearl of Great Price. These "standard works," the written canons of our faith, are complementary rather than competitive; each supports and corroborates the others.

Because the Church has four books of divine scripture, some observers have misunderstood our attitude toward the Bible. Saul (later known as Paul) probably had similar feelings when he heard the early New Testament Saints tell of their faith in Jesus Christ; the new revelations and experiences seemed to be a threat to and

159

a replacement of the Old Testament. But Paul's resentment gave way to understanding; he not only became converted to the "new" doctrine and history but even wrote a large portion of what is now called the New Testament. Paul learned that it is not necessary to reject the Old Testament in order to accept and believe the New Testament.

Similarly, acceptance of the Book of Mormon and other Latter-day Saint scripture does not mean rejection of the Bible. As one becomes familiar with all of the revelations God has given, he understands and reveres each volume all the more.

For people living in the first centuries of the Christian era, the Old Testament and the New Testament were two separate collections of sacred writings. Only with the passage of time have modern Christian people come to think of the Bible as one book. With that change in attitude, the connotation of the word *Bible* has unfortunately changed from plural ("the books") to singular ("the Book"). The singular meaning of *Bible* is too restrictive and is historically inaccurate; the original meaning—which does not exclude the possibility of additional books being added to the canon—is more correct.

Latter-day Scriptures Testify the Bible Is True

The Book of Mormon is a second witness of the Bible. Book of Mormon prophets possessed the Old Testament, from Genesis to Jeremiah, and frequently quoted from it, affirmatively and repeatedly referring to many specific events and personalities in various parts of those scriptures.

The Book of Mormon also witnesses to the truthfulness of the New Testament. Book of Mormon prophets saw in vision the life, ministry, and atoning sacrifice of Jesus Christ. They wrote of a series of glorious visits by Jesus himself to the American continent after his resurrection and ascension. They also teach of faith, prayer, fasting, repentance, baptism, revelation, visions, and other biblical themes.

In these and other ways the Book of Mormon not only supports the biblical record but actually confirms its ancient existence and historical authenticity. Even more important, the Book of Mormon joins with the Bible to serve as an ancient witness for God and Jesus Christ. Its subtitle, "Another Testament of Jesus Christ," clearly states its purpose.

The Book of Mormon preserves an ancient prophecy by Joseph in Egypt in which the Bible and the Book of Mormon "shall grow together, unto the confounding of false doctrines and laying down of contentions, and establishing peace." The mission of the Prophet Joseph Smith, described in this same prophecy, was not only to bring forth more of the words of the Lord unto the children of men but also "to the convincing them of my word, which shall have already gone forth among them." (2 Nephi 3:11–12.)

Promise of a Restoration of Lost Material

Scholars and some clergy have long recognized that there are errors, variations, omissions, and minor contradictions in the Bible. As is evident in its many versions and translations, the Bible lacks certain clarity and completeness which it once enjoyed. This is the condition referred to in our eighth article of faith: "We believe the Bible to be the word of God as far as it is translated correctly."

Referring to the "lost books"—scriptural books mentioned in the Bible that are now missing—the Prophet Joseph Smith said, "It seems the Apostolic Church had some of these writings, as Jude mentions or quotes the Prophecy of Enoch, the seventh from Adam." (*History of the Church,* 7 vols., 2d ed. rev., ed. B. H. Roberts [Salt Lake City: The Church of Jesus Christ of Latter-day Saints, 1932–51], 1:132.) On another occasion, the Prophet noted: "From sundry revelations which had been received, it was apparent that many important points touching the salvation of men, had been taken from the Bible, or lost before it was compiled." He wrote further: "I believe the Bible as it read when it came from the pen of the original writers. Ignorant translators, careless transcribers, or designing and corrupt priests have committed many errors." (*Teachings of the Prophet Joseph Smith,* sel. Joseph Fielding Smith [Salt Lake City: Deseret Book Co., 1938], pp. 9–10, 327.)

The Book of Mormon tells of the original plainness and accuracy of the Bible and of the loss of certain precious parts. But it also prophesies a restoration of these parts in the latter days. In vision, Nephi saw the Bible going forth among the nations of the earth in its imperfect form—and the subsequent latter-day restoration of scripture:

"And after it [the Bible] had come forth unto them I beheld other books, which came forth by the power of the Lamb, from the Gentiles unto them, unto the convincing of the Gentiles and the remnant of

161

the seed of my brethren, and also the Jews who were scattered upon all the face of the earth, that the records of the prophets [the Old Testament] and of the twelve apostles of the Lamb [the New Testament] are true.

"And the angel spake unto me, saying: These last records, . . . shall establish the truth of the first, which are of the twelve apostles of the Lamb, and shall make known the plain and precious things which have been taken away from them. . . .

" . . . and the words of the Lamb shall be made known in the records of thy seed [the Book of Mormon], as well as in the records of the twelve apostles of the Lamb [the New Testament]; wherefore they both shall be established in one; for there is one God and one Shepherd over all the earth." (1 Nephi 13:39–41.) The restoration of the lost material has come through the Book of Mormon, the Doctrine and Covenants, the Pearl of Great Price, and the Joseph Smith Translation of the Bible, which are among the "other books" spoken of by Nephi.

The textual variants have not negated the original truth of the Bible nor removed the essential message of God's dealings with his children and the redemptive mission of Jesus Christ. From latter-day scripture we learn that the most serious changes in the Bible do not consist so much of erroneous statements as the loss of extensive portions of the text.

Church Leaders Testify the Bible Is True

All of the presidents and the other leaders of the Church have strongly advocated our use of the Bible. Joseph Smith was a student of the Bible all his life; it was from reading James 1:5 and feeling its power at the young age of fourteen that he was led to pray vocally and subsequently to receive his first vision from the Lord. He later spoke of the truth of the "sacred volume," the Bible, in these words:

"He that can mark the power of Omnipotence, inscribed upon the heavens, can also see God's own handwriting in the *sacred volume:* and he who reads it oftenest will like it best, and he who is acquainted with it, will know the hand [of the Lord] wherever he can see it." (*Teachings of the Prophet Joseph Smith,* p. 56; italics added.)

President Brigham Young often spoke of his confidence in the Bible. "We have a holy reverence for and a belief in the Bible," he said. "The doctrines contained in the Bible will lift to a superior condition all who observe them; they will impart to them knowledge, wisdom, charity, fill them with compassion and cause them to feel after the wants of those who are in distress, or in painful or degraded circumstances. They who observe the precepts contained in the Scriptures will be just and true and virtuous and peaceable at home and abroad. Follow out the doctrines of the Bible, and men will make splendid husbands, women excellent wives, and children will be obedient; they will make families happy and the nations wealthy and happy and lifted up above the things of this life." (*Discourses of Brigham Young*, sel. John A. Widtsoe [Salt Lake City: Deseret Book Co., 1954], pp. 124–25.)

In recent years, the First Presidency has issued statements in support of National Bible Week, encouraging members of the Church everywhere to read the Bible and to teach it to their children.

Use of the Bible in Church Instructional Classes

The Lord specified to the Prophet Joseph Smith in 1831 that the elders and teachers of the Church "shall teach the principles of my gospel, which are in the Bible and the Book of Mormon, in the which is the fulness of the gospel." (D&C 42:12.) This command has been in force in the Church continually since that time and is conspicuous in the procedures of the Church in missionary work, in Sunday worship, and in the curriculum of Church schools.

Every Latter-day Saint missionary studies and teaches from the Bible regularly. The missionary lessons make repeated use of the Bible in teaching the doctrines of Jesus Christ.

Instructions sent from Church headquarters have asked every local bishop to place a copy of the Bible and the other standard works on the pulpits and in the libraries of every meetinghouse throughout the Church so they may be available for frequent use. (See *Bulletin*, Feb. 1982, no. 20.)

All Church members are encouraged to study the scriptures individually and as families. Every fourth year the course of study for priesthood quorums and Sunday School and Relief Society classes is the Old Testament. The following year's course of study is the New Testament. Similarly, high-school-age seminary students study the Old and the New Testament every four years. On the college and university level, Bible courses are offered every semester.

During the years when the Bible is not the principal book studied in Church curriculum programs, the curriculum follows the other standard works. These other scriptures are so intertwined with biblical history and doctrine, however, that the Bible is in constant use throughout the Church.

Latter-day Saint Edition of the Bible

Until 1979, the Church had purchased the Bible from various publishers, chiefly, but not exclusively, Cambridge University in England. In 1979, however, the Church officially published for the first time its own edition of the King James Version with chapter headings, footnotes, a reference system, a dictionary, and a topical guide. The production and use of this edition is convincing evidence of the Church's high regard for the Bible.

The Topical Guide, a significant feature of the Latter-day Saint edition of the Bible, deserves special notice. It is perhaps the greatest literary evidence of the harmony of the scriptures. Although each book of scripture is a separate record originating in different parts of the world, among different peoples, under differing circumstances, and at different times, all four books were inspired by the same God for the same purposes — and they are witnesses for each other. In the Topical Guide, some 3,495 gospel topics are listed alphabetically, followed by the numerous passages that have a bearing on the subject. These passages are listed in each instance first from the Old Testament, next from the New Testament, and then from the Book of Mormon, Doctrine and Covenants, and Pearl of Great Price. The reader soon becomes aware of the unity and harmony of the four standard works as they support and complement one another.

On 15 October 1982 the Layman's National Bible Committee presented an award to the Church at ceremonies held in Salt Lake City. The citation reads:

"Presented to The Church of Jesus Christ of Latter-day Saints. In appreciation of outstanding service to the Bible cause through the publication of its own new edition of the King James Version which features interpretive chapter headings, a simplified footnote system and the linking of references to all other LDS scriptures — thereby greatly enhancing the study of the Bible by its membership."

President Gordon B. Hinckley, upon accepting the award on behalf of the Church, explained that the Bible project was developed to "help the people become better Bible scholars." He said that the Latter-day Saints read, believe, and love the Bible, and that they are trying to live in accordance with its teachings and to "have a

164

personal witness that Jesus is the Christ." (*Church News,* 23 Oct. 1982, p. 3.)

There can be no question about the attitude of the Church toward the Bible: (1) It is one of the four standard works that serve as guides for faith and doctrine. (2) It is a true and authentic ancient record, but (3) it is not the *only* record God has caused to be written. (4) Many important concepts once in the Bible but now missing from it have been restored through the Book of Mormon and other latter-day revelations. (5) These additional scriptures prove that the Bible is true; thus, the Bible's position is stronger than if it had to stand alone. (6) The use of the Bible has been constant in the Church from the beginning in 1830 and is on the increase, along with the study of all the sacred scriptures.

CHURCH
HISTORY

QA

Do the various accounts by the Prophet Joseph Smith of his first vision demonstrate the validity of that event, or do they cast doubt on the Prophet's integrity?

Milton V. Backman, Jr., professor of Church history, Brigham Young University

One of the most significant religious events in the history of the world occurred in the spring of 1820 in a beautiful grove near the Finger Lakes of western New York. While engaged in a fervent quest for religious truth, Joseph Smith beheld a glorious vision that altered his life and inaugurated a new religious era, the dispensation of the fulness of times.

On at least four different occasions, Joseph Smith either wrote or dictated to scribes accounts of his sacred experience in 1820. Possibly he wrote or dictated other histories of the First Vision; if so, they have not been located. The four surviving recitals of this theophany were prepared by or rendered through different scribes, at different times, from a different perspective, for different purposes, and to different audiences.[1] It is not surprising, therefore, that each of them emphasizes different aspects of the Prophet's experience. When Latter-day Saints today explain this remarkable vision to others, their descriptions often vary according to the audience or the circumstances that prompt their reports. If one were relating the incident to a group of high priests, for example, he would undoubtedly tell it somewhat differently from the way he would tell it to individuals who had never heard of the restoration of the gospel or of Joseph Smith.

In an important way, the existence of these different accounts helps support the integrity of the Latter-day Saint prophet. It indicates that Joseph did not deliberately create a memorized version that he related to everyone. In the legal profession, for example, attorneys and judges recognize that if a witness repeats an incident by using precisely the same language, the court might challenge the validity of such a statement.

Indeed, there are long-standing precedents for differing accounts of the same spiritual experience. For example, the Four Gospels do not correspond exactly concerning the great events at the Garden's empty tomb. There are variations in the number of women and angels who were present and whether the angels were sitting or standing. Although the Prophet Joseph Smith in his inspired translation clarified some of these details (and others cited below), minor disparities remain in the four descriptions of this event (compare Matthew 28 with Mark 18; Luke 24; and John 20). The differences, however, are not important—they may have resulted from incorrect transmissions or translations, or they may be the result of recording the event from different perspectives. The glorious fact remains that the tomb was empty because Jesus had risen as the first fruits of the Resurrection.

Accounts of the Savior's appearance to Paul on the road to Damascus, related to us in Acts by Luke and by Paul in his letters, also vary. To cite one example, in Acts 8:7, we read that others traveling with Paul heard a voice but saw no man. In Acts 22:9, we read that others saw the light but did not hear the voice.

A description of an event found in John 12 is similar in some respects to the New Testament account of Paul's vision. According to John, while Jesus was in Jerusalem a "voice" was heard from heaven. While some perceived that the noise was like thunder, others thought that an angel had spoken. (See John 12:28–29.)

It is the great reality that is important, not the somewhat differing perceptions of it. Although the description by Matthew of the death of Judas (Matthew 27:5) is different from the description in Acts (Acts 1:18), and although the Gospels differ on the message inscribed on the cross and the words that Jesus spoke just before his death (compare Matthew 27:37; Mark 15:34; Luke 23:38, 43; and John 19:19–21), we should not become so engrossed with differences that we fail to comprehend the basic message conveyed in the Gospels. Of most importance in the descriptions of the Crucifixion is that Jesus, while on the cross, was completing the Atonement.

Like Paul, Joseph Smith did not relate all the details of his profound experience of 1820 at any one time. When Paul found that his gentile ministry was in question, he recalled (years after his vision) how the Lord had outlined his mission to the non-Jewish nations at the time of his first vision. (See Acts 26:16–18.) Similarly, in the most complete account of the First Vision (one prepared in 1838 as part of the history of the Church), the Prophet concluded that "many other things did [the Savior] say unto me, which I cannot write at this time." (Joseph Smith–History 1:20.) As a matter of fact, we do not have a full account today of the First Vision. At no time did the Prophet disclose everything that he learned during his vision near Palmyra. Nevertheless, as with the four Gospels and the three versions of Paul's experience on the road to Damascus, by combining all known accounts of the First Vision written by the Prophet, we may gain a more complete understanding of his theophany of 1820.

Considering the social and literary climate of his times, we can also better understand why the young Joseph Smith possibly did not write an account of the First Vision until the early 1830s. Many people living in nineteenth-century America did not publish autobiographies or histories until many years after the events that shaped their lives had transpired. The possibility of Joseph Smith's keeping a diary in 1820 at age fourteen seems remote.[2] Still, as aptly explained by Dean C. Jessee, research historian for the Joseph Fielding Smith Institute for Church History at Brigham Young University, the apparent time lag between the First Vision and its recording is more presumed than real. "Considering the youth of the Prophet, the frontier conditions in which he lived, his lack of academic training, the absence of any formal directive to motivate him to write, and the antagonistic reception he received upon first relating the experience, it is not strange that he failed to preserve an account of his First Vision during the decade between 1820 and 1830. However, once directed by an 1830 revelation to keep a history, Joseph acted with all dispatch that time-consuming responsibilities and frustrating difficulties would allow."[3] The first known recording by Paul of his experience on the road to Damascus was written about twenty-four years after his vision.[4]

Although no published reports of the First Vision appeared during the 1820s and 1830s, the Prophet included descriptions of his sacred experience in the grove in all four accounts of the rise of the restored Church that he wrote or dictated during the ten-year span from 1832 to 1842. And when Joseph published for the first time two different versions of the history of the Church (a brief sketch and then a more detailed history) in 1842, he included in both accounts a description of this vision.

While the wording in Joseph's accounts of the First Vision is different, the basic truths disclosed in each of his recitals involve a rich harmony in many details. One can better understand and appreciate the different emphases in these testimonies by examining their individual historical setting, by considering Joseph's efforts to write history, and by noting his attempts to improve the form in which the basic message of the Restoration was conveyed to others.

The 1832 Account

The earliest known written account of the First Vision was included in an autobiography Joseph wrote in 1832. The narrative begins with the following introduction:

"A History of the life of Joseph Smith Jr. an account of his marvilous experience and of all the mighty acts which he doeth in the name of Jesus Ch[r]ist the son of the living God . . . and also an account of the rise of the church of Christ."[5]

In this sketch of the Prophet's life there is a reference to his birth in Vermont in 1805, his move to New York when he was about ten, his quest for religious truth, and his experience in the grove. There is also a description in this autobiography of events that led to the coming forth of the Book of Mormon.

For many years historians were perplexed concerning the date of this manuscript. A few years ago, however, Dean C. Jessee determined that this manuscript, which was written in part by Joseph's scribe, Frederick G. Williams, was prepared between 20 July 1832 and 1 December 1832 (possibly during the month of November). Although Frederick G. Williams wrote down the introduction of this autobiography as dictated by Joseph Smith, Joseph himself wrote the portion dealing with the First Vision. This is the only recounting of Joseph's sacred experience in 1820 that is in his own handwriting.

Since the 1832 history is one of the earliest known manuscripts written by Joseph Smith, this record provides many clues to Joseph's formal education. Joseph admitted that because of the poverty of his large family he was "deprived of the bennifit of an education. Suffice it to say," he continued, "I was mearly instructid in reading writing and the ground rules of Arithmatic which constuted my whole literary acquirements."[6]

Most children living in the area of Palmyra and Manchester, New York, during the second and third decades of the nineteenth century attended school on an average of seven or eight months each year. Absenteeism in these one-room schools, where children from five to sixteen gathered, was high, and Joseph said that he was among those whose formal education was sometimes neglected. When he listed his educational attainments, he did not mention spelling. A comparison of the spelling in the 1832 account with forms recommended in the popular grammars of the age indicates that by that time Joseph (like most of his contemporaries) had not learned to spell a number of words as prescribed by some secular authorities. Moreover, some of the sentences in that recital were not complete. Others were not in the best literary form, and there was little punctuation in the manuscript. Such natural mistakes, however, take nothing from the powerful, spiritual, and uplifting tone of the 1832 account. In fact, in some ways the 1832 account is the most powerful and convincing of all the accounts.

During the winter of 1832–33, and for several years thereafter, Joseph studied grammar in an attempt to improve his capacity to express himself. His later writings reveal that both his spelling and style improved considerably.

While Joseph was attempting to write history, he was also receiving many revelations. A comparison of the 1832 account with some of the revelations recorded in that same year indicates that Joseph the man did not have the same ability of expression that was evident when Joseph the Prophet unfolded the will of God in the form of latter-day revelations.

Although most experiences recorded by Joseph Smith in his 1832 autobiography were included in later histories that he wrote, some details were omitted in his published works that were recorded in this early manuscript. Most of the themes that were not published in the nineteenth century pertained to personal events or feelings or referred to the work and mission of the Savior, which were described in greater detail in ancient and modern scriptures. Similar events in the life of Joseph Smith that were recorded about 1838, such as his operation in New Hampshire while he was a boy and his conversation with his mother following the First Vision, were also excluded from Joseph's initial publication of the "History of the Church."

One example of an event in Joseph's life that was not included in the other accounts of the First Vision written by the Prophet was his extended quest for religious truth. For about three years (from about age twelve to age fifteen), he was searching for religious truth, especially God's plan of salvation, which involves the remitting of sin. During this investigation, he wrote, there were times when he thought that no society or denomination was built upon the gospel of Jesus Christ. The First Vision, therefore, did not occur after a brief quest but took place following a two- or three-year inquiry initiated by Joseph's concern for the welfare of his soul.

Joseph Smith was not satisfied with the programs of redemption taught by the religious leaders in the community where he lived. After investigating the basic beliefs of various denominations, he stated that he "cried unto the Lord for mercy for there was none else to whom" he could go. While calling upon the Lord, the young man testified, "I was filld with the spirit of God and the Lord opened the heavens upon me and I saw the Lord and he spake unto me saying Joseph my son thy sins are forgiven thee. go thy way walk in my statutes and keep my commandments behold I am the Lord of glory I was crucifyed for the world that all those who believe on my name may have Eternal life."

After learning that Jesus was crucified "for the world," and that all who believed in him would have eternal life, Joseph was instructed that the Savior would return "quickly" in "the cloud clothed in the glory" of the Father. Following this sacred experience, Joseph declared that he rejoiced, and his soul was filled with love for many days.

By way of summary, the 1832 account is the only known recital of the First Vision in which Joseph told of his prolonged quest for religious truth, his earnest desire to secure a forgiveness of sins, his utmost concern because of the sins of mankind, his learning about the nature of the Atonement and the reality of the Second Coming, and his rejoicing following his spiritual experience. Although Joseph also referred to the conflicting doctrines that he encountered, recalled his investigation of the different religious societies, and mentioned that he learned that God's true church was not upon the earth, in this account he concentrated on his personal quest to secure a remission of sins.

Because Joseph was describing in 1832 an event that occurred twelve years earlier, it may have been difficult for him to remember certain details, such as the exact date of this vision. The account was undoubtedly a first draft in which Joseph was attempting to record various impressions. Moreover, Joseph did not revise this account in preparation for publication, nor did he attempt to clarify statements that possibly needed revising. His main interest, as far as time was concerned, was merely to explain that the vision occurred in his teenage years. If in his preliminary effort to record events in his life he inserted between two lines that the event occurred during his "16th" rather than his fifteenth year, he just intended to make a correction for a more carefully prepared history that was begun in 1838. (The "16th" is an insertion that is difficult to read. It is possible that the insertion is really "15th," which then would harmonize with his later more carefully prepared drafts.)

A few concepts were included in Joseph's later recitals of the First Vision that were not mentioned in the 1832 autobiography. In all accounts (except the 1842 account) prepared by the Prophet after 1832, for example, Joseph discussed the powerful force of opposition that he encountered prior to his seeing the pillar of light. Moreover, in the other three histories, Joseph specifically referred to the appearance of two personages. This does not mean that in 1832 Joseph said that *only* one personage appeared or in any way disclaimed the appearance of two personages. In fact, Joseph Smith may have referred to the Father in his 1832 account when he declared that he "cried unto the Lord" and the "Lord opened the heavens," even though Joseph was referring to the Son when he wrote that the Lord spoke to him. The Prophet (and other early General Authorities) used the word *God,* meaning the Father, and *Lord* interchangeably, such as in the prayer written in the Liberty Jail. (See D&C 121:1–4.) Nevertheless, in this initial effort to record the spiritual effect of the vision on him, Joseph focused on the message that the Savior unfolded to him. Even though the accounts emphasize different ideas and details, the various versions do not contradict each other in this important point.

In 1832 Joseph Smith and Sidney Rigdon beheld a glorious vision in which they saw Christ on the right hand of the Father and angels worshiping God and the "Lamb." After being commanded during this theophany to write an account of their experience, they did not concentrate on having seen the Father but bore a powerful witness of the Savior and emphasized that which they learned during the remarkable vision. Incidentally, this account was recorded and published less than six months after the event occurred. (D&C 76:14, 20–24, first printed in *The Evening and the Morning Star,* Independence, Missouri, July 1832.)

The 1835 Account

On 9 November 1835 Joseph related his early vision to a visiting Jewish minister named Robert Matthews, alias Robert Matthias, who said his priestly name was Joshua. A brief summary of this conversation, which mentioned the First Vision and the coming forth of the Book of Mormon, was recorded in Joseph's Kirtland diary by one of his scribes, Warren Cowdery. Later this account was copied from Joseph's journal and placed in the manuscript history that

Joseph began in 1838. In 1843, however, Willard Richards, who had been called by Joseph to edit his history, copied the early portions of the manuscript and omitted that which Joseph had told Matthews concerning his early visions. By that date a more detailed version (the 1838 account) of these events had been written and published.[7]

One concept was mentioned in the 1835 recital that was not included in any other account of the First Vision written or dictated by the Prophet. Joseph informed Matthews that he not only saw two personages during this vision but beheld "many angels."

In this November 9th diary account Joseph Smith also declared (if Warren Cowdery recorded correctly this statement) that one personage appeared and then another. There is no contradiction in this statement and the 1838 account in which the Prophet testified that he looked up and beheld two personages. The latter account might have been one in which the time element was reduced.

In a brief reference to the First Vision in this same diary (which because of its brevity is not included as one of the four recitals emphasized in this article), Joseph apparently told a visitor in Kirtland on 14 November 1835 that "he received the first visitation of angels" when he was about fourteen.[8] Apparently, in his discussions with some nonmembers, the Prophet hesitated to identify the personages who had appeared to him.

Following his sacred experience of 1820 the young prophet was persecuted for telling others that he had seen a vision and was visited by two glorious personages. Recognizing that many would not accept nor appreciate this sacred experience, Joseph Smith was cautious about what he related to others. Summaries of this event addressed to nonmembers and related before and after the Prophet had identified the personages do not always mention that the Father or the Son appeared.[9]

Moreover, a similar pattern of expression is found in the Old Testament where *God* and *Angel* are used interchangeably. (See Genesis 48:15–16.) In this vein, the Prophet taught others that the resurrected Christ was an angel. One kind of being in heaven, he said, is an angel or personage who is resurrected with a body of flesh and bones.[10] To support this concept, Joseph quoted the Savior when he said to his disciples, "Handle me and see, for a spirit hath not flesh and bones, as ye see me have." (D&C 129:1–2.) Early Latter-day Saint leaders who knew that Christ had instructed Joseph during his vision of 1820 sometimes declared that an angel told Joseph Smith not to join any of the churches. In their sermons, these same leaders used the term *Lord* to identify the Father and the Son and used the words *Lord, Christ, personage, messenger,* and *angel* interchangeably. An examination of twenty-one sermons delivered by six different leaders in early Utah, all of whom were well acquainted with Joseph Smith and his teachings, reveals that eleven talks mentioning the First Vision identify the appearance of two personages. In other sermons these same leaders declared in essence that an angel told Joseph not to join any of the churches. In one instance, Orson Pratt, in the same sentence, says that Joseph Smith was visited by an angel from God and by two personages. Obviously, these leaders, like the Prophet himself, sometimes testified that the Father and Son appeared in 1820 and at other times emphasized the message that the one personage delivered.[11]

The 1838 Account

The third known account of the First Vision recorded by the Prophet was included in his "History of the Church." Although Joseph Smith commenced dictating this history in 1838, the earliest known manuscript of this work is in the handwriting of James Mulholland, who was serving as scribe for the Prophet in 1839, thus indicating that the manuscript was probably copied by Mulholland in that year. It is evident that the Prophet intended this narrative to become the basic source for Church literature, and it was carefully prepared with the intention of publishing the information. This account was undoubtedly more carefully considered than either of the first two. It was this version of the First Vision that first appeared in the 15 March and 1 April 1842 issues of *Times and Seasons* and was republished in the *Millennial Star* in June. Nine years later, Franklin D. Richards published extracts from the *Times and Seasons* account of this history in the first edition of the Pearl of Great Price, and this record, which includes Joseph's testimony concerning the First Vision, was published in subsequent editions of that book.

A comparison of the manuscript in Mulholland's handwriting with the account of the First Vision appearing in the *Times and Seasons* indicates many changes in punctuation and a few changes in spelling. Since Joseph Smith was editor of the *Times and Seasons* in the spring of 1842, he must have been responsible for the changes that occurred when early portions of his manuscript history were first published. The Prophet introduced this account, which appeared in serial form, by writing: "In the last number I gave a brief history of the rise and progress of the Church. I now enter more particularly into that history, and extract from my journal."[12]

Although nearly all changes in the Prophet's early history were made during his life and while he was editor of the *Times and Seasons,* a few minor alterations in wording and punctuation were made in later publications. After the Pearl of Great Price had been accepted by the Church in 1880 as scripture, Elder James E. Talmage was appointed by the First Presidency to prepare a new edition of that work, which became the 1902 edition. At that time, Elder Talmage modified a few words in Joseph's description of the historical setting of the First Vision. For example, to improve the style and grammar, the tense of several verbs was changed, an *either* appeared instead of *both,* and *to* replaced an *unto.* An *endeavoring* and *passage of scripture* were also added.

Another change in the 1902 edition (originally in the 1891 edition) of the Pearl of Great Price was the omission of a phrase that had appeared in parentheses in Joseph's manuscript history and in early publications of that work. This was the comment concerning Joseph's attitude immediately prior to his entering the Sacred Grove — "(for at this time it had never entered into my heart that all were wrong)." This statement was reinserted in the 1981 edition.

There appears to be a possible discrepancy between a statement recorded in the 1832 account — that Joseph decided by searching the scriptures that no denomination was "built upon the Gospel . . . as recorded in the New Testament" — and a comment in the 1838 account — that "at this time it had never entered into my heart that all were wrong." If there is a contradiction in these accounts, then the 1838 account should be considered as the more reliable history. The young Joseph Smith, like many others then and now, was possibly not precise in his use of all words.

But perhaps the statements are not contradictory. Through a study of the Bible (an intellectual analysis) Joseph Smith may have decided that all the churches he knew of were wrong. At the time he entered the grove, however, and at other times, he may have believed in his heart that God's true church existed somewhere — he just didn't know where. It is often difficult to understand a writer's real intent and the precise meaning of all his phrases, especially if the writer was unskilled and wrote during an era earlier than our own.

Additional revisions in the account of the First Vision were made in the 1921 edition of the Pearl of Great Price. Several paragraphs were added that had been included as notes in the manuscript history. This information had been recorded in that work during Joseph's life, as evidenced by a notation in Willard Richards's diary under the date of December 1842. Note B, which appears on pages 133 and 134 of the manuscript history, describes Joseph's conversation with his mother following his sacred experience in the grove.

The 1838 description of the historical setting of the First Vision is nearly twice as long as his 1835 summary. The account of what he learned in the Sacred Grove is about the same length as the 1832 recital, but though the emphasis is different, it is not contradictory. In 1838 Joseph was writing a history of the Church, rather than an autobiography and brief history, and instead of concentrating on his quest for a remission of sins, he emphasized his search for God's true church.

This concept of Joseph's investigating the various faiths, his dilemma concerning which church was right, and his learning that the fulness of the gospel was not upon the earth were discussed in nearly all the accounts. But in the 1838 (and an 1842) history of the Church, Joseph did not mention that Christ informed him that his sins were forgiven. Instead of developing this theme, Joseph in 1838 described in greater detail the instructions of the Savior concerning the churches of his age. For example, in 1832 Joseph wrote that Jesus informed him that the people of the world had turned aside from the gospel, that they were not keeping his commandments, and that they drew near to him with their lips while their hearts were far from him. Six years later Joseph elaborated on this concept by writing:

"I was answered that I must join none of them, for they were all wrong, and the Personage who addressed me said that all their Creeds were an abomination in his sight, that those professors were all corrupt, that: 'they draw near to me with their lips but their hearts are far from me, They teach for doctrines the commandments of men, having a form of Godliness but they deny the power thereof.' He again forbade me to join with any of them and many other things did he say unto me which I cannot write at this time."[13]

The 1838 account was also the only history written by the Prophet in which he described in some detail the religious excitement and contention that occurred in the place where he lived, the uniting of some members of his family with the Presbyterians, the attraction of others to the Methodist faith, and the joining of great multitudes of different religious parties in that "whole region of country." This was also the only account in which he specified that the event occurred in the spring of 1820.

Moreover, this testimony is the only account prepared by the Prophet in which he specifically identified the Father as one of the two personages who appeared to him. In the two recitals related to non–Latter-day Saints (the 1835 and an 1842 account), Joseph described the appearance of two personages without identifying them. Meanwhile, other individuals, members and nonmembers, during the early 1840s wrote accounts of the First Vision based on what they had learned from the latter-day prophet and reported that Joseph testified that during his first vision he beheld the Father and the Son.[14]

The 1842 Account

The last known account of the First Vision written by Joseph Smith was included in what is known as the Wentworth Letter. At the request of John Wentworth, editor of the *Chicago Democrat,* Joseph Smith was invited to write a history of the Latter-day Saints for one of Wentworth's friends, George Barstow, who was preparing a history of New Hampshire. After writing a brief history of the Church, Joseph inserted thirteen unnumbered statements of belief that are known as the Articles of Faith. Although the manuscript of this history has not been located, the account was published in the 1 March 1842 issue of the *Times and Seasons,* the issue that immediately preceded Joseph's publication of his manuscript history in serial form.

One of the noticeable differences in the wording in the Wentworth Letter from other recitals of the First Vision pertains to what Joseph learned during his communication with Deity. Instead of writing, as Joseph had done in 1838, that Christ informed him that all creeds were an abomination in God's sight, the Prophet declared in his 1842 account that the personages told him that "all religious denominations were believing in incorrect doctrines, and that none of them was acknowledged of God as his church and kingdom. And I was expressly commanded to 'go not after them.' "[15]

Joseph concluded this recital with a statement that was implied but not specifically declared in the other three accounts: " . . . at the same time receiving a promise that the fulness of the gospel should at some future time be made known unto me."

In conclusion, an examination of the four accounts of the First Vision reveals several important concepts concerning the writing of

Church history. Recognizing the importance of preserving what had transpired, Joseph Smith devoted many hours during the 1830s and early 1840s to recording events that he had witnessed. While describing his sacred experience of 1820, he sometimes emphasized one theme and at other times concentrated on other major concepts. Although the precise wording of what he learned from the Savior is different in all the accounts, the same essential message was included in all except the 1835 recital—that God's true church was not upon the earth in 1820. Of utmost importance was not the specific language in which the truths were unfolded but the truths themselves.

Since the 1838 recital was included in the Pearl of Great Price, an investigation of the publications of this history helps one better understand principles concerning the formation of scriptures. Joseph Smith was responsible for many changes in punctuation, spelling, and other similar revisions in his manuscript history. After a portion of this history was canonized in the Pearl of Great Price, additional textual refinements were made by editors acting under the authorization of Church leaders. These revisions were apparently made in the interests of grammatical quality, clarification, and consistency. Several short paragraphs were also added that had been included as notes in the manuscript history prior to the Prophet's martyrdom. All these alterations were in harmony with precedents set by Joseph Smith in his textual revisions of latter-day scriptures. In no instance was there a change in the basic message recorded in the manuscript history concerning the historical setting of the First Vision or the truths unfolded during this remarkable experience. But changes were made in an effort to convey the truths unfolded by God in the latter days in the best and clearest language that mortals could fashion.[16]

Notes

1. Accounts of Joseph's recitals of the First Vision (and accounts prepared by Joseph's contemporaries) have been published in the appendix of Milton V. Backman, Jr., *Joseph Smith's First Vision* (Salt Lake City: Bookcraft, 1980). Some of these accounts also have been reprinted in Dean C. Jessee, *The Personal Writings of Joseph Smith* (Salt Lake City: Deseret Book Co., 1984), pp. 5–6, 75–76, 199–200, 213. A harmony of the writings of the Prophet on the First Vision appears in Milton V. Backman, Jr., *Eyewitness Accounts of the Restoration* (Orem, Utah: Grandin, 1983).

2. Why would Joseph have been keeping a diary at a time when

other members of his family and nearly all farmers in his economic class in western New York did not? The poverty of his family prevented him from attending school as frequently as other children did, and his continual labor in the fields was not conducive to advanced learning, let alone diary-keeping. Social historians have long understood that there are few writings from the childhood and youth of even the most prominent of the elite who lived before 1900. Norman F. Cantor and Richard I. Schneider (*How to Study History* [New York: Thomas Y. Crowell Co., 1967], p. 72) have shown that the availability of diaries, journals, and private correspondence is most determined by changes in the level of literacy and education, by technology, and by social and intellectual fashion. It was not until the late nineteenth century that it became a middle class fashion to write detailed letters and keep diaries.

3. Dean C. Jessee, "The Early Accounts of Joseph Smith's First Vision," *BYU Studies* 9 (Spring 1969): 294.

4. Richard L. Anderson, "Parallel Prophets: Paul and Joseph Smith," *Brigham Young University Fireside and Devotional Speeches* (Provo, Utah: Brigham Young University Publications, 1983), pp. 178–79.

5. Joseph Smith History, Letter books, Church Historical Department.

6. Spelling and punctuation of this and other manuscripts cited in this article have been preserved in the form in which the information was originally recorded.

7. Joseph Smith, Kirtland Diary, 9 November 1835, Church Historical Department; Manuscript History, 9 November 1835, Book A–1 and Book B–1, Church Historical Department.

8. Jessee, *Personal Writings of Joseph Smith,* p. 84.

9. See Backman, *Joseph Smith's First Vision,* pp. 158–59, 168–69, 176 for accounts of the First Vision related to nonmembers.

10. Joseph Smith, *History of The Church of Jesus Christ of Latter-day Saints,* 7 vols., 2d rev. ed., ed. B. H. Roberts (Salt Lake City: The Church of Jesus Christ of Latter-day Saints, 1932–51), 4:425; Andrew F. Ehat and Lyndon B. Cook, *The Words of Joseph Smith: The Contemporary Accounts of the Nauvoo Discourses of the Prophet Joseph* (Provo, Utah: Brigham Young University Religious Studies Center, 1980), p. 77.

11. In *Journal of Discourses,* 26 vols. (London: Latter-day Saints' Book Depot, 1855–86), 2:170–71; 2:196–97; 7:220–21; 8:346; 11:1–2; 12:67; 12:302; 12:352–54; 13:65–67; 13:77–78; 14:140–41; 15:180–82; 18:239; 20:167; 21:65; 21:161–65; 22:29; 24:371–73; 25:155–57.

12. *Times and Seasons,* 15 Mar. 1842, p. 726.

13. Backman, *Joseph Smith's First Vision,* p. 163; see also Joseph Smith–History 1:19, in Pearl of Great Price, 1981, p. 49.

14. Backman, *Joseph Smith's First Vision,* pp. 170–77.

15. Ibid., pp. 168–69.

16. Richard P. Howard, *Restoration Scriptures: A Study of Their Textual Development* (Independence, Mo.: Herald Publishing House, 1969), pp. 51–52.

QA

Did Joseph Smith's contemporaries provide accounts of the First Vision as given to them by Joseph Smith, and, if so, are these accounts consistent with his own accounts of the First Vision?

Milton V. Backman, Jr., professor of Church history, Brigham Young University

In 1834, one year following the organization of the Pontiac (Michigan) Branch, Joseph Smith and several witnesses to the Book of Mormon bore powerful affirmations to the branch members of their spiritual experiences. While summarizing the Prophet's testimony, Edward Stevenson, a convert who attended these meetings, reminisced, "The Prophet testified with great power concerning the visit of the Father and Son, and the conversation he had with them. Never before did I feel such power as was manifested on these occasions."[1]

Many others who were either close associates of Joseph Smith or who interviewed him also declared that the Prophet informed them of that sacred experience. These contemporaries bore witness that Joseph identified the personages who appeared to him and that he told them of the message he received from the Father and the Son.[2]

Orson Pratt's Accounts

An early convert who may have referred to that historical event more frequently in his sermons and writings than any other contemporary of Joseph Smith was Orson Pratt. Throughout the decade of the 1830s and during the winter of 1839–40, Orson Pratt was one of the Prophet's most attentive students. Shortly after his baptism in September 1830, the nineteen-year-old convert traveled more than two hundred miles to meet the Prophet, who, in December of that year, ordained him an elder. When Joseph moved to Kirtland, Ohio,

Orson Pratt followed. While there, he lived for nearly two months in the Prophet's home and worked with him. He was one of the early members of the School of the Prophets and spent many hours in 1833 listening as the Prophet unfolded to the school the history and doctrines of the restored faith. In the early 1830s he traveled with Joseph to western Missouri and in 1835 was called to be an Apostle of the Lord.

Orson Pratt's contact with Joseph Smith continued in 1839 and early 1840. During the late spring and early summer of 1839, Orson lived near the Mississippi River not far from the residence of Joseph Smith. Later that year he served a brief mission with the Prophet in Philadelphia before traveling on to Edinburgh, Scotland, where he preached for about nine months, "raised up a Church of over 200 Saints . . . [and] published a pamphlet now entitled REMARKABLE VISIONS."[3]

This missionary pamphlet was published in the fall of 1840 and contained the first account of the First Vision to appear in print.[4] It included a description of Joseph Smith's early visions, from his initial theophany near Palmyra to the early appearances of Moroni and his experience with the Three Witnesses to the Book of Mormon. Elder Pratt reprinted the work twice in 1841 and again in 1842 (called the third American edition). In the American editions, the work was enlarged to include an account of the restoration of the priesthood.

A comparison of Orson Pratt's pamphlet with Joseph Smith's historical writings reveals that most of the major concepts included in the Prophet's histories (especially in the 1838 account) were included in Elder Pratt's work. Since there are no direct quotations in the Pratt pamphlet, and since the literary style is very different from Joseph's pre-1840 writings, Orson Pratt undoubtedly based his history on what he had learned from the teachings rather than the writings of Joseph.

In a sermon delivered in 1859 in which he discussed the First Vision, Elder Pratt said, "I will give you a brief history as it came from his own mouth. I have often heard him relate it."[5] Consequently, by publishing this pamphlet, Orson Pratt not only gave to the world an excellent summary of Joseph Smith's early visions but also bore witness to their authenticity.

The following selection, giving background of the First Vision and an account of the vision itself, with original spelling and punctuation retained, is from the 1840 edition of *Remarkable Visions*. Concepts similar to statements included in Joseph Smith's writings are reproduced in italics, and after each statement (in parentheses) is the approximate date when Joseph Smith first recorded that information himself. The relatively few differences in the accounts are probably due either to literary embellishments or to details related to Orson that were never recorded by Joseph.[6]

"*Mr Joseph Smith, jun., who made the following important discovery, was born in the town of Sharon, Windsor county, Vermont, on the 23d of December, A.D. 1805. When ten years old, his parents with their family, moved to Palmyra, New York* (1838); *in the vicinity of which he resided for about eleven years, the latter part in the town of Manchester. Cultivating the earth for a livelihood was his occupation, in which he employed the most of his time. His advantages, for acquiring literary knowledge, were exceedingly small; hence, his education was limited to a slight acquaintance with two or three of the common branches of learning.* He could *read* without much difficulty, and *write* a very imperfect hand; and had a very limited understanding of the ground rules of *arithmetic* (1832).[7] These were his highest and only attainments; while the rest of those branches, so universally taught in the common schools throughout the United States, were entirely unknown to him.

"When somewhere about fourteen or fifteen years old, *he began seriously to reflect upon the necessity of being prepared for a future state of existence.* . . . *He perceived that it was a question of infinite importance and that the salvation of his soul depended upon a correct understanding of the same* (1832). . . . *If he went to the religious denominations to seek information, each one pointed to its particular tenets, saying—'This is the way, walk ye in it?'* (1838) . . . *It, also, occurred to his mind, that God was not the author of but one doctrine, and therefore could not acknowledge but one denomination as his church* (1842); and that such denomination must be a people who believe, and teach, that one doctrine (whatever it may be,) and build upon the same. He then reflected upon the immense number of doctrines, now, in the world, which had given rise to many hundreds of different denominations. *The great question to be decided in his mind, was—if any one of these denominations be the Church of Christ, which one is it?* (1838) . . . *He, accordingly, commenced perusing the sacred pages of the Bible, with sincerity, believing the things that he read. His mind soon caught hold the following passage:—'If any of you lack wisdom, let him ask of God, that giveth to all men liberally, and upbraideth not; and it shall be given him.'—James i.5* (1838) . . . *It was like a light shining forth in a dark place.* . . . *He, now, saw that if he* inquired of God, there was, not only, a possibility, but a probability; yea, more, a certainty, that he should obtain a knowledge, which, of all the doctrines, was the doctrine of Christ; and, which, of all the churches, was the church of Christ. *He, therefore, retired to a secret place, in a grove* but a short distance from his father's house *and knelt down* (1838), and began to call upon the Lord (1832, 1838). *At first he was severely tempted by the powers of darkness, which endeavoured to overcome him; but he continued to seek for deliverance, until darkness gave way from his mind.* (1838) . . . *And, while thus pouring out his soul, anxiously desiring an answer from God, he, at length, saw a very bright and glorious light in the heavens above;* which, at first, seemed to be at a considerable distance. . . . *He continued praying, while the light appeared to be gradually descending towards him;* and, as it drew nearer, it increased in brightness, and magnitude, so that, by the time that it reached the tops of the trees, the whole wilderness, for some distance around, was illuminated in a most glorious and brilliant manner. He expected to have seen the leaves and boughs of the trees consumed, as soon as the light came in contact with them; but, perceiving that it did not produce that effect, he was encouraged with the hopes of being able to endure its presence. It continued descending, slowly, until it rested upon the earth, and he was enveloped in the midst of it. When it first came upon him, it produced a peculiar sensation throughout his whole system; and, immediately, his mind was caught away, from the natural objects with which he was surrounded;

"*And he was enrapped in a heavenly vision, and saw two glorious personages* (1838, 1842) *who exactly resembled each other in their features or likeness* (1842). *He was informed, that his sins were forgiven* (1832). *He was also informed upon the subjects, which had for some time previously agitated his mind, viz. — that all the religious denominations were believing in incorrect doctrines* (1832, 1838, 1842); *and, consequently that none of them was acknowledged of God, as his church and kingdom* (1832). *And he was expressly commanded, to go not after them* (1838); *and he received a promise that the true doctrine — the fulness of the gospel, should, at some future time, be made known to him* (1842); *after which, the vision withdrew, leaving his mind in a state of calmness and peace, indescribable* (1832).*"

On subsequent occasions Orson Pratt declared that it was the Father and the Son who spoke to Joseph during his first vision. While serving as editor of the *Millennial Star,* Elder Pratt wrote an article entitled "Are the Father and Son Two Distinct Persons?" He included scriptural evidences and events from Church history to support his belief in the separate nature of these members of the Godhead. While using Church history as a tool to teach doctrine, Elder Pratt declared that Joseph Smith and Sidney Rigdon saw Christ "on the right hand of God" in February 1832 (see D&C 76) and that Joseph Smith saw "both the Father and Son" during his first vision.[8]

In sermons delivered after he migrated to the Great Basin, Elder Pratt informed others of sacred experiences related to him by the Prophet. In an 1859 sermon, Orson Pratt declared Joseph Smith told him that when he was between fourteen and fifteen years of age "he beheld a vision . . . [and] saw two glorious personages; and one, pointing to the other, said, 'Behold my beloved son! hear ye him.' Then he was instructed and informed in regard to many things pertaining to his own welfare, and commanded not to unite himself to any of these churches. He was also informed that at some future time the fulness of the Gospel should be made manifest to him, and he should be an instrument in the hands of God of laying the foundations of the kingdom of God."[9]

Orson Hyde's Testimony

Another close friend of Joseph Smith who published a pamphlet describing the First Vision before the Prophet published his own historical writings was Orson Hyde. Throughout most of the 1830s, Elder Hyde lived in Kirtland near the Prophet's home, and after his baptism on 30 October 1831, he was called to be a missionary. His first two companions were Joseph's brothers, Hyrum and Samuel.

In 1833 he was invited by the Prophet to be one of the teachers in the School of the Prophets. Because of his faith and ability, he was also called in 1835 to be one of the original members of the Quorum of the Twelve Apostles. His association with the Prophet was enhanced when he had several opportunities during the 1830s to travel with the Prophet.

After gathering with other Saints in Nauvoo, Elder Hyde was called on a mission to Palestine, where he dedicated the Holy Land for the gathering of the Jews. While Elder Hyde was returning home in August 1842, he published a missionary pamphlet in Frankfurt, Germany, entitled, *A Cry from the Wilderness, a Voice from the Dust of the Earth*.[10] Although a principal source for this work was Orson Pratt's *Remarkable Visions*, the Hyde tract also includes an introduction and foreword not found in the earlier work and contains more detailed explanations.

In his *Cry from the Wilderness*, Elder Hyde described Joseph's search for truth, his introduction to James's admonition on prayer, his prayer in the woods near his father's house, the presence of the adversary, and the appearance of light following the darkness. While describing Joseph's vision, Elder Hyde wrote that Joseph saw two glorious personages who resembled each other in stature and likeness. They informed him that he should not join any religious party, for they had all erred concerning doctrine, and that none of them was considered by God to be his church and kingdom. He was directed to wait until a later date when the true doctrine of Christ and the fulness of the gospel would be revealed to him. After the vision closed, Elder Hyde concluded, Joseph's soul was filled with peace and calmness.

Other Descriptions of the First Vision

Latter-day Saints were not the only contemporaries who described the First Vision as related to them by Joseph Smith. A nonmember editor of the *Pittsburg Gazette* interviewed the Prophet in Nauvoo and then published an article on him. The editor discussed the reformation that preceded the First Vision, the young boy's quest to know which church to join, and Joseph's compliance with James's admonition on prayer. Then he described the First Vision as related by Joseph Smith:

"I saw a light," he quoted Joseph Smith as saying, "and then a glorious personage in the light, and then another personage, and the first personage said to the second, Behold my beloved Son, hear him. — I then addressed this second person, saying, O Lord, what Church shall I join? He replied, 'don't join any of them, they are all corrupt.' "[11]

Alexander Neibaur, a convert who gathered with the Saints in Nauvoo, described in his journal what Joseph told him during a dinner conversation. Brother Neibaur wrote that the Prophet said he had been "struck" by a passage on prayer in the Bible and so went into the woods to pray. After his tongue cleaved temporarily to the roof of his mouth, he saw a fire which gradually drew nearer to him. He "saw a personage in the fire, light complexion, blue eyes. . . . [Another] person came to the side of the first. Mr. Smith then asked, must I join the Methodist Church. No, they are not my

People, [they] have gone astray. There is none that Doeth good, not one, but this is my Beloved Son harken ye him."[12]

President John Taylor was another contemporary "intimately acquainted" with Joseph who described the First Vision as it was related to him by the Prophet. "I have travelled with him [Joseph Smith]," he wrote. "I have been with him in private and in public; I have associated with him in councils of all kinds; I have listened hundreds of times to his public teachings, and his advice to his friends and associates of a more private nature. I have been at his house and seen his deportment in his family. . . . I was with him . . . when he died, when he was murdered in Carthage. . . . I testify before God, angels, and men that he was a good, honourable, virtuous man . . . that his private and public character was unimpeachable — and that he lived and died as a man of God."[13]

Recalling that which Joseph told him, Elder Taylor said: "I can tell you what he told me about it. He said that he was very ignorant of the ways, designs and purposes of God, and knew nothing about them; he was a youth unacquainted with religious matters or the systems and theories of the day. He went to the Lord, having read James' statement. . . . He believed that statement and went to the Lord and asked him, and the Lord revealed himself to him together with his Son Jesus, and, pointing to the latter, said: 'This is my beloved Son, hear him.' He then asked in regard to the various religions with which he was surrounded. He enquired which of them was right, for he wanted to know the right way and to walk in it. He was told that none of them was right, that they had all departed from the right way."[14]

Elder Taylor not only declared that he personally learned from Joseph Smith the basic truths unfolded during the First Vision but proclaimed that Joseph Smith's 1838 history discussing events preceding the organization of the Church was accurate.

In October 1880, during the Church's Fiftieth Semiannual General Conference, members of the Church sustained Elder Taylor as prophet, seer, and revelator. Following this sustaining, President George Q. Cannon, First Counselor in the First Presidency, acting under the direction of President Taylor, presented to the assembly a new edition of the Doctrine and Covenants and the Pearl of Great Price, which contained Joseph Smith's 1838 account of the First Vision. He proposed that those present accept the books and their contents "as from God, and binding upon us as a people and as a Church." Then President Joseph F. Smith, Second Counselor in the

First Presidency, moved that the membership accept the books as containing "revelations from God to the Church." By unanimous vote, leaders and members agreed that the First Vision and other material in the Pearl of Great Price and the Doctrine and Covenants was inspired of God.[15]

By this sustaining action, the First Presidency, the Twelve Apostles (most of whom had been personally acquainted with Joseph Smith), and other Church members testified that the portion of Joseph Smith's 1838 history that described his 1820 vision was a reliable description of an actual historical event.

From 1830 to the present, General Authorities and other Latter-day Saints throughout the world have borne firm testimony of the authenticity of Joseph Smith's teachings and writings regarding the First Vision. President Spencer W. Kimball, for example, has declared that "nothing short of this total vision to Joseph could have served the purpose to clear away the mists of the centuries. Merely an impression, a hidden voice, a dream could [not] have dispelled the old vagaries and misconceptions.

"The God of all these worlds and the Son of God, the Redeemer, our Savior, in person attended this boy. He saw the living God. He saw the living Christ.

"Of all the great events of the century, none compared with the first vision of Joseph Smith."[16]

Notes

1. Joseph Grant Stevenson, "The Life of Edward Stevenson" (Master's thesis, Brigham Young University, 1955), pp. 19–20; Edward Stevenson, *Reminiscences of Joseph, the Prophet, and the Coming Forth of the Book of Mormon* (Salt Lake City, 1893), p. 4.

2. Accounts were written in 1832, 1835, 1838, and 1842. The Prophet did not publish his 1832 account of the experience, and it remained as a draft only. The 1835 account was recorded in his Kirtland diary, but the Prophet did not include it in his published *History of the Church*. The 1838 account was part of a history that Joseph Smith initiated in the spring of 1838 and completed sometime before November 1839. This history was originally published in the *Times and Seasons* in 1842 and was included in the 1878 edition of the Pearl of Great Price, which was accepted by the Church as scripture in 1880. The 1842 account, known as the Wentworth Letter, was the last prepared by the Prophet. It was published in March 1842 shortly before his 1838 history commenced publication in serial form.

3. "History of Orson Pratt," *Millennial Star*, 11 Feb. 1865, p. 88.

4. A reference to the publication of this missionary pamphlet "by Orson Pratt" appeared in Joseph Smith's history under the date December 1840 with the following notation: "Edinburgh, September." (*History of the Church*, 7 vols., 2d ed. rev., ed. B. H. Roberts [Salt Lake City: The Church of Jesus Christ of Latter-day Saints, 1932–51], 4:254.)

5. In *Journal of Discourses*, 26 vols. (London: Latter-day Saints' Book Depot, 1855–86), 7:220.

6. Joseph Smith's accounts of the First Vision have been published in the Appendix of Milton V. Backman, Jr., *Joseph Smith's First Vision* (Salt Lake City: Bookcraft, 1980).

7. Joseph Smith wrote in his 1832 history that because of poverty, he was forced to labor hard to help support his family and he and his brothers and sisters were deprived of the benefits of an education. "Suffice it to say," he added, "I was mearly instructid in reading writing and the ground rules of Arithmatic which constuted my whole literary acquirements." (In *The Personal Writings of Joseph Smith*, comp. Dean C. Jessee [Salt Lake City: Deseret Book Co., 1984], p. 4.)

8. *Millennial Star*, 15 Sept. 1849, pp. 281–84; 15 Oct. 1849, pp. 309–12.

9. In *Journal of Discourses*, 7:220–21.

10. There are different translations of the title and contents of the Hyde pamphlet. A copy of this publication is in the Church Historical Department, The Church of Jesus Christ of Latter-day Saints, Salt Lake City, Utah.

11. *New York Spectator*, 23 Sept. 1843.

12. Journal of Alexander Neibaur, 24 May 1844, Historical Department, The Church of Jesus Christ of Latter-day Saints, Salt Lake City, Utah.

13. *Three Nights' Public Discussion* (Liverpool: John Taylor, 1850), pp. 23–24.

14. In *Journal of Discourses*, 21:161.

15. *Millennial Star*, 15 Nov. 1880, pp. 723–24.

16. Spencer W. Kimball, *The Teachings of Spencer W. Kimball*, ed. Edward L. Kimball (Salt Lake City: Bookcraft, 1982), pp. 428, 430.

QA

What is the historical context of Joseph Smith's concern about which church was true? Did Joseph write a reliable account of the historical setting?

Milton V. Backman, Jr., professor of Church history, Brigham Young University

Joseph Smith not only wrote an accurate account of the truths unfolded during the First Vision but also aptly described the historical setting of that vision.

Joseph's interest in organized religion was intensified by the religious awakening that occurred in the area where he lived. "In the second year after our removal to Manchester," he explained, "there was in the place where we lived an unusual excitement on the subject of religion. It commenced with the Methodists, but soon became general among all the sects in that region of country. Indeed, the *whole district of country seemed affected by it, and great multitudes united themselves to the different religious parties."* (Joseph Smith–History 1:5; italics added.)

An uncommon development in world history occurred in the young nation during the early nineteenth century. Religious liberty was advancing, becoming a legal reality. Following the transplanting to the thirteen colonies of all major religions of Western Europe and the rise of new faiths in the young nation, religious pluralism increased. In fact, there was greater religious diversity in the United States than in any other Christian land. Moreover, most Americans in the early Republic were not active members of a religious community. Many immigrants to this land gradually lost their identity with organized religion. Expanding into the frontier, most inhabitants lived on isolated farms and found it difficult to attend church with any degree of regularity. Following a long decrease in the ratio of church members to population, this decline reached its lowest level around 1800, when only about 7 percent of the citizens in the United States were active members of a church.[1] A combination of increased religious liberty, unusual religious pluralism, and a population that had lost its identity with organized religion created a unique environment. Seeds for a powerful revival had been planted.

One of the most extended, widespread, and consequential religious awakenings in history began in America about 1800 and reached a climax during the 1830s and 1840s. Amid a fruitful field, Methodist circuit riders, Baptist farm preachers, and itinerant Presbyterian ministers sought to carry their forms of Protestantism to others. During this Second Great Awakening, vast numbers confessed Christ, many claimed that they were saved, and the increase (in percentage) of church membership resulting from conversions was greater than at any other time in American history. Between 1800 and 1820, church membership increased from around 7 percent to 11 percent (also the ratio in the Manchester-Palmyra area in 1820), and during the next four decades it increased to about 23 percent.[2]

Joseph Smith's search for truth occurred during this powerful religious enlivenment. According to his account, the excitement that influenced him commenced with the Methodists and spread to others. Indeed, he emphasized, great multitudes joined churches in the whole region of country. In 1819 and 1820 the Methodist and Baptist faiths were the fastest growing religious communities in the United States, and there were in those years more reports of revivals in upstate and western New York than in any other state. Accounts of religious upsurges and increases in membership in New York appeared in periodicals and newspapers, including the *Palmyra Register*. Unusual meetings and revivals were also advertised by itinerant preachers and traveling businessmen. After learning the locations of prospective revivals, many people traveled to these neighborhoods in anticipation of witnessing an unusual growth of religiosity.[3]

Contemporaries of Joseph Smith affirmed his testimony regarding the spiritual awakening that occurred at the time of the First Vision. Brigham Young, who was living in Mendon, New York, about forty miles from the Smith farm in 1820, reminisced: "I very well recollect the reformation which took place in the country among the various denominations of Christians, the Baptists, Methodists, Presbyterians, and others — when Joseph was a boy . . . of fourteen. . . . And in the midst of these revivals among the religious bodies, the invitation, 'Come and join our church,' was often extended to Joseph."[4]

Daniel Wells, born in western New York in 1814, recalled religious conditions in that region of country during the era of Joseph Smith's quest for truth. "The days of my youth," he explained, "were days of religious excitement — the days of revivals, which so pervaded that section of country at that time — and I can well apprehend the effect these things must have had on the mind of

193

Joseph. . . . I know how those revivals affected young minds in the neighbourhood in which I lived."[5]

Notes

1. Milton V. Backman, Jr., *American Religions and the Rise of Mormonism* (Salt Lake City, Utah: Deseret Book Co., 1965), pp. 277, 283, 301, 309; Backman, *Joseph Smith's First Vision*, pp. 76–78.

2. Backman, *Joseph Smith's First Vision*, pp. 68, 76, 78.

3. One contemporary of Joseph Smith, David Marks, traveled in 1821 to Brutus and Camillus, twenty to thirty miles from his father's house, to attend meetings because he learned that there was a great revival in that area. Marks referred to an area which included towns thirty miles from his home as the "vicinity of Junius." When Joseph Smith discussed the increased number of church members in his 1838 History, he not only described conditions in Palmyra village but aptly described an awakening that led to increased church membership in a much larger geographical area, or in the "whole region of country." Marilla Marks, ed., *Memoirs of the Life of David Marks* (Dover, N.H., 1846), pp. 17, 32.

For a more detailed discussion of the awakening of 1819–20, see Backman, *Joseph Smith's First Vision*, pp. 80–89.

4. Brigham Young, in *Journal of Discourses*, 26 vols. (London: Latter-day Saints' Book Depot, 1855–86), 12:67.

5. Daniel Wells, in *Journal of Discourses*, 12:71–72.

QA

What changes have been made in the name of the Church? Its full designation does not appear in the revelations until 1838. (See D&C 115:4.)

Richard Lloyd Anderson, professor of religion and history, Brigham Young University

The changes that have been made in the name of the Church can be found by comparing the name of the Church on the title pages of the first three printings of the revelations: "The Church of Christ" (*Book of Commandments*, 1833), "The Church of the Latter Day Saints" (Doctrine and Covenants, 1835), and "The Church of Jesus Christ of Latter Day Saints" (Doctrine and Covenants, 1844).

The Savior told the Nephites that his church should be called in his name. (See 3 Nephi 27:8.) As a result, the restored Church's official title from 1830 to 1834 was "The Church of Christ." That title is found in the revelation on the organization and government of the Church (D&C 20:1) and in early minute books. During this period, however, members of the Church regularly called themselves "saints"; the word *saint* is used approximately three dozen times in the Doctrine and Covenants before 1834. On 3 May 1834, official action modified the name of the Church. In a priesthood conference presided over by Joseph Smith, a motion passed "by unanimous voice" that the Church be known as "The Church of the Latter Day Saints." (See *The Evening and the Morning Star*, May 1834, 2:160.) This alteration was not seen as a deemphasis of Christ; on the contrary, it was done in hopes that the name of the Church would more clearly reflect the fact that Christ was at its head.

In the same issue of the Kirtland newspaper in which the announcement appeared, an editorial explained that the change stemmed from a misleading nickname: the "Mormonite" church. The new name also had these advantages: (1) Since American Christians, including Congregationalists and reformers, frequently designated themselves as "The Church of Christ," that title did not distinguish the restored gospel from a host of Protestant sects. (2) Because Paul and Peter had used the Greek word *saint* ("a holy person") to refer to believers in Christ, the term *Latter-day Saints* implied that Church members were modern followers of Christ. Thus it also asserted the claim of restoration.

Just as the term *saint* flourished when the official name was "The Church of Christ," the name of Christ regularly supplemented the official name of "The Church of the Latter Day Saints." For example, in 1835, the church was referred to as "the church of Christ" and the twelve apostles were commissioned as special "witnesses of the name of Christ." (D&C 107:59, 23.) The Saints certainly did not feel that the Church was leaving out the name of Christ.

Sometimes during this period the first and second titles would be combined—"the church of Christ of Latter Day saints"—as they were in priesthood minutes (*Messenger and Advocate*, Feb. 1836, 2:266) and in the publication of the first high council minutes (see headnote to D&C 5, 1835 edition).

A vivid illustration of the way members then understood the official name of the Church is found in a letter from John Smith, the Prophet's uncle, to his son Elias before the latter was converted.

Writing 19 October 1834, Uncle John answered the question of why the name could be changed:

"The Church of Christ is the Church of Saints and always was. This is the reason why the apostle directed letters sometimes to the Church of God, others to the Church, and again to the Brethren, sometimes to the Saints, always meaning the Church of Christ." (Archives, University of Utah, Salt Lake City, Utah.)

Thus, the final version of the Church's name was no radical shift from the previous practice of using both "Christ" and "Saints" in designating the restored Church and its members. Revealed on 26 April 1838 (D&C 115:4), the full title, "The Church of Jesus Christ of Latter-day Saints," is striking by comparison to the names of the scores of churches that obscure their Christianity under the label of their founders or of some characteristic belief or aspect of church organization. It is a highly effective name, for while it is distinctive, it indicates that Jesus is at its head. It is also descriptive of divine restoration. And it is more than a name—it is a public commitment to a holy life through the Savior's power.

QA

Was the Church legally incorporated at the time it was organized in the state of New York?

Larry C. Porter, director, Church History Area, Religious Studies Center, Brigham Young University

Section 20 of the Doctrine and Covenants speaks of the newly evolving "Church of Christ" as being "regularly organized and established agreeable to the laws of our country." (D&C 20:1.) In 1969 and 1970 I spent several months looking for evidence that the Church had been incorporated according to the laws of the state of New York. Though I could not locate the incorporating document, I found several accounts that show that the organizers of the Church were aware of the legal requirements for incorporation and made a conscientious attempt to meet them.

David Whitmer, a contemporary and a close associate of the Prophet Joseph Smith, showed that he recognized the legal requirements for the organization when he stated: "On the 6th of April,

1830, the church was called together and the elders acknowledged according to the laws of New York." (*Kansas City Daily Journal*, 5 June 1881.) The "laws" David Whitmer was referring to were "An Act to provide for the Incorporation of Religious Societies," passed by the New York State Legislature on 5 April 1813. Section III of that act reads, in part:

"III. And be it further enacted, that it shall be lawful for the male persons of full age, belonging to any other church, congregation or religious society, now or hereafter to be established in this state, and not already incorporated, to assemble at the church meeting-house, or to the place where they statedly attend for divine worship [in this case, the Peter Whitmer, Sr., farmhouse in Fayette Township], and, by plurality of voices, to elect any number of discreet persons of their church, congregation or society, not less than three, nor exceeding nine in number [Joseph Smith chose six—Oliver Cowdery, Joseph Smith, Jun., Hyrum Smith, Peter Whitmer, Jun., Samuel H. Smith, and David Whitmer] as trustees, to . . . transact all affairs relative to the temporalities thereof. . . . That on the said day of election, two of the elders or church wardens, and if there be no such officers, then two of the members [Joseph Smith, Jun., and Oliver Cowdery] of said church, congregation or society, to be nominated by a majority of the members present, shall preside at such election, receive the votes of the electors, be the judges of the qualifications of such electors, and the officers, to return the names of the persons who, by plurality of voices, shall be elected to serve as trustees for said church [the six men named above] . . . in which certificate, the name or title by which the said trustees and their successors shall forever thereafter be called and known [The Church of Jesus Christ]." (See *History of the Church*, 7 vols., 2d ed. rev., ed. B. H. Roberts [Salt Lake City: The Church of Jesus Christ of Latter-day Saints, 1932–51], 1:76, 79.)

With this knowledge of the legal requirements, I went in search of the elusive document. Mr. John S. Genung, trustee and historian of the Waterloo Library and Historical Society, Waterloo, New York, helped me make a systematic examination of possible repositories. Since the *Laws of the State of New York* (III, p. 214) indicated that the incorporation certificate should be initiated and recorded in the county, by the county clerk, there is no evidence that such a certificate would be filed with the state offices at Albany, nor in the offices of Fayette Township.

Accordingly, we began with the Seneca County Courthouse at

Waterloo. Mr. Thomas B. Masten, Jr., the county clerk, allowed us access to the materials deposited in the clerk's offices. The records there showed only three religious societies incorporated in 1830: "January 7, 1830, Trinity Church of Ovid; January 12, 1830, Seneca Falls Society of ME [Methodists]; November 24, 1830, 1st Baptist Church, Lodi." *(Miscellaneous Record Book B.)* No record was found that even approximated the title or time of founding of the LDS Church. If the incorporation certificate of "The Church of Jesus Christ" or "The Church of Christ" had been duly filed with the county clerk of Seneca County, it should have appeared in this listing.

I was then allowed to examine the records in the downstairs vault and an adjoining storage room. Again, the desired record was not found; however, the vault did contain a ledger entitled "Court of Common Pleas, 1827–1831." As the Act of 1813 stipulated that a certificate of incorporation could be issued by "one of the judges of the court of common pleas," I studied this record at length but found no appropriate entry.

Seneca County is one of the few two-shire counties in the United States; that is, it has two county seats — one at Waterloo in the north and one at Ovid in the south. At the time the LDS Church was organized, both of these seats were operative on a "sharing" basis. Every six months, country records were shuttled back and forth by wagon, depending on whose term of jurisdiction was then incumbent. On 2 February 1830, the Seneca County Court of Common Pleas met at Waterloo. On 11 May 1830, it convened in Ovid. If they had not gone into Waterloo earlier, the organizers of the LDS Church could have gone to Ovid, New York, 14.6 miles south of the Whitmer farm, to validate their certificate of incorporation.

So Mr. Genung arranged for me to meet with Undersheriff Gerald B. Brewer at the courthouse in Ovid. Today, with Waterloo the site of Seneca County government, only a small office is maintained by the undersheriff at the old courthouse in Ovid. Undersheriff Brewer opened his shelves for inspection. A few old ledgers still remained in a basement room, but none pertained to the incorporation of religious societies.

My next step was to see if any of the New York branches of the Church had been registered. Because the law required religious societies within each county to register their particular congregations, the various branches of the Church might have applied for a certificate of incorporation in their respective locations. Byron C.

Blazey, Ontario County clerk, Canandaigua, New York; Leonard Schlee, Wayne County clerk, Lyons, New York; John P. McGuire, Chenango County clerk, Norwich, New York; and Howard Davis, Broome County clerk, Binghamton, New York, all gave me access to their offices and storage facilities. In no instance was there record of an incorporation proceeding for any LDS Church religious society during 1830–31.

In a last attempt to turn up any lead, I searched records in the Fayette Town Hall, the Waterloo Town Hall, and the state archives at Albany—all to no avail.

My extensive examination of the primary sources thus pointed to at least two possible explanations: first, the organizers of the Latter-day Saint Church met all the legal requirements and submitted their application for incorporation, but through some technicality or omission the certificate was never recorded in the appropriate record book. Or second, the organizers made an attempt to meet the prerequisites of the law, but the press of initial business and local opposition somehow stayed them from formally executing the document in a court of law during the ten months the Prophet remained in New York.

Given the circumstances, I doubt that the original certificate of incorporation in Seneca County will ever be found; however, it is possible that the elusive document is still in existence and will be discovered in an obscure place. The legal preliminaries were met by the Prophet Joseph, but we don't know if they were ever completed.

QA

I've been reading the *Journal of Discourses* with a great deal of interest and pleasure, but I notice that they are not printed by the Church. How authoritative should I consider them to be?

Gerald E. Jones, director, LDS Institute of Religion, Stanford University, Stanford, California

Many queries come from students concerning the *Journal of Discourses*, first published in England between 1853 and 1886. The original intent of their publication was to provide income for George D. Watt, their stenographer and publisher. Many Church members in

England desired to read the sermons delivered by the General Authorities of the Church in Utah, and Brother Watt's books filled that need. He obtained clearance from the First Presidency 1 June 1853. Addressed to Elder Samuel Richards, missionary printer in England and to "the Saints abroad," this statement introduced the first volume:

"Dear Brethren—It is well known to many of you, that Elder George D. Watt, by our counsel, spent much time in the midst of poverty and hardships to acquire the art of reporting in Phonography [shorthand], which he has faithfully and fully accomplished; and he has been reporting the public Sermons, Discourses, Lectures delivered by the Presidency, the Twelve, and others in this city, for nearly two years, almost without fee or reward. Elder Watt now proposes to publish a *Journal* of these reports, in England, for the benefit of the Saints at large, and to obtain means to enable him to sustain his highly useful position of Reporter. You will perceive at once that this will be a work of mutual benefit, and we cheerfully and warmly request your cooperation in the purchase and sale of the above named *Journal,* and wish all the profits arising therefrom to be under the control of Elder Watt." (Signed by Brigham Young, Heber C. Kimball, and Willard Richards.)

The first four volumes were reported by Elder Watt, but after that other reporters are included—one a sister, Julia Young. Brother Watt reported through volume 12, when David W. Evans became the prime reporter. He was followed by George W. Biggs, a secretary to the First Presidency.

In considering the reliability of the *Journal of Discourses,* we should remember certain circumstances.

Though the First Presidency endorsed the publication of the *Journal,* there was no endorsement as to the accuracy or reliability of the contents. There were occasions when the accuracy was questionable. The accounts were not always cleared by the speakers because of problems of time and distance. This was especially true during the persecution of the 1880s, which finally forced the cessation of publication.

We should remember that the times were different then. A principal concern of the early Saints was physical survival. Sermons often dealt with the practical problems of the time and so may seem quaint in our day, even if much of the advice is still valid.

Doctrinally, members of the Church were growing and learning. Most adults were converts who had to unlearn and relearn many doctrines. They were learning things that our children learn in Primary and Sunday School. Remarks were frequently impromptu. Close, friendly audiences frequently invited informal discussion of varied topics. There was occasional speculation about doctrines that have since been determined unimportant or even misleading.

The general membership of the Church has progressed in knowledge of gospel principles, which is as it should be. In our organizations, we have been taught the gospel for more than one hundred years now. Because of modern revelation and because of "line-upon-line, precept-upon-precept" progression, we have answers that were not yet given when the *Journal of Discourses* was published.

We also should be aware of priorities in our studies. It seems to me that we should first become very familiar with the four books of scripture accepted as standard works. The words of our current living prophet are also most valuable for us in our time. The official statements of the First Presidency are standards for doctrine and practice in the Church. We should be familiar with the manuals and courses of study provided for us in our day. For further inspiration and instruction by the General Authorities, we should study general conference addresses, beginning with the most current and moving back in time.

Even after digesting these materials, some persons may still have time and inclination to peruse the *Journal of Discourses*. We can be grateful that records of the early sermons were kept to help us understand the growth of the Church and the testimonies of our early leaders. If we find the time to read them, however, we should avoid getting caught up in their uniqueness and should concentrate on the inspiring thoughts and experiences related to us by choice men.

Having taught seminary and institute classes for more than thirty years, I have tried to follow my own advice. Because I also love to read, I have read the scriptures many times, all of the general conference reports, and finally, all volumes of the *Journal of Discourses*. Frankly, one of the main reasons I read the *Journal of Discourses* was so I could answer students' questions about them with some knowledge of what they were about. Though I enjoyed reading them, gained some new insights, and was inspired by the spirit of the early Brethren, except for the needs of students, there was no practical benefit that I could not have obtained from current conference talks with less effort, much greater clarity, and more economy. For me, the most pertinent discussion of gospel doctrines and answers to life's problems and source of spiritual inspiration in today's world comes from the standard works and our living prophets.

Doctrines and Principles

QA

The Savior said that we should be perfect, even as he and our Father in Heaven are perfect. (See 3 Nephi 12:48.) Are we expected to achieve perfection in this life? If so, how can I avoid becoming discouraged with myself while I try to achieve it?

Gerald N. Lund, zone administrator, Church Educational System

First, we need to ask, "Do we have to be perfect in order to achieve exaltation?" Whether we answer this question yes or no depends on how we define the word *perfect*. One definition of *perfect* is "never having flaw or error." In that sense, only one person in all of human history—our Savior—has been perfect. Not once in all his mortal life—not as a child, not as an adult—was he out of harmony with the Father's will. In this sense, we clearly do not have to be *perfect* to be saved. Otherwise, there would be no hope for any of us, for as Paul said, "All have sinned, and come short of the glory of God." (Romans 3:23.)

But *perfect* can also mean "having all flaws and errors removed." A better question might be, "Do we have to be *perfected* to be exalted?" Here the scriptural answer is a resounding yes. In numerous references, the Lord says that no unclean thing can enter into his presence. (See 1 Nephi 10:21; Alma 7:21; 3 Nephi 27:19; Moses 6:57.) Obviously, then, we must repent of those flaws identified as sins and become clean before we can be exalted. But what of other flaws, those that don't qualify as sins but are nevertheless imperfections?

The Prophet Joseph Smith said that our very faith rests in knowing that the attributes of God, such as his love, mercy, power, and knowledge, are all held in perfection. (See *Lectures on Faith*, 5:1.) An imperfect God would indeed be a contradiction in terms. At some point, then, if we are to become like God, we must become perfect, without any flaw or error.

But must we achieve that state in this life? Here the prophets have spoken plainly. In the great sermon known as the King Follett discourse, the Prophet Joseph taught:

"When you climb up a ladder, you must begin at the bottom,

and ascend step by step, until you arrive at the top; and so it is with the principles of the Gospel—you must begin with the first and go on until you learn all the principles of exaltation. But it will be a great while after you have passed through the veil before you will have learned them. It is not all to be comprehended in this world; it will be a great work to learn our salvation and exaltation even beyond the grave." (*Teachings of the Prophet Joseph Smith,* sel. Joseph Fielding Smith [Salt Lake City: Deseret Book Co., 1977], p. 348.)

President Joseph F. Smith confirmed this idea:

"We do not look for absolute perfection in man. Mortal man is not capable of being absolutely perfect. Nevertheless, it is given to us to be as perfect in the sphere in which we are called to be and to act, as it is for the Father in heaven to be pure and righteous in the more exalted sphere in which he acts. We will find in the scriptures the words of the Savior himself to his disciples, in which he required that they should be perfect, even as their Father in heaven is perfect; that they should be righteous, even as he is righteous. I do not expect that we can be as perfect as Christ, that we can be as righteous as God. But I believe that we can strive for that perfection with the intelligence that we possess, and the knowledge that we have of the principles of life and salvation." (*Gospel Doctrine,* 5th ed. [Salt Lake City, Deseret Book Co., 1939], p. 132.)

President Joseph Fielding Smith spoke with equal clarity on the same subject:

"Salvation does not come all at once; we are commanded to be perfect even as our Father in heaven is perfect. It will take us ages to accomplish this end, for there will be greater progress beyond the grave, and it will be there that the faithful will overcome all things, and receive all things, even the fulness of the Father's glory. I believe the Lord meant just what he said: that we should be perfect, as our Father in heaven is perfect. That will not come all at once, but line upon line, and precept upon precept, example upon example, and even then not as long as we live in this mortal life, for we will have to go even beyond the grave before we reach that perfection and shall be like God.

"But here we lay the foundation." (*Doctrines of Salvation,* 3 vols., comp. Bruce R. McConkie [Salt Lake City: Deseret Book Co., 1954–56], 2:18.)

While these statements make it clear that full perfection is not achievable in mortality, each also suggests that we should always strive for perfection in our lives. Perfection is our eternal goal: it is what we must eventually achieve if we are to become like our Father. A purpose of mortality is to come as close to perfection as possible before we die.

So how can we keep perfection as our goal without becoming so discouraged or depressed with our failings that we lose hope and give up trying to perfect ourselves? I would like to suggest seven practical ideas that can help us maintain the balance between eternal goals and mortal realities.

1. Remember that one of Satan's strategies, especially with good people, is to whisper in their ears: "If you are not perfect, you are failing." This is one of his most effective deceptions, for it contains some elements of truth. But it *is* deception nonetheless. While we should never be completely satisfied until we *are* perfect, we should recognize that God is pleased with every effort we make—no matter how faltering—to better ourselves. One of the most commonly listed attributes of God is that he is long-suffering and quick to show mercy. He wants us to strive for perfection, but the fact that we have not yet achieved it does not mean we are failing.

2. Feelings of failure are natural and common to most people. Elder Neal A. Maxwell put it this way:

"I speak, not to the slackers in the Kingdom, but to those who carry their own load and more; not to those lulled into false security, but to those buffeted by false insecurity, who, though laboring devotedly in the Kingdom, have recurring feelings of falling forever short. . . .

"The first thing to be said of this feeling of inadequacy is that it is normal. . . . Following celestial road signs while in telestial traffic jams is not easy, especially when we are not just moving next door—or even across town." *(Ensign,* Nov. 1976, p. 12.)

Even such great men as Moses, Enoch, and Gideon were reluctant to believe they were capable of doing what God called them to do. To their credit, they tried anyway—and with the Lord's help, they succeeded. (See Exodus 4:10; Moses 6:31; Judges 6:15.)

3. The Lord himself has warned us about being unrealistic in our expectations. To a young prophet, deeply contrite over losing 116 pages of sacred manuscript, the Lord said: "Do not run faster or labor more than you have strength." (D&C 10:4.) And after a lengthy and powerful call to repentance, King Benjamin gave this counsel: "And see that all these things are done *in wisdom and order;* for it is not requisite that a man should run faster than he has strength. And again, it is expedient that he should be diligent, that

thereby he might win the prize; therefore, all things must be done in order." (Mosiah 4:27; italics added.)

4. Remember that the scriptures are replete with examples of great men and women who moved toward perfection *through missteps, in spite of failings, and having to overcome their weaknesses.* For example, the author of the second Gospel is the same Mark who earlier had left his missionary service, deserting Paul and Barnabas. (See Acts 12:25; 13:13; 15:37–38.) The same Corianton who was severely chastized for being immoral on his mission (see Alma 39:3–5, 11) was later listed among the faithful who helped bring peace to the Nephites (see Alma 49:30). Finally, the people of Melchizedek at one point had "waxed strong in iniquity and abomination; yea, *they had all gone astray;* they were full of all manner of wickedness." (Alma 13:17; italics added.) But "they did repent" (v. 18) and went to join the city of Enoch (see JST Genesis 14:34).

5. The Lord not only looks at our works, but he also takes into account the desires of our hearts. (See Alma 41:3; D&C 88:109; 137:9.) This means that even if we don't always perfectly translate our good desires into action, these desires will be included in our final evaluation. Elder Bruce R. McConkie described what it takes to be saved:

"What we do in this life is chart a course leading to eternal life. That course begins here and now and continues in the realms ahead. We must determine in our hearts and in our souls, with all the power and ability we have, that from this time forward we will press on in righteousness; by so doing we can go where God and Christ are. If we make that firm determination, and are in the course of our duty when this life is over, we will continue in that course in eternity. That same spirit that possesses our bodies at the time we depart from this mortal life will have power to possess our bodies in the eternal world. If we go out of this life loving the Lord, desiring righteousness, and seeking to acquire the attributes of godliness, we will have that same spirit in the eternal world, and we will then continue to advance and progress until an ultimate, destined day when we will possess, receive, and inherit all things." ("The Seven Deadly Heresies," in *Speeches of the Year, 1980* [Provo: Brigham Young University, 1981], pp. 78–79.)

6. "Hanging in there," in modern vernacular, is one of the most important keys to becoming perfected. That is what the scriptures mean by enduring to the end. Some people live out years of righteousness and then, when life takes a downward turn or becomes

boring, tedious, and monotonous, they become discouraged and decide that striving for perfection is no longer worth it. After a remarkable life of faith and commitment, King David lost his exaltation because he did not continue in his set course.

Somehow, some of us get it into our heads that if we are not making great, dramatic leaps forward spiritually, we are not progressing. Actually, for most of us, the challenge of living the gospel is that progress comes in almost imperceptible increments. It is very seldom that we can look back over one day and see great progress. Becoming like God takes years and years of striving and trying again.

We must also keep in mind that just because we are striving to better ourselves does not mean all problems, challenges, and setbacks will disappear. Elder Gordon B. Hinckley, quoting columnist Jenkins Lloyd Jones, reminded us that life will always have its challenges:

"Anyone who imagines that bliss is normal is going to waste a lot of time running around shouting that he's been robbed. The fact is that most putts don't drop, most beef is tough, most children grow up to be just people, most successful marriages require a high degree of mutual toleration, most jobs are more often dull than otherwise. Life is like an old time rail journey . . . delays, sidetracks, smoke, dust, cinders, and jolts, interspersed only occasionally by beautiful vistas, and thrilling bursts of speed. The trick is to thank the Lord for letting you have the ride." (Address to Religious Educators, Sept. 1978, p. 4.)

7. Finally, to overcome the discouragement we feel when we see our failings and imperfections, we should remember that we learn and progress in spiritual things in much the same way we learn and progress in physical things. We are not disappointed when a baby learns to crawl before he walks. It is the natural order of things. Likewise, no one expects a student to understand calculus until he has first learned the numbers, then the laws of addition and subtraction, and then the mysteries of algebra and trigonometry. President Spencer W. Kimball noted that "working toward perfection is not a one-time decision but a process to be pursued *throughout one's lifetime*." (*Ensign*, Oct. 1978, p. 6; italics added.) So why is it that we demand instant perfection? Why should we expect to run spiritual four-minute miles until we have jogged hundreds upon hundreds of times around the spiritual tracks of our lives? Why do we expect to work spiritual calculus before we have mastered the

spiritual multiplication tables? And why should we be disappointed when we cannot play spiritual symphonies if we have not yet learned to play the spiritual scales?

Perfection is our goal. But let us not be thrown off course when we do not fully achieve it in this life. And most of all, let us, as we strive for that lofty goal, remember the Lord's promise to those of us who so keenly sense our weaknesses and inadequacies: "And if men come unto me I will show unto them their weakness. I give unto men weakness that they may be humble; and my grace is sufficient for all men that humble themselves before me; for if they humble themselves before me, and have faith in me, then will I make weak things become strong unto them." (Ether 12:27.)

QA

What was in the creeds of men that the Lord found abominable, as he stated in the First Vision?

Hoyt W. Brewster, Jr., manager, curriculum planning and development, Church Curriculum Department

On at least four occasions, the Prophet Joseph Smith wrote or dictated an account of his first vision. Only one of these, a brief account recorded in 1835 by Warren Cowdery, makes no mention of false creeds then being taught among men. (See Milton V. Backman, Jr., *Joseph Smith's First Vision* [Salt Lake City: Bookcraft, 1980]; see also Backman, "Joseph Smith's Recitals of the First Vision," *Ensign,* Jan. 1985, pp. 8–17.)

In an account dictated in 1832 to Frederick G. Williams, the Prophet Joseph related how the Savior had told him that "the world lieth in sin at this time and none doeth good." The Lord further said, "They draw near to me with their lips while their hearts are far from me." (Backman, *First Vision,* p. 157.)

The account currently found in the Pearl of Great Price was written in 1838. In this record young Joseph asked Deity "which of all the sects was right." The Son of God answered that "they were all wrong; . . . that all their creeds were an abomination in his sight; that those professors were all corrupt; that: 'they draw near to me with their lips, but their hearts are far from me, they teach for doctrines the commandments of men, having a form of godliness, but they deny the power thereof.' " (Joseph Smith–History 1:18–19.)

In an 1842 account known as the Wentworth Letter, the Prophet wrote, "Two glorious personages . . . told me that all religious denominations were believing in incorrect doctrines, and that none of them was acknowledged of God as his church and kingdom." (Backman, *First Vision,* p. 169.)

From these accounts of the Prophet's experience in the Sacred Grove that spring morning of 1820, it is clear that God the Father and his Son were greatly displeased with the doctrines being taught in the churches. Perhaps one important reason the Lord was displeased is that the precepts of men lack saving power. Anciently, the apostle Paul warned that perilous times would come in which many man-made, apostate practices would prevail. He warned that those who advocated such practices would have "a form of godliness" but would deny "the power thereof." His exhortation was "from such turn away." (2 Timothy 3:5; see also Joseph Smith–History 1:19.) Any creed, doctrine, philosophy, precept, practice, ordinance, or teaching that deliberately or inadvertently leads people from the *saving power* of Christ and his gospel is an abomination. In this sense, anything that deviates from truth or the divine authority of God, even slightly, lacks godliness; from such we should turn away.

The Lord revealed to the Prophet Joseph Smith that the power of godliness is manifest in the ordinances of his priesthood. "Without the ordinances thereof, and the authority of the priesthood, the power of godliness is not manifest unto men in the flesh." (D&C 84:20–21.) Gospel ordinances that resemble in *form* those that Deity has declared necessary for salvation but that lack divine priesthood *authority,* are not accepted by God and therefore lack the power to save souls. Furthermore, no matter how sincere a person's intentions may be in performing or receiving a gospel ordinance, if the ordinance is performed without authority recognized by God, it has no power to save. As a result, God's work—which is "to bring to pass the immortality and eternal life of man" (Moses 1:39)—is hindered. Thus, anything that hinders God's work, intentionally or not, is an abomination.

Elder John A. Widtsoe made the following observation regarding the abominations spoken of in the First Vision:

"Jesus said to Joseph that all the churches were wrong, and that their creeds were an abomination in his sight, that those professors were all corrupt. This statement has given a great deal of offense. It should not amaze us, however, if we consider that Joseph went in search of truth. There was doubt in his mind. *All untruth is an abomination.* Clear the world of untruth, and the world will be a better place. The ministers were not necessarily corrupt personally; but since they preached untruth and professed untruth, they were corrupt teachers. There is a fine distinction between a man who is misled and one who deliberately teaches untruth. The statement made by the Savior should not be misunderstood. Truth is the only holy thing; and if it is violated or changed, those who teach it become corrupt and abominable." ("Joseph Smith — The Significance of the First Vision," *The Annual Joseph Smith Memorial Sermons* [Logan, Utah: Institute of Religion, 1966], 1:28; italics added.)

The scriptures appropriately counsel us to give no heed to "fables, and commandments of men, that turn from the truth." (Titus 1:14.)

Latter-day Saints do not intend to give offense by speaking of the false creeds and beliefs of others as abominations. But we must be unyielding in tenaciously holding to the truth. There is but *"one Lord, one* faith, *one* baptism." (Ephesians 4:5; italics added.)

We acknowledge that the sincere, dedicated efforts of teachers and ministers of other faiths accomplish much good in the world. For example, Sidney Rigdon served as a minister of another church before becoming acquainted with the restored gospel of Jesus Christ. After his conversion, the Lord said to him, "My servant Sidney, I have looked upon thee and thy works. I have heard thy prayers, and prepared thee for a greater work." (D&C 35:3.)

Sidney Rigdon had obviously rendered a valuable service in his previous ministry but was able, after accepting the restored gospel and receiving divinely restored priesthood power, to go forth in a "greater work," teaching the revelations of God and administering the saving ordinances of the gospel.

Surely promoters of righteousness, which include many ministers of other churches, are among the honorable men and women of the earth. Yet revelation reminds us that even the "honorable men of the earth" will be among those who fall short of exaltation in the celestial kingdom if they have not accepted the principles and saving ordinances of the gospel of Jesus Christ, which are available only through his restored church. (See D&C 76:75–78.)

Personal righteousness and good intentions are not sufficient to save souls in the celestial kingdom of God. The Savior himself, differentiating between rewards, said, "He that receiveth a prophet in the name of a prophet shall receive a prophet's reward; and he that receiveth a righteous man in the name of a righteous man shall receive a righteous man's reward." (Matthew 10:41.) If one were to follow the teachings of an honorable, righteous minister who lacked authority to administer the saving ordinances of the gospel, he would receive the reward of that righteous man but fall short of full salvation. The Lord clearly stresses over and over the necessity of certain ordinances to receive salvation. (See John 3:5; D&C 132:18–19.)

In rejecting false creeds and unauthorized ordinances, we do not pass judgment on people. We recognize that there are good, moral, upright people in all churches. Elder James E. Talmage observed that "when we say that the Lord is not pleased with those churches, we do not mean that he is not pleased with the members thereof. . . . The church as such may be wholly corrupt because of the false claims that are being made for it, and yet within that church as members there may be people who are doing their best." (In Conference Report, Oct. 1928, p. 120.)

Elder Boyd K. Packer, of the Quorum of the Twelve Apostles, noted:

"We know there are decent, respectable, humble people in many churches, Christian and otherwise. In turn, sadly enough, there are so-called Latter-day Saints who by comparison are not as worthy, for they do not keep their covenants.

"But it is not a matter of comparing individuals. . . .

"Good conduct without the ordinances of the gospel will neither redeem nor exalt mankind; covenants and the ordinances are essential. We are required to teach the doctrines, even the unpopular ones." (*Ensign,* Nov. 1985, p. 82.)

We do not ask people to abandon any truths they now possess. Our desire is to share the whole truth of the gospel of Jesus Christ with all mankind and to make the full power of salvation available to each individual.

In declaring this message, we would do well to keep the admonitions of two of God's servants in mind. The Nephite prophet Alma counseled his son Shiblon to "use boldness, but not overbearance" in preaching the word of God. (Alma 38:12.) On the other hand, the words of the apostle Paul should be on the lips and in the hearts of all Latter-day Saints: "For I am not ashamed of the gospel of Christ: for it is the power of God unto salvation to every one that believeth." (Romans 1:16.)

Thus, while we boldly declare that the precepts of men are an abomination in the sight of God, we humbly acknowledge the sacred trust we have to share the fulness of the gospel and invite all mankind to come unto Christ. To do less would be to come under condemnation. To have the truth, to be the custodians of the saving ordinances, and to be unwilling to share them with others would itself be an abomination to the Lord.

Perhaps a final thought regarding truth and abomination should be considered. Members of Christ's kingdom here on earth, who have received the saving ordinances of the gospel through proper priesthood authority, must not be smug or complacent with their membership. The Lord himself declared that The Church of Jesus Christ of Latter-day Saints is "the only true and living church upon the face of the whole earth, with which I, the Lord, am well pleased, speaking unto the church collectively and not individually." (D&C 1:30.)

Membership in the Lord's church here on earth does not guarantee exaltation in his kingdom hereafter. We must keep the sacred covenants entered into with God and seek in all things to do his will. Receiving all the authorized ordinances is essential to salvation, but so is obedience in keeping the commandments and covenants associated with those ordinances. The words of an ancient prophet remind us that once we have gotten onto the strait and narrow path, we "must press forward with a steadfastness in Christ," that if we "press forward, feasting upon the word of Christ, and endure to the end," the Father promises us eternal life. (2 Nephi 31:19–20.)

It makes little difference whether one has followed abominable creeds or abandoned true doctrines. Either way lacks saving power, and the result is the same: the individual falls short of exaltation: "For what doth it profit a man if a gift is bestowed upon him, and he receive not the gift? . . . That which . . . abideth not by law, but seeketh to become a law unto itself, and willeth to abide in sin . . . cannot be sanctified by law, neither by mercy, justice, nor judgment." (D&C 88:33, 35.)

QA

How do Latter-day Saints support the doctrine of Melchizedek Priesthood authority from the Bible?

James A. Carver, principal, Moab Seminary, Moab, Utah

Critics sometimes question the Latter-day Saint doctrine of priesthood authority by citing two passages of scripture, one in Matthew and one in Hebrews. Interestingly, Latter-day Saints use these same references to support the doctrine of the priesthood. Fortunately, however, because of modern-day revelation, Latter-day Saints are not dependent upon the Bible alone for their complete understanding of this and other doctrines.

The first passage of scripture, Matthew 16:13–19, has been used by Catholics to support its position that a continuous chain of authority extends from the apostle Peter to the present pontiff:

"When Jesus came into the coasts of Caesarea Philippi, he asked his disciples, saying, Whom do men say that I the Son of man am? . . .

"And Simon Peter answered and said, Thou art the Christ, the Son of the living God.

"And Jesus answered and said unto him, Blessed art thou, Simon Bar-jona: for flesh and blood hath not revealed it unto thee, but my Father which is in heaven.

"And I say also unto thee, That thou art Peter, and upon this rock I will build my church; and the gates of hell shall not prevail against it.

"And I will give unto thee the keys of the kingdom of heaven: and whatsoever thou shalt bind on earth shall be bound in heaven: and whatsoever thou shalt loose on earth shall be loosed in heaven."

Joseph Smith explained that the rock upon which the church would be built was revelation. (See *Teachings of the Prophet Joseph Smith,* sel. Joseph Fielding Smith [Salt Lake City: Deseret Book Co., 1938], p. 274.) Indeed, revelation was the issue at hand. Peter knew that Jesus was the Christ through revelation: "Flesh and blood hath not revealed it unto thee, but my Father which is in heaven."

The Bible also supports this interpretation. A textual analysis of this passage clearly demonstrates that although the keys of the kingdom were given to Simon Peter, the church was not built upon him. It was built, instead, upon Christ, the "rock" of revelation.

The Greek text, for example, makes it clear that the "rock" in verse 18 was not Peter. The Greek word used for *Peter* is *petros,* a masculine noun meaning a small rock or stone. The Greek word for *rock* ("upon this rock") is *petra,* a feminine noun meaning bedrock. Thus, the Greek text reads like this: "Thou art Peter [*petros,* small rock], and upon this rock [*petra,* bedrock] I will build my church."

Who is this *petra,* this bedrock? The answer is given explicitly in 1 Corinthians 10:1–4:

"All our fathers were under the cloud, and all passed through the sea;

"And were all baptized unto Moses in the cloud and in the sea;

"And did all eat the same spiritual meat;

"And did all drink the same spiritual drink: for they drank of that spiritual Rock that followed them: and *that Rock was Christ."* (Italics added.)

The Greek word for *Rock* in the passage above, as in the verse in Matthew, is *petra* (bedrock). There is no question that Christ is the "Rock" the Church was to be built upon, rather than Peter. Paul told the Corinthians that "other foundation can no man lay than that is laid, which is Jesus Christ." (1 Corinthians 3:11.)

But what is the importance of the relationship between the bedrock and the stone? And what part does revelation play in this relationship?

When Simon Peter was first introduced to Jesus, the Lord changed Simon's name to "Cephas, which is by interpretation, A stone." (John 1:42.) In the Joseph Smith Translation, a clarifying word is given: "Cephas, which is, by interpretation, *a seer,* or a stone." (Italics added.)

The reason for Simon's new name does not become clear until the experience at Caesarea Philippi, quoted earlier. Elder Bruce R. McConkie explained: "In promising him the keys of the kingdom, our Lord [told] Peter that the gates of hell shall never prevail against the rock of revelation, or in other words against seership. (Matthew 16:18.) Seers are specially selected prophets who are authorized to use the Urim and Thummim and who are empowered to know past, present, and future things. 'A gift which is greater can no man have.' (Mosiah 8:13–18.)" (*Doctrinal New Testament Commentary,* 3 vols. [Salt Lake City: Bookcraft, 1965–73], 1:133.)

The events at the Mount of Transfiguration were essential for the new role Peter would play. Just as the mount was a rock of revelation, it was by revelation that Peter knew Jesus to be "the Christ, the Son of the living God." The small rock (Peter) was to become a "seer" who would receive revelation from the large rock (Jesus Christ)—the Rock of Revelation. He would be the one to hold the keys of the kingdom and represent the Lord upon the earth. He would feed the sheep. (See John 21:15–17.)

Jesus did not say to Peter that there would always be a seer upon the earth to hold the keys of the kingdom, but that the "gates of hell" would not prevail against "this rock"—*petra*, or the Rock of Revelation. "In this instance," wrote Elder McConkie, "Jesus is telling Peter that the gates of hell shall never prevail against the rock or revelation; that is, as long as the saints are living in righteousness so as to receive revelation from heaven, they will avoid the gates of hell and the Church itself will remain pure, undefiled, and secure against every evil. But when, because of iniquity, revelation ceases, then the gates of hell prevail against the people." (*New Testament Commentary*, 1:389.)

Catholics do not embrace the principle of modern-day revelation; the popes are not considered "seers" who receive revelation from the Rock. Protestants accept the conclusion that the church was not built upon Peter, but they fail to recognize the significance of the role of the *petros*, the seer who holds the keys of the kingdom. Latter-day Saints are indeed blessed to understand the full implications of this important event in the Bible. President Ezra Taft Benson is that needed seer in our day—a prophet, seer, and revelator.

Now let's move to the second passage of scripture in question. The seventh chapter of Hebrews is used by many Protestants to argue that there is no need for a priesthood function in the church apart from Jesus, that he alone held the Melchizedek Priesthood.

When Luther rebelled against the Catholic priesthood, he developed the idea of a "priesthood of all believers" and taught the notion "that no man needed a priest to mediate between him and God except Christ, who is the perfect priest for all men."[1] In essence, Luther said there is no priesthood function performed except by Christ. A Christian does not need the priesthood, he said, nor does he need a priesthood bearer other than Christ in order to be saved.

In his epistle to the Hebrews, Paul refers explicitly to the Melchizedek Priesthood, assuming that his readers already understand its function. His purpose in writing the epistle is to prove the superiority of the higher covenant (gospel law) to the lesser covenant (Mosiac law). In chapter 7, he continues to follow this pattern by showing that the Melchizedek Priesthood, which administers the higher law, is superior to the Aaronic or Levitical Priesthood, which administers the lesser law.

There is much information about the priesthood in this chapter, the concept that perfection comes through the Melchizedek Priesthood (vv. 11–12), that the Melchizedek Priesthood is not restricted to one lineage (vv. 13–15), that the priesthood is eternal (vv. 16–17), that it is received with an oath and a covenant (vv. 20–21), and that Christ's priesthood function continues eternally (vv. 27–28).

This chapter could best be understood as a typology, with Melchizedek, the great priest, being a "type" of Christ and the order of the priesthood held by Melchizedek and his people being typical of the order of the priesthood held by Jesus Christ and his disciples.

Verse 24 is perhaps the one most often misunderstood, and it has caused considerable debate. The confusion is over the Greek word translated as *unchangeable:* "But this man, because he continueth ever, hath an unchangeable priesthood."

The confusion is illustrated by the alternate translation for *unchangeable* which the King James translators have given in the footnote or margin: "Or, which passeth not from one to another." (This alternate translation has been omitted in the Latter-day Saint edition.) This translation supports Luther's contention that the administration of the priesthood has occurred only in Christ, that his priesthood did not pass to others, that there is no formal priesthood in the church. A number of commentaries and some lexicons have attempted to defend this alternate translation as being correct, in spite of the fact that there is no attestation (verified evidence of usage) for the translation and no contextual basis for that interpretation.

Unchangeable is translated from the Greek word *aparabaton.* The usage of that word in ancient Greek has been examined for years — and no scholar that I know of has found any reliable example of the word being used to mean "cannot pass from one to another." On the other hand, the translation "unchangeable" or "immutable" has numerous attestations. Thus, according to known Greek usage, the best translation would be "unchangeable." For example, that is the conclusion in Kittel's *Theological Dictionary of the New Testament:* "We should keep to the rendering 'unchangeable' the more so as the active sense ('non-transferable') is not attested elsewhere."[2] Moulton's and Milligan's *The Vocabulary of the Greek Testament*, a compilation of attested Greek usage, says: "It is clear that the technical use, compared with late literary, constitutes a very strong case against the rendering 'not transferable.' "[3]

The context itself of the chapter in Hebrews welcomes the translation "unchangeable" but cannot tolerate the idea of "non-transferable." The author began chapter 7 by stressing the eternal nature of the priesthood. Melchizedek "abideth a priest continually" (v. 3); he still "liveth" (v. 8); another priest is made "after the power of an endless life" (v. 16); "Thou art a priest for ever" (vv. 17, 21); "But this man, because he *continueth ever*, hath an unchangeable priesthood" (v. 24; italics added).

There is nothing in the context to suggest that the priesthood is "nontransferable." It is eternal; it will never depart from a priesthood holder except through transgression. In one sense, one never passes his priesthood to another; it is his, "unchangeable," or eternal. But that doesn't mean that he can't bestow the priesthood on another man when authorized to do so.

The priesthood is organized into an "order." Christ was a priest "after the order of Melchisedec." (V. 21.) The fact that Melchizedek had an "order of the priesthood" indicates that more than Jesus held the priesthood. If Christ had been the only one to hold the Melchizedek Priesthood, there would have been no "order." The scriptures themselves attest that such an order did exist in New Testament times. Not only were the apostles ordained to their position by the Savior (see John 15:16), but others were also given the priesthood (see Acts 13:3; Titus 1:5).

Supportive of these conclusions is evidence from the Ante-Nicene Fathers. Ignatius, bishop of Antioch, who died A.D. 135, stated that "the priesthood is the *very highest point of all good things among men*, against which whosoever is made enough to strive, dishonors not man, but God, and Christ Jesus, the First-born, and the only High Priest, by nature, of the father."[4]

Here Ignatius suggests that Christ is indeed the only high priest *of the father*. He says nothing, however, about those who have received the Melchizedek Priesthood—"the Holy Priesthood, after the Order of the Son of God" (D&C 107:3)—and are ordained as high priests *of the Son*. He also distinguishes between Christ's right to the priesthood *by nature*, and man's receipt of priesthood *by ordination*. It is Christ's priesthood by nature, but for others it is the "highest point of all good things" that they can attain.

Theophilus, a later bishop of Antioch, circa A.D. 168, said in reference to the man Melchizedek: "At that time there was a righteous king called Melchisedek, in the city of Salem, which now is Jerusalem. This was the first priest of all priests of the Most High God. . . . And from his time priests were found in all the earth."[5] Certainly in the mind of Theophilus there was an "order" of Melchizedek.

The knowledge of an order of the Melchizedek Priesthood has faded from the biblical text. But modern revelation has restored many plain and precious truths about the priesthood that are vital to our salvation and eternal life. The priesthood is essential. It is the power of God that leads us to perfection.

There are other biblical passages that might allude to the priesthood, but the two discussed here are the passages that have been misunderstood by many Bible students. For a much more complete understanding of the priesthood held by Melchizedek, see Joseph Smith Translation Genesis 14:25–40, in the appendix of the Latter-day Saint edition of the Bible. For additional references on the priesthood, see the various headings in the Topical Guide under the listing "Priesthood," also in the Latter-day Saint edition of the Bible.

Notes

1. See William Hordern, *A Layman's Guide to Protestant Theology*, New York: Macmillan Co., 1955, pp. 29–30.

2. Grand Rapids, Mich.: Wm. B. Eerdmans Publishing Co., 1967, p. 743.

3. Grand Rapids, Mich.: Wm. B. Eerdmans Publishing Co., 1982, p. 53.

4. See Alexander Roberts and James Donaldson, eds., *The Ante-Nicene Fathers*, 10 vols. [Grand Rapids, Mich.: Wm. B. Eerdmans Publishing Co., 1979], 1:90; italics added.

5. See *Ante-Nicene Fathers*, 2:107.

QA

Why do we observe the Sabbath on Sunday when the biblical Sabbath seems to have been observed on the seventh day?

Robert J. Matthews, dean, Religious Education, Brigham Young University

The Sabbath has several purposes. It is a holy day specified in the scriptures as a day not only of rest but also of worship. The word *sabbath* is derived from the Hebrew *shabbath,* meaning "to break off" or "to desist," and in this can be seen the idea of rest.

But in the best sense, rest does not mean idleness; it signifies rather a change of emphasis. In plain terms, "keeping the Sabbath day holy" means to cease or to rest from the secular labors of the week and to use the specified day in worshiping God and doing good to our fellow beings. It is a day for spiritual works and refreshment as compared to the secular accomplishments of other days.

The various dimensions of the Sabbath are sometimes spoken of separately in the scriptures. For example, one mention of the Sabbath is found in Exodus 16:23 and has to do with instructions for the Israelites to gather a double amount of manna the day before the Sabbath so that such labor should not be performed on the Sabbath.

Exodus 20:8–11 and 31:12–17 deal with a different aspect of the Sabbath, however, and emphasize that the Lord rested on the seventh day after having created the world. These passages reconfirm the event told in Genesis 2:1–3, reminding us that the Sabbath was inaugurated in the very beginning. No doubt the sacredness of the Sabbath day was known to the true believers from the time of Adam, although the Bible is not very clear on this point. The scriptures appear to establish the Sabbath at the time of Moses, but that is probably due more to an incompleteness of the earlier record than to an absence of teaching at the time of the early patriarchs.

Still another dimension is shown after the exodus from Egypt, wherein the Sabbath is used to commemorate Israel's deliverance from bondage. (See Deuteronomy 5:12–15.)

And in the last days the Lord has explained that another purpose of the Sabbath is "that thou mayest more fully keep thyself unspotted from the world" by keeping it holy in the way he has commanded us. (D&C 59:9.)

In New Testament times the Sabbath day was called the "Lord's day" (Revelation 1:10) and was observed on the first day of the week (see Acts 20:7), honoring the resurrection of Jesus Christ from the tomb. In the present dispensation the Lord called the day of worship "my holy day" in a revelation given to the Prophet Joseph Smith on Sunday, 7 August 1831. (D&C 59:9–10.) Since Jesus is Jehovah, the Creator and the God of Israel, the different aspects of the Sabbath all bear witness of the same Lord Jesus Christ but emphasize different features of his ministry.

221

When the Pharisees criticized the disciples for picking ears of corn on the Sabbath, Jesus explained to the Pharisees that "the Sabbath was made for man, and not man for the Sabbath.

"Wherefore the Sabbath was given unto man for a day of rest; and also that man should glorify God, and not that man should not eat;

"For the Son of Man made the Sabbath day, therefore the Son of Man is Lord also of the Sabbath." (JST Mark 2:25–27.)

Not only does this explanation manifest a practical view of the Sabbath but it also illustrates its multiple nature: the Sabbath is for man's benefit, it is a day of rest, it is a day of worship, and Jesus is the maker of the Sabbath and the Lord thereof in any age of the world.

Public and Private Worship

Proper observance of the Sabbath is a sign and even a test that distinguishes the covenant people of the Lord from those who follow the ways of the world. (See Exodus 31:13–18; Nehemiah 13:15–22; Isaiah 56:1–8; 58:13–14; Jeremiah 17:19–27.) In this respect it serves a purpose similar to the Word of Wisdom and tithing, which soon divide the believers from the nonbelievers in their performance.

Sabbath observance entails more than simply staying at home. It also involves public worship. It was and is a day for the believers to meet together for worship and for instruction. The New Testament informs us that Jesus, "as his custom was," frequently went to the synagogue on the Sabbath day. (Luke 4:16.)

The most extensive revelation in the current dispensation that deals with the Sabbath day is recorded as Doctrine and Covenants 59. In this communication the Lord emphasized the public nature of Sabbath worship by indicating that one should "go to the house of prayer" on the Lord's holy day and "pay thy devotions unto the Most High." (D&C 59:9–10.)

Which Day Is the Sabbath?

The Sabbath has eternal significance. The Old Testament declares the Sabbath is to be observed as a "perpetual covenant" (see Exodus 31:13–17), which does not necessarily mean that it should be forever on the same day but rather that the Sabbath is a covenant for eternity—that is, of eternal significance—and is needed by mortals in every generation for their frequent spiritual rejuvenation. The context of the passage seems to make that point clear. It is evident from the Bible that the sacred day was the seventh day of the week during Old Testament times, whereas in the New Testament it was observed on the first day of the week by the church after the resurrection of Jesus Christ from the grave.

Traditionally The Church of Jesus Christ of Latter-day Saints has recognized Sunday as the day of worship, according to the pattern given in Doctrine and Covenants 59. Nevertheless, in the Middle East today, some branches of the Church observe the Sabbath on days other than Sunday, consistent with the custom of the countries in which they are located. That is necessary so meetings can be held at a time when the members of the Church can be present.

Because the Sabbath is for man and not man for the Sabbath, with its purpose not only to be a day of rest for the individual but also to be a day of spiritual instruction and public worship, it is important that the Sabbath day be observed at a time when the people can attend. The significant fact seems not to be *which* day is observed so much as *how* and *why* the day is observed and that the local group of believers observe the same day each week.

In the Church the matter of Sabbath-day observance can be settled quite effectively from the fact that the twelve successive Presidents of the Church from the Prophet Joseph Smith to President Ezra Taft Benson have all seen fit to observe Sunday as a proper day and have thus set the pattern. The important factor is that the programs of the Church are under the direction of the holy priesthood and have the approval of the President of the Church—the prophet, seer, and revelator, and the Lord's representative on earth. When rare exceptions to the established day have seemed necessary, the proper priesthood authority makes the decision.

QA

How can Jesus and Lucifer be spirit brothers when their characters and purposes are so utterly opposed?

Jess L. Christensen, director, LDS Institute of Religion, Utah State University, Logan, Utah

On first hearing, the doctrine that Lucifer and our Lord, Jesus Christ, are brothers may seem surprising to some, especially to those unacquainted with latter-day revelations. But both the scriptures and the prophets affirm that Jesus Christ and Lucifer are indeed offspring of our Heavenly Father and, therefore, spirit brothers. Jesus Christ was with the Father from the beginning. Lucifer, too, was an angel "who was in authority in the presence of God," a "son of the morning." (See Isaiah 14:12; D&C 76:25–27.) Both Jesus and Lucifer were strong leaders with great knowledge and influence. But as the First-born of the Father, Jesus was Lucifer's older brother. (See Colossians 1:15; D&C 93:21.)

How could two such great spirits become so totally opposite? The answer lies in the principle of agency, which has existed from all eternity. (See D&C 93:30–31.) Of Lucifer, the scripture says that because of rebellion "he became Satan, yea, even the devil, the father of all lies." (Moses 4:4.) Note that he was not created evil but *became* Satan by his own choice.

When our Father in Heaven presented his plan of salvation, Jesus sustained the plan and his part in it, giving the glory to God, to whom it properly belonged. Lucifer, on the other hand, sought power, honor, and glory only for himself. (See Isaiah 14:13–14; Moses 4:1–2.) When his modification of the Father's plan was rejected, he rebelled against God and was subsequently cast out of heaven with those who had sided with him. (See Revelation 12:7–9; D&C 29:36–37.)

That brothers would make dramatically different choices is not unusual. It has happened time and again, as the scriptures attest: Cain chose to serve Satan; Abel chose to serve God. (See Moses 5:16–18.) Esau "despised his birthright"; Jacob wanted to honor it. (Genesis 25:29–34.) Joseph's brothers sought to kill him; he sought to preserve them. (Genesis 37:12–24; 45:3–11.)

It is ironic that the agency with which Lucifer rebelled is the very gift he tried to take from man. His proposal was that all be forced back into God's presence. (See Moses 4:1, 3.) But the principle of agency is fundamental to the existence and progression of intelligent beings: as we make wise choices, we grow in light and truth. On the other hand, wrong choices — such as the one Satan made — stop progress and can even deny us blessings that we already have. (See D&C 93:30–36.)

In order for us to progress, therefore, we must have the opportunity to choose good or evil. Interestingly, Satan and his angels — those who opposed agency — have become that opposition. As the prophet Lehi taught, "Men are free according to the flesh;

and all things are given them which are expedient unto man. And they are free to choose liberty and eternal life, through the great Mediator of all men, or to choose captivity and death, according to the captivity and power of the devil; for he seeketh that all men might be miserable like unto himself." (2 Nephi 2:27.)

Although the Father has allowed Satan and his angels to tempt us, he has given each of us the ability to rise above temptation. (See 1 Corinthians 10:13.) He has also given us the great gift of the Atonement.

When the Lord placed enmity between Eve's children and the devil, Satan was told that he would bruise the heel of Eve's seed but her seed would bruise his head. (See Moses 4:21.) President Joseph Fielding Smith explained that "the 'God of peace,' who according to the scriptures is to bruise Satan, is Jesus Christ." (*Answers to Gospel Questions,* 5 vols. [Salt Lake City: Deseret Book Co., 1957], 1:3.) Satan would bruise the Savior's heel by leading men to crucify Him. But through his death and resurrection, Christ overcame death for all of us; and through his atonement, he offers each of us a way to escape the eternal ramifications of sin. Thus, Satan's machinations have been frustrated, and eventually he will be judged, bound, and cast into hell forever. (See Revelation 20:1–10; D&C 29:26–29.) The Hebrew word for *bruise* means "to crush or grind." Therefore, the very heel that was bruised will crush Satan and will help us overcome the world and return to our Father. As we use our agency to choose good over evil, the atonement of Christ prepares the way for us to return to our Father in Heaven.

We can only imagine the sorrow of our Heavenly Father as he watched a loved son incite and lead a rebellion and lose his opportunity for exaltation. But we can also imagine the Father's love and rejoicing as he welcomed back the beloved son who had valiantly and perfectly fought the battles of life and brought about the great Atonement through his suffering and death.

QA

How do we endure to the end? The idea seems to imply putting up with a bad situation (life) until death brings release. What do the prophets really mean when they speak of enduring to the end?

Gordon M. Thomas, Welfare Serves multiregion agent, Salt Lake South Multiregion

Nephi gave us a good description of what enduring to the end involves. He wrote that "unless a man shall endure to the end, *in following the example of the Son of the living God,* he cannot be saved." (2 Nephi 31:16; italics added.) Enduring, in this sense, means remaining faithful to the commandments and to the covenants we make with God to live a Christlike life. And living such a life, as Nephi taught brings joy, not sorrow. (See 1 Nephi 8:10–12; 11:21–23; 2 Nephi 2:25.) "Behold," wrote the apostle James, "we count them happy which endure." (James 5:11.)

In this vein, President Joseph Fielding Smith suggested that enduring to the end involves the acquisition of those attributes that bring happiness. "We must endure to the end," he said. "We must so live as to acquire the attributes of godliness and become the kind of people who can enjoy the glory and wonders of the celestial kingdom." *(Ensign,* Nov. 1971, p. 5.)

While some may see enduring to the end as suffering through the challenges of daily life until death introduces them to a better world, Latter-day Saints are given a different perspective. Brigham Young said, "Every trial and experience you have passed through is necessary for your salvation." *(Discourses of Brigham Young,* sel. John A. Widtsoe [Salt Lake City: Deseret Book Co., 1954], p. 345.) Such a perspective, as Elder Neal A. Maxwell pointed out, enables us, even in the most pressing of circumstances, to pass "the breaking point without breaking, having cause to be bitter — as men measure cause — without being bitter." *(A Time to Choose* [Salt Lake City: Deseret Book Co., 1972], p. 42.)

Challenges are a normal part of life, not the exception or a punishment. Joy comes as we learn to conquer these obstacles, not simply dutifully put up with them.

It has been said by some that heaven is just a change of address. That statement may be partially correct in respect to our feelings. We will not leave this life and find we have made dramatic changes

226

in our attitudes and desires. If we have endured well, we will be in the habit of being righteous and happy, and we will have earned the right to be with others who have also learned this lesson. Enduring well makes us worthy and ready for a joyful, celestial life.

When we endure to the end in righteousness, no blessing will be withheld from us. There are those who feel that all will be better in the celestial kingdom if they can just endure—or get by—in this life. Yet those who just "get by" may not be found in that kingdom. (See D&C 76:71, 79.) We must pattern our lives after the life of the Savior.

Our enduring, therefore, must be active, not passive. Many of us go through life expecting others to make us feel happy. Yet the power for achieving happiness is not in others; it is in ourselves. And we get that power through the help of God. Others may help us and serve us, but if we are waiting for some person or some future event to bring us happiness, we may never find it. We can accept conditions as they exist, or we can accept the responsibility to change either the situation or our attitude about it.

One thing that can help is staying close to the Spirit through prayer. We should pray to endure, to live by the Spirit, to accept the will of the Lord in our lives. I believe the real miracle will come when we can totally submit to his will. Then God is free to grant us those things that will benefit us the most.

When I was serving as a bishop, a sister in my ward was critically injured when her car was struck by a train. There were many anxious days and weeks in the hospital. Blessings were given as each crisis arose. One evening her husband said it was time to accept the Lord's will. That seemed to be the turning point in her recovery. A sister who was as close to death as she could be is now living a normal life.

Another thing we can do to endure is not to dwell on the misfortunes of the past. Looking forward with new resolve is more effective than continually looking back. If you have made a poor decision that requires action in the future, then face up to it and correct it. Of course, if the past requires repentance, that certainly must be done also.

At times in some lives there may arise a situation that seems "impossible," such as being married to someone you can't get along with. Is our only choice, then, to "endure" in quiet desperation? A situation this serious generally takes a long time to develop. It may also take a long time and a great deal of effort to resolve. It may require the help of a bishop or a trusted counselor.

I have a general attitude in life that helps me remain happy in rough times. I have found that I tend to avoid those activities I don't enjoy doing. Now, I have duties in my life which may not be pleasant. My plan then is *not to avoid the activity but to change my attitude about it.* I also know that a bad time will not last forever. I know I will be happy next month. And if I'll be happy next month, why not next week? or tomorrow? Why not today? I find that with this approach I can appreciate just about every day.

Nephi, addressing the members of the Church in his day, showed us the key to enduring righteously:

"And now, my beloved brethren, after ye have gotten into this strait and narrow path, I would ask if all is done? Behold, I say unto you, Nay; for ye have not come thus far save it were by the word of Christ with unshaken faith in him, relying wholly upon the merits of him who is mighty to save.

"Wherefore, ye must press forward with a steadfastness in Christ, having a perfect brightness of hope, and a love of God and of all men. Wherefore, if ye shall press forward, feasting upon the word of Christ, and endure to the end, behold, thus saith the Father: Ye shall have eternal life." (2 Nephi 31:19–20.)

Thus, for members of the Church, enduring to the end includes several steps:

Pressing forward with a steadfastness in Christ

Having a perfect brightness of hope

Having a love of God

Having a love of all men

Feasting upon the word of Christ

Relying wholly upon the merits of him who is mighty to save

The promise is that when we do these things, we will endure well and inherit eternal life.

INDEX

Address to All Believers in Christ, 41
Adieu, definition of, 16–17
Agency, fundamental principle of, 224–25
Ancient American Setting for the Book of Mormon, 68
Anderson, Richard Lloyd, 39, 194
Applegarth, Bill, 77
Augustine, 96

Backman, Milton V., Jr., 169, 183, 192
Baptism: for the dead, 106–9; necessity for, 121–22, 157; covenant of, 158–59
Baptize, definition of, 17
Bennett, John C., 43
Bible: definition of, 17–18; Book of Mormon companion to, 30–31; typographical errors in the, 37–38; insufficiency of, to effect gathering, 138–39; Church's attitude toward, 159–65; Book of Mormon testifies of, 160–61; materials lost from, 161–62; Latter-day Saint edition of, 164–65
Biggs, George W., 200
Birth of Christ, 3–5
Blazey, Byron C., 198–99
Blumell, Bruce D., 54
Book of Mormon: on birth of Christ, 3–5; on the Godhead, 5–11; some ordinances not contained in, 11–15; language of the, 16–18; Hebrew characteristics in the, 21–26; authenticity of the, 27–33; changes in editions of the, 33–39; witnesses testify of, 39–46; defines hell, 46–50; B. H. Roberts's testimony of the, 61–72; joins Bible to effect gathering, 139–42; bears witness of Bible, 160–61. *See also* Gold plates; Moroni's promise

Brandt, Edward J., 16

229

Brewer, Gerald B., 198
Brewster, Hoyt W., 210
Brunson, Seymour, 108
Bulloch, Brent, 143

Cannon, George Q., 189
Carver, James A., 215
Celestial kingdom, Joseph Smith's vision of, 108
Christensen, Jack, 68
Christensen, Jess L, 223
Christianity, primitive: fall of, 94–95; formal church organization in, 100–102
Christians, true, definition of, 155–59
Church, formal organization of, by Christ, 100–102
Church of Jesus Christ of Latter-day Saints: responding to questions about, 151–54; as Christian church, 155–59; changes in name of, 194–96; legal organization of, 196–99
"Confession of Oliver Overstreet," 40
Cowdery, Oliver: copies Book of Mormon, 35; death of, 39; spurious documents about, 40–44; never denied Book of Mormon, 44–45

Creeds, abominable, 210–14

Davis, Howard, 199
Dead, salvation for, 106–9
Defence in a Rehearsal of My Grounds for Separating Myself from the Latter Day Saints, 40–44
Doctrine and Covenants, 1981 additions to, 77–78
Doxey, Roy W., 5, 50

E. B. Grandin Company, 36
Enduring to the end, 208–9, 225–28
Eternal, definition of, 83–84
Evans, David W., 200
Ezekiel, 129–32, 135–38, 141

Faith, necessity for, 121
First Vision: four accounts of, by Joseph Smith, 169–72, 210–11; 1832 account of, 172–75; 1835 account of, 175–77; 1838 account of, 178–80; 1842 account of, 180; Orson Pratt's accounts of, 183–87; Orson Hyde's account of, 187–88
Cry from the Wilderness, A, 187–88; various testimonies of, 188–90; historical setting of, 192–94
Fudge, George H., 103

Gathering of Israel, 137–42, 144–45
Genealogical records, 103–5
Gentiles, 146
Genung, John S., 197
Gilbert, John H., 36
Gilliland, Steve F., 151
God: nature of, 5–11; condescension of, 28–29, privilege of seeing, 78–82; anthropomorphic concept of, 93, 98; is a spirit, 97
Godhead, Book of Mormon on the, 5–11
Gold plates: weight of the, 50–52; not placed in museum, 52–54
Goodson, John, 36
Gospel: definition of, 11–12; unchanging nature of, 110–12; restoration of, prophecies concerning, 143–44; teaching basics of, 152–53
Greek influence in early church, 95

Grant, Heber J., 63, 68
Griggs, C. Wilfred, 116

Harris, Martin, 39, 51
Hatch, Edwin, 95
Hebrew characteristics in the Book of Mormon, 21–26
Hell defined in Book of Mormon, 46–50
Hinckley, Gordon B., 97, 164–65, 209
Howe, Eber D., 43, 55–58
Hurlbut, Philastus, 55–59

Hyde, Orson, 187–88

Iba, Stephen K., 83
Ignatius, 219
Investigating the Book of Mormon Witnesses, 43
Israel: failure of, to endure God's presence, 81–82; scattering and gathering of, 136–42
Ivins, Anthony W., 68

Jerusalem: land of, 3–4; at, 4
Jessee, Dean C., 171, 172
Jesus Christ: birth of, 3–5; nature of, 8–9; atonement of, 11; Book of Mormon teaches of, 28, 29; physical resurrection of, 93–94; second coming of, 146–47; is spirit brother of Lucifer, 223–25
Johnson, Joel H., 43
Jones, Gerald E., 199
Joseph, stick of, 141–42
Journal of Discourses, 199–201
Judah, house of, 145–46

Kimball, Heber C., 111
Kimball, Spencer W., 190, 209

Language of the Book of Mormon, 16–18

Last days, Book of Mormon warns about, 31–32, Old Testament prophecies of, 143–48
Law of Moses, 122–23, 125
Lucifer, 223–25
Lloyd, Wesley, 67
Ludlow, Daniel H., 11, 18
Lund, Gerald N., 205
Luther, Martin, 217

McConkie, Bruce R., 49–50, 124, 208, 216
McLellin, William E., 43
McGuire, John P., 199
Mallowan, Max, 130, 133, 134, 135
"Manuscript Story—Conneaut Creek," 55–56
Marriage: eternal, 113–16; Paul's views on, 116–20
Mason, Dr. James, 85
Masten, Thomas B., Jr., 198
Matthews, Robert J., 33, 110, 159, 220
Maxwell, Neal A., 207, 226
Melchizedek Priesthood: not prerequisite to seeing God, 78–79; biblical support for, 215–20
Meservy, Keith, 129
Messenger and Advocate, 42–43
Millet, Robert L., 106
Misunderstandings, correcting, 151–52
Mormonism Unvailed, 55–60
Mulholland, James, 177
Moroni's promise, 18–21

Neal, R. B., 40
Neibaur, Alexander, 188–89
Nelson, William O., 93
Neoplatonism, 94
New Witnesses for God, 64
Nibley, Hugh, 60, 68
Nyman, Monte S., 52

Ogden, D. Kelly, 3
Old Testament, topics of Restoration in, 143–48
Oppenheim, Leo, 132
Ordinances: revealed in all dispensations, 110–12; necessity for, 121

Packer, Boyd K., 213
Page, Hyrum, 42
Parsons, Robert E., 120
Pearl of Great Price, 189–90
Perfection, working toward, 205–10
Petersen, Melvin J., 78
Peterson, H. Donl, 46
Porter, Larry C., 196
Pratt, P. P., 36
Pratt, Orson, 183–87
Priesthood: power of, involved in seeing God, 79–80, 82; authority of, 211; of all believers, 217
Promise, Moroni's, 18–21

Rasmussen, Ellis T., 27
Remarkable Visions, 184
Revelation, church built on rock of, 215–17
Revivals, religious, 192–94
Richards, Franklin D., 177
Rice, L. L., 55
Rigdon, Sidney, 33–34, 41, 55–59, 175, 212
Romney, Marion G., 84
Roberts, B. H.: writings of, 60–61, 64–74; questions and answers about, 61–72
Robinson, Ebenezer, 36

Sabbath day, 220–23
Sadducees, 113–15
Salvation: for the dead, 106–9; role of works in, 120–26

Schlee, Leonard, 199
Section headings in Doctrine and Covenants, 77–78
Seers, 216
"Shepherd of Hermas," 108
Smith, Don Carlos, 36
Smith, Emma, 51
Smith, Ethan, 55, 59–60, 68
Smith, John, 195–96
Smith, Joseph: on birth of Christ, 4; modern teachings of, 15; testimony of origins of the Book of Mormon, 26; as translator, 34–35; leadership of, challenged, 39; describes gold plates, 51; theories of fraud and, 56–60; affirms corporeal nature of God, 98; on salvation for dead, 108–9; testifies of Bible, 162; wrote four accounts of First Vision, 169–72; search of, for religious truth, 173–74; on gradual climb to exaltation, 205–6
Smith, Joseph F., 189–90, 206
Smith, Joseph Fielding, 111, 206, 225, 226
Smith, William, 51
Sorenson, John L., 68
Spaulding manuscript, 54–60
Spaulding, Solomon, 54
Sperry, Sidney B., 21–22, 68
Spirit: God is more than a, 9–11; world, 48
Stevenson, Edward, 183
Sticks, Ezekiel's prophecy about, 129–42
Study helps in Doctrine and Covenants, 77–78
"Study of the Book of Mormon," 63–72

Talmage, James E., 63, 67, 178, 213

Taylor, John, 189
Temple, ordinances of, among
   ancients, 110–12
Tertullian, 95
Testimony, bearing, to
   nonmembers, 153
Theophilus, 220
Thomas, Gordon M., 225
Tobacco: harmful effects of, 85–88;
   smokeless, 88–89
Transfiguration, 80–81
Trinity, traditional views on, 93,
   95–96
Tvedtnes, John A., 21

View of the Hebrews, 55–60, 69–72

United order, 83–84

Watt, George D., 199–200
Wax writing boards, 130–34
Weaknesses, overcoming, 208

Welch, John W., 60
Wells, Daniel, 193–94
Wentworth Letter, 180, 211
Weyland, Jack, 155
Whitmer, David, 39, 41–42, 196–97
Whitmer, Elizabeth Ann, 39–40
Widtsoe, John A., 68, 211–12
Williams, Frederick G., 172, 210
Williams, R.J., 134
Woodford, Robert J., 99
Word of Wisdom, statistical
   support for, 85–89
Works, role of, in salvation, 120–
   26, 156–59

Yarn, David H., Jr., 113
Young, Brigham, 44, 57–58, 162–
   63, 193, 226
Young, Julia, 200

Zion, prophecies concerning, 147–
   48